"Progress on many SDGs is not on track, especially for SDG2. In this book, many well-known scholars and practitioners contribute timely knowledge to support action and accelerate progress towards SGD2."

Dr Shenggen Fan, Director General, International Food Policy Research Institute

"This book is written by a global leader who spans the worlds of academia, policy and programmes, excelling in each. Professor Sheryl Hendriks has produced a beautifully balanced book on the challenges of delivering food security and nutrition. The book highlights the many complexities of doing so, but also highlights the many opportunities and solutions. It is a must read for all who need to understand the centrality of well-functioning food systems for sustainable development."

Dr Lawrence Haddad, Executive Director, Global Alliance for Improved Nutrition (GAIN) and 2018 World Food Prize Laureate

"This book comes at a time when Africa is rising, yet millions remain on the periphery of two decades of positive gains. Reflecting on emerging transdisciplinary approaches to addressing food security, the book provides innovative approaches to tackling Africa's beleaguering food security challenges. It offers practical policy interventions and raises questions concerning developing consensus about Africa's quest for a food secure continent. This book is a tremendous research and teaching resource for African food security professionals. Sheryl Hendriks, who has for two decades adorned the food security CAADP face across Africa, has unquestionably ignited new debates around food security in Africa."

Prof Richard M. Mkandawire PhD. Dr.hc, Director, Africa Secretariat Alliance for African Partnership (AAP) and Chairperson of the Malawi National Planning Commission

"Food security and nutrition analysis and understanding is, and continues to be, a very complex field that challenges the world; particularly vulnerable populations and Development and Humanitarian professionals. Therefore, the fight against hunger and related malnutrition demands a cadre of well-trained professionals, equipped to deal with shocks, stresses and resulting acute food shortages. This book aptly provides a wealth of analytical tools and insights that guide professionals committed to understanding the core elements of food insecurity and the contemporary realities related to inadequate food intake."

Angelline Rudakubana, Director, WFP Africa Office, Representative to the African Union and the United Nations Economic Commission for Africa (UNECA), Addis Ababa - Ethiopia

FOOD SECURITY POLICY, EVALUATION AND IMPACT ASSESSMENT

This book offers an essential, comprehensive, yet accessible reference of contemporary food security discourse and guides readers through the steps required for food security analysis.

Food insecurity is a major obstacle to development and achievement of the Sustainable Development Goals. It is a complex issue that cuts across traditional sectors in government and disciplines in academia. Understanding how multiple elements cause and influence food security is essential for policymakers, practitioners and scholars. This book demonstrates how evaluation can integrate the four elements of food security (availability, access, nutrition and resilience) and offers practical tools for policy and programme impact assessment to support evidence-based planning.

Aimed at researchers, postgraduates and those undertaking professional development in food studies, agricultural economics, rural development, nutrition and public health, the book is key reading for those seeking to understand evidence-based food security analysis.

Sheryl L. Hendriks is Professor and Head of the Department of Agricultural Economics, Extension and Rural Development and Director of the Institute for Food, Nutrition and Well-being, University of Pretoria, South Africa.

EARTHSCAN FOOD AND AGRICULTURE

Governing Sustainable Seafood
Peter Oosterveer and Simon Bush

Farming Systems and Food Security in Africa
Priorities for Science and Policy Under Global Change
Edited by John Dixon, Dennis P. Garrity, Jean-Marc Boffa, Timothy Olalekan Williams, Tilahun Amede with Christopher Auricht, Rosemary Lott and George Mburathi

Consumers, Meat and Animal Products
Policies, Regulations and Marketing
Terence J. Centner

Gender, Agriculture and Agrarian Transformations
Changing Relations in Africa, Latin America and Asia
Edited by Carolyn E. Sachs

A Global Corporate Trust for Agroecological Integrity
New Agriculture in a World of Legitimate Eco-states
John W. Head

Geographical Indication and Global Agri-Food
Development and Democratization
Edited by Alessandro Bonanno, Kae Sekine and Hart N. Feuer

Multifunctional Land Uses in Africa
Sustainable Food Security Solutions
Elisabeth Simelton and Madelene Ostwald

Food Security Policy, Evaluation and Impact Assessment
Edited by Sheryl L. Hendriks

For further details please visit the series page on the Routledge website:
http://www.routledge.com/books/series/ECEFA/

FOOD SECURITY POLICY, EVALUATION AND IMPACT ASSESSMENT

Edited by Sheryl L. Hendriks

First published 2020
by Routledge
2 Park Square, Milton Park, Abingdon, Oxon OX14 4RN

and by Routledge
52 Vanderbilt Avenue, New York, NY 10017

Routledge is an imprint of the Taylor & Francis Group, an informa business

© 2020 selection and editorial matter, Sheryl L. Hendriks; individual chapters, the
contributors

The right of Sheryl L. Hendriks to be identified as the author of the editorial
material, and of the authors for their individual chapters, has been asserted in
accordance with sections 77 and 78 of the Copyright, Designs and Patents Act
1988.

All rights reserved. No part of this book may be reprinted or reproduced or
utilised in any form or by any electronic, mechanical, or other means, now
known or hereafter invented, including photocopying and recording, or in any
information storage or retrieval system, without permission in writing from the
publishers.

Trademark notice: Product or corporate names may be trademarks or registered
trademarks, and are used only for identification and explanation without intent to
infringe.

British Library Cataloguing-in-Publication Data
A catalogue record for this book is available from the British Library

Library of Congress Cataloging-in-Publication Data
A catalog record has been requested for this book

ISBN: 978-1-138-49708-5 (hbk)
ISBN: 978-1-138-49709-2 (pbk)
ISBN: 978-1-351-01982-8 (ebk)

Typeset in Bembo
by Taylor & Francis Books

Dedicated to those left behind by previous development efforts and who we, the contributors of this book, are committed to helping on the path to sustainable food security.

CONTENTS

List of figures	*xii*
List of tables	*xiv*
List of boxes	*xv*
Preface and acknowledgements	*xvi*
List of contributors	*xix*
List of acronyms and abbreviations	*xxviii*
Foreword	*xxxi*

PART I
The fundamentals of food security policy assessment in the era of the SDGs

1

1 Food security policy analysis as a key element in attaining SGD2
and addressing food policy failures of the past   3
Sheryl L. Hendriks

2 How the understanding of food security and nutrition shapes
policy analysis   9
Sheryl L. Hendriks

3 Understanding the depth and severity of food security as a
continuum of experiences   14
Sheryl L. Hendriks

4 Contemporary policy issues related to food availability   21
Sheryl L. Hendriks

x Contents

5 Contemporary policy issues related to poverty and inequality
and the imperatives to improve access to food 31
Nic J.J. Olivier, Francette Gouws and Nico J.J. Olivier

6 Contemporary policy issues and the imperatives to reduce
malnutrition 41
*Beulah Pretorius, Suresh C. Babu, Angela M McIntyre and
Hettie C. Schönfeldt*

7 Mitigating negative nutrition transitions: Cultivating diversity in
food systems 53
Angela M. McIntyre

8 Contemporary policy issues in food assistance 61
Steven Were Omamo, Lorenzo Motta and Chelsea Graham

PART II
Practical guidance on in the components of evidence-based food security policy analysis 75

9 Assessing the coherence of broader development policies for
food security 77
Nic J.J. Olivier and Nico J.J. Olivier

10 The policymaking process: Introducing the Kaleidoscope Model
for food security policy analysis 88
*Steven Haggblade, Suresh C. Babu, Danielle Resnick and
Sheryl L. Hendriks*

11 Developing and applying a theory of change assessment 100
Angela M. McIntyre

12 The essential elements of assessment, monitoring and evaluation
to determine the impact of policies and programmes 109
Sheryl L. Hendriks and Hunadi Mapula Nkwana

13 Identification of risks and vulnerable populations 121
Filippo Fossi

14 Institutional arrangements for governance, coordination and
mutual accountability 132
Moraka N. Makhura and Nosipho Mabuza

15 Gender and food security 142
Elizabeth Mkandawire

Contents **xi**

16 Inclusion and engagement with Indigenous Peoples   155
    Carol Kalafatic

PART III
Measurement and information systems   **167**

17 Measuring food insecurity   169
    Carlo Cafiero

18 The Integrated Phase Classification approach as an example of
    comprehensive system approaches   206
    Jannie Armstrong, Leila Oliveira, Kaija Korpi-Salmela and Jose Lopez

PART IV
Practical insights for implementation, monitoring and
evaluation   **219**

19 Shaping food security agendas: Notes from the field on
    challenges, solutions and promising ideas   221
    Angela M. McIntyre, Jannie Armstrong, Suresh C. Babu,
    Yergelem Beraki, Duncan Boughton, Boaz B. Keizire,
    Michael Roberto Kenyi Legge, Lailà Lokosang, Bongeka Mdleleni,
    Rufaro Musvaire, Leila Oliveira, Luca Russo, Jeanette Sprinkhuizen
    and Duncan Stewart

20 What next for evidence-based food security policy analysis?   230
    Sheryl L. Hendriks

Index   *232*

FIGURES

3.1	The SGDs and how they are all linked to food	15
3.2	The food security continuum	16
3.3	Continuums of food insecurity, coping strategies and interventions	18
3.4	Continuums of magnitude and intensity of food insecurity	19
4.1	Conceptual framework of the food system	23
4.2	The increasing number of extreme weather-related crises between 1996 and 2016	25
6.1	Impacts of malnutrition over the life course	44
8.1	Integrated Food Security Phases Classification	62
8.2	Food crisis risk factors	64
8.3	A functional and contextual view of food systems	66
8.4	The good year, the bad year, and the last mile	67
8.5	Systemic problems in food systems	69
8.6	WFP interventions across the food system in Kenya	70
8.7	Managing good years, bad years and the last mile	72
9.1	An illustration of the interrelationship between global, regional and national elements of the framework determining policy development	81
9.2	The governance (policy, regulatory, strategic and implementation) loop	82
9.3	The policy development loop/cycle	83
10.1	The Kaleidoscope Model	90
10.2	Policy system schematic	92
10.3	Circle of influence	93

11.1	Generic theory of change model	103
11.2	Theory of change for increasing micronutrient consumption through biofortified crops	106
12.1	Differentiating between causes, context and consequences	110
12.2	Differentiating between inputs, outcomes and impacts	111
13.1	The spheres of vulnerability	124
13.2	How changes in the environment affect the elements of the food system in different ways	125
14.1	Inclusive Sustainable Partnerships for Development (ISP4D)	137
18.1	IPC's analytical framework	208
18.2	The IPC Acute Food insecurity table for area classification	212
18.3	The IPC Household Group Reference Tables	213

TABLES

5.1	Food entitlement failures and social protection responses	38
6.1	Summary of policy discourse and policy change related to nutrition over the decades	47
8.1	WHO severity indices for wasting and stunting	63
8.2	Summary of food assistance-based responses and solutions to systemic problems in food systems	71
9.1	Summary of national instruments linked to the institutions responsible for the approval and/or implementation of these instruments	85
10.1	Kaleidoscope Model hypotheses about key drivers of policy change	95
10.2	KM hypothesis tests (percentage of cases in which variables proved significant)	97
12.1	List of potential indicators	116
13.1	Typology of risks and response options	123
13.2	Summary of main vulnerability estimates	127
15.1	Integrated framework for gender analysis in nutrition policy	150
17.1	Properties and potential appropriate use of food security indicators	199

BOXES

Working definition of Indigenous Peoples and characteristics most
shared by them   156
Agricultural systems and landscapes shaped and managed by
Indigenous Peoples   157

PREFACE AND ACKNOWLEDGEMENTS

Despite considerable effort to end hunger over the last six decades, it is on the rise again. Deprivation that results in hunger and malnutrition plunders opportunities from the lives of close to 11 per cent (one person in 10) of the world's population, disproportionately concentrated in developing nations. Regardless of the strong commitment by world leaders to end hunger, food insecurity remains a complex challenge of our time. Overcoming the scourge of food insecurity will take comprehensive national policies, coordinated programmes and mutual accountability for action in inclusive development efforts across.

This book seeks to address a fundamental gap in the training of professionals in academia and in practice to deal with the challenges of food security. It is fitting that the drafting of this manuscript is inspired by the professionals from across Africa I have had the privilege to train; starting with the first transdisciplinary postgraduate training programme in food security established at the former University of Natal in 1999. Since then, I have not only trained or supervised students and professionals from across the African continent, but I have learnt enormously from each participant in the process. Many serve the global food security agenda in important roles and positions. I applaud their ongoing commitment to making a difference in their contexts.

The core framework for this book is drawn from a module in Food Security Policy Analysis that I have taught at the University of Pretoria since 2011. The module also forms part of the enormously successful Collaborative Masters in Agricultural and Applied Economics (CMAAE). Initially, the module covered the elements of the Comprehensive Africa Agricultural Development's Framework for Food Security (CAADP FAFS). The foundational content has evolved through experience gained from various capacity development engagements including: the EU-FAO Improved Global Governance for Hunger Reduction Programme, Africa Lead's CAADP capacity programme, the IFPRI/Regional Strategic Knowledge

Support System (ReSAKSS) National Agriculture and Food Security Investment Plan Task Force, IFPRI, the CMAAE and the USAID Feed the Future Innovation Lab for Food Security Policy (FSP-IL).

While useful for training, this manuscript is not a textbook. It seeks to capture the broad areas of knowledge needed by anyone, anywhere working in food security. It presents the contemporary knowledge on the four dimensions of food security and the essential considerations for food security policy analysis, programme evaluation and policy and programme impact assessment. It acts as a complement to numerous texts that provide the technical detail for empirical techniques.

The foreword is written by one of my mentors in development – Dr Ousmane Badiane, who along with Jeff Hill and Prof Richard Mkandawire drew me into the CAAAP programme in 2006. The chapters are authored by 25 brilliant thinkers and practical experts drawn from a network built throught engagement in international think tanks, panels and programmes. Here concepts are challenged, complexity is unpacked and solutions to the intractable problems are sought

The authors represent two networks. Firstly, the global network of equally dedicated colleagues who are committed to ending hunger and identifying pathways to sustainable food security for people and communities across the world, which include people I have worked with from: the CAADP process, the Global Agriculture and Food Security Programme, the United Nations Committee on World Food Security's High Level Panel of Experts on Food Security and Nutrition (HLPE), the IFPRI Copact 2023 Technical Advisory Team, the Malabo Montpellier Panel, the InterAcademy Partnership (IAP) Programme for Food and Nutrition Security and Agriculture and, closer to home, my colleagues from the University of Pretoria and its Institute for Food, Nutrition and Well-being. Chapters 9, 10, 13, 14 and 15 draw on stimulating research conducted through the FSP-IL. Second, some authors represent the alumni of my postgraduate programmes at the Universities of KwaZulu-Natal and Pretoria who serve in important roles in the global food security network.

When Tim Hardwick of Earthscan Routledge first offered an opportunity to author a book, I immediately knew that this was an opportunity to share the content of my module and simultaneously enhance the core content by harnessing the incredibly deep experience and insights of these networks of professionals in academia, policy-making and development practice.

I thank each author and co-author for their generous contribution of intellectual acumen and experience to the chapters. I am grateful to Tim Hardwick and Amy Johnston for the opportunity to publish and their guidance through the publishing process. I express my deep gratitude to the comments of the anonymous reviewers who helped shape the final content of the book. I thank Angela McIntyre for her most valued role as Editorial Assistant and personal encourager. Thanks go to Elizabeth Mkandawire, Nosipho Mabuza and Ntombizethu Mkhwanazi for help with the task of documenting the references. The credit for the cover photo goes to my younger son, Aidan Hendriks.

xviii Preface and acknowledgements

To my amazing family, Roelie, Kevin and Aidan, thank you for your incredible patience, support and the sacrifices you make in sharing me with the global community committed to ensuring food security.

Sheryl L. Hendriks

CONTRIBUTORS

Sheryl L. Hendriks is Professor and Head of the Department of Agricultural Economics, Extension and Rural Development and Director of the Institute for Food, Nutrition and Well-being, University of Pretoria, South Africa. She has extensive experience in food security policy analysis, programme design and monitoring and evaluation. She was a founding member of the Committee on World Food Security's High Level Panel on Food Security and Nutrition. She is a member of the Malabo Montpellier Panel. She actively supports food policy reform in African countries. She has made a significant contribution to capacity building for food security in Africa professionals from over 18 African countries, establishing a large network of graduates.

Jannie Armstrong works with the Integrated Phase Classification's Global Support Unit, supporting an activity aimed at developing graduate-level course curriculum on the IPC for use at universities worldwide. He received his doctorate and MSc in food policy from City University (UK), and has consulted extensively on food security and nutrition for FAO, WFP, World Fish and others. Based in Lusaka, Zambia, he has lived and worked in Asia, Africa and Europe for the past 25 years. He is a member of the World Public Health Nutrition Association, and holds a particular research and professional interest in food security policy.

Suresh C. Babu is a Senior Fellow and a program leader at the International Food Policy Research Institute (IFPRI) in Washington, DC and Extraordinary Professor of Agricultural Economics at the University of Pretoria, South Africa. Babu was a research economist at Cornell University before joining IFPRI in 1992. He has held visiting or honorary professorships at American University, Washington, DC; Indira Gandhi National Open University, India; University of Kwazulu-Natal, South Africa and Zhejiang University, China. He is on the editorial boards of

xx List of contributors

several leading journals. He received a PhD and MS in Economics from Iowa State University, which also awarded its Outstanding Young Alumnus Award for his services to global development.

Yergelem Beraki is a Food Security Officer at FAO Sub-regional Office for Eastern Africa. He has more than 20 years' experience in providing professional support to countries in Eastern and Greater Horn of Africa sub-region on various capacity development areas that concerns food and nutrition security. In recent years he has been involved in designing and implementing capacity development programmes that focused on food security and nutrition (FSN) analysis and food security policy and strategy development at national levels as well as capacity development support and on creation of the inter-sectoral food security and nutrition coordination framework at national and sub-national levels.

Duncan Boughton is an Agricultural Economist and Professor in International Development, at Michigan State University, USA. He has led Michigan State University's work in Myanmar since October 2012. Since January 2015 he has directed the USAID Burma and LIFT funded Food Security Policy Project in collaboration with the International Food Policy Research Institute (IFPRI). He has over 30 years of professional experience in policy analysis to raise smallholder farmer incomes in Southeast Asia and Sub-Saharan Africa, and has undertaken long-term assignments in the Philippines, The Gambia, Mali, Malawi, Mozambique and Myanmar. His work has focused on agricultural research and technology transfer for smallholder farmers, value chain development, policy analysis and outreach to host country senior government decision makers and capacity building of local staff. Duncan received his BSc and MSc from the University of Reading in the United Kingdom and his PhD at Michigan State University.

Carlo Cafiero is a senior economist and statistician at the FAO in Rome, Italy, where he leads the team in charge of producing food security and nutrition statistics at global, regional and country levels. He is also FAO focal point for the indicators used to monitor SDG Target 2.1. He previously taught statistics and agricultural economics and policy at the Graduate School of Agriculture of the University of Naples Federico II, Italy. His research interests have spanned risk management in agriculture, the econometrics of storable commodity prices and measurement issues in the fields of food security and nutrition. He received a PhD in agricultural and natural resource economics from the University of California at Berkeley, a Doctoral degree in agricultural policy from the University of Naples Federico II, Italy and a MS in agricultural economics from the University of Arizona.

Filippo Fossi is a food security analyst with 20 years of experience in Africa, Asia and Latin America. He worked for FAO, WFP, donors and international NGOs, in project coordination and vulnerability analysis. He carried out a number of risk assessments, food security analysis, programme designs and evaluations. He currently lives in South Africa, where he is a FEWS NET consultant for Southern Africa and is PhD candidate at the University of Pretoria.

Chelsea Graham is Knowledge Manager for Airbel, Innovation Center at the International Rescue Committee in NYC, USA. She worked for the World Food Programme in Rome from 2013 to 2018, with assignments in countries such as Afghanistan, Rwanda and Mozambique. Her final position with the WFP was Programme Policy Officer with the Food Systems Service, where she worked on World Food Assistance papers from 2018 and 2017, as well as key policy and strategy document. She holds an MSc in Sociology from the London School of Economics and Political Science and a BA in Communications from the American University of Rome.

Francette Gouws is a pupil advocate with the KwaZulu-Natal Society of Advocates (Durban) and part-time researcher at the Institute for Food, Nutrition and Well-being, University of Pretoria. She holds a BCom LLB LLM (International Law) from the University of Pretoria. Her fields of specialisation include international law, constitutional law; general litigation; commercial law and policy and legal research, review and drafting.

Steven Haggblade is Professor of International Development in the Department of Agricultural, Food and Resource Economics at Michigan State University, East Lansing, USA. He has worked overseas for most of his career, holding long-term assignments in Botswana, Bangladesh, Cameroon, Madagascar and Zambia. His professional research and publications have focused on agricultural and rural development policies, including extensive work on value chains and the rural nonfarm economy. His long-term advisory and research assignments abroad working on agricultural policy issues and reform agendas has contributed to the development of the Kaleidoscope Model of policy change.

Michael Roberto Kenyi Legge is a FAO Consultant in Juba, South Sudan. He holds a BScAgric (Genetics) and MSc in Food Security. He is a PhD candidate at the Institute of Peace, Development and Security Studies, University of Juba, South Sudan. Michael has a wide experience in agriculture, food security and nutrition policy development, planning, programme design, monitoring and evaluation. He maintains excellent institutional relations with the international development partners on matters related to resource mobilisation, governance, accountability and coordination mechanisms of food security and nutrition.

Carol Kalafatic is an Honorary Research Fellow at the Centre for Agroecology, Water and Resilience, Coventry University, UK. Since 1991, she has worked as an educator and policy advocate with Indigenous Peoples. She served two terms on the High Level Panel of Experts on Food Security and Nutrition (one term as Vice-Chair). She has served as Associate Director, Cornell University's American Indian

xxii List of contributors

Program; Founding coordinator Right to Food Program; International Indian Treaty Council; Coordinator of the Indigenous Peoples' Caucus at UN Commission on Sustainable Development; and Indigenous Peoples' Focal Point of the International Planning Committee for Food Sovereignty. Carol was the lead author of the framework for the UN FAO *Policy on Indigenous and Tribal Peoples* and Indigenous and Tribal Peoples: Building on Biological and Cultural Diversity for Food and Livelihood Security. She currently works with communities in Alaska and the Yukon to protect wild salmon.

Boaz B. Keizire holds an MSc in Agricultural Economics and a BSc in Economics from Makerere University, Uganda, and a Diploma in Fisheries Policy, Planning and Management from United Nations University, Iceland. Boaz has spent over 15 years working in the areas of Agriculture and Natural Resource Policy, Planning and Analysis and Rural Development. Previously he worked as a Head of Agriculture and Food Security and Team Leader CAADP at the African Union Commission in Ethiopia and Head of Agriculture and Natural Resource Planning, at the National Planning Authority in Uganda and Principal Economist in Uganda. Boaz has been instrumental in using country specific models and examples to change the quality of leadership of CAADP at the African Union Commission.

Kaija Korpi-Salmela is a Food Security Specialist with the Food and Agriculture Organisation (FAO) and is based in Tampere, Finland. She has worked on food security and vulnerability analysis for the past 15 years, initially in Eastern and Central Africa, and later on, globally. Since 2012 she has worked on the global Integrated Food Security Phase Classification (IPC) initiative with an emphasis on technical development of the IPC classification system and the three types of IPC classifications (IPC Acute Food Insecurity, IPC Chronic Food Insecurity, and IPC Acute Malnutrition Classification).

Lailà Lokosang is an Advisor for Food and Nutrition Security to the African Union's Comprehensive Africa Agriculture Development Programme (CAADP). He was Director for Monitoring and Evaluation, National Bureau of Statistics, South Sudan (2007–2011). Lailà has held several positions in the management of information systems, community health, livelihoods surveillance and disaster risk analysis in Sudan and Malawi. He holds a PhD in Statistics, MSc in Food Security and BSc in Statistics and Demography. He was the Founding President of Medical Informatics Association of Malawi (2005–2006) and is the Co-Chair of the EU–AU Working Group on Food Security and Sustainable Agriculture of the EU–AU Research and Innovation Partnership (from 2007).

Jose Lopez is a senior programme manager and food security analyst at the Food and Agriculture Organisation of the United Nations (FAO) in Rome, Italy, where he leads the Integrated Food Security Phase Classification (IPC) Global Support Unit. He has over 20 years work experience in humanitarian and food security programming and food security and nutrition analysis in East, West, central Africa and Central Asia. Prior to joining the IPC initiative, he was FAO Resilience Coordinator for Eastern Africa Sub-Region, supporting evidence-based decision making through resilience, food security and nutrition analysis. As Regional Food Security Adviser for ECHO in East and Central Africa, Jose has also provided technical assistance to countries in designing food assistance strategies and responses. He holds a PhD in Molecular Biology and a Masters in Biochemistry and Nutrition.

Nosipho Mabuza is a Research Assistant with the Institute for Food, Nutrition and Well-being and a PhD candidate in the Department of Agricultural Economics, Extension and Rural Development at the University of Pretoria, South Africa. Her research interests focus on public agriculture investment, food security policy analysis and monitoring and evaluation. Most recently, she has been involved in the assessment of the policy landscapes, institutional coordination structures and monitoring and evaluation frameworks of 11 African national agriculture and food security and nutrition investment plans (NAIPs) to determine if these can support or constrain progress. These studies were carried out as part of the USAID's Feed the Future Food Security Policy Innovation Lab.

Moraka N. Makhura is a Senior Lecturer focusing on Agriculture, Rural & Economic Development at the University of Pretoria, South Africa. He was project Team Leader for the Committee on World Food Securitys High Level Panel of Experts report on *Multi-stakeholder partnerships to finance and improve food security and nutrition in the framework of the 2030 Agenda*. He is Director of Makhureng One Company. He has served at the Land Bank, the Development Bank of Southern Africa (DBSA) and the Limpopo Department of Agriculture. He has a PhD in Agricultural Economics. Makhura has served as the President of Agricultural Economics Association of SA (AEASA), and as a member of several Boards and Committees.

Bongeka Mdleleni is a Deputy Director responsible for African Multilateral Relations in the South African Department of Agriculture, Forestry and Fisheries. She is also a Comprehensive African Agriculture Development Programme (CAADP) Focal point for South Africa. Among her responsibilities she has coordinated South Africa's review of on-going agricultural development efforts in preparation of the domestication of CAADP and coordinated the preparation of South Africa's Biennale Review report on the progress made in implementing the 2014 Malabo Declaration. She holds a Masters of Business Leadership from the University of South Africa.

Angela M. McIntyre is a Researcher with the Institute of Food, Nutrition and well-being at the University of Pretoria. She has 25 years of policy, program and research experience in food security, public health, peace and security. She has worked with community-based organisations, governments and United Nations agencies, development partners and post-secondary learning institutions in sub-Saharan Africa and North America. Angela holds a Bachelor of Arts in Anthropology (Winnipeg), a Master of

xxiv List of contributors

Public Health (Liverpool) and a Masters of Science in Environmental Management (London). She currently works as a senior health promotion specialist at the First Nations Health Authority in British Columbia, Canada, supporting Indigenous community-led food security and chronic disease prevention initiatives.

Elizabeth Mkandawire is a Postdoctoral Fellow and Coordinator of the UN Academic Impact Hub for SDG2 at the Institute for Food, Nutrition and Well-being, University of Pretoria, South Africa. Her research experience and publications have focused on gender and food security policy analysis. She has been involved in supporting the development of National Agriculture Investment Plans in several African countries and has made significant contributions to policy processes in Malawi.

Lorenzo Motta is a Research and Analytics Consultant for the Food Systems Unit at the United Nations World Food Programme (WFP) in Rome, Italy, which he joined in 2016. He has consulted in Thailand for the United Nations Economic and Social Commission for Asia and the Pacific (UN ESCAP), and has carried out research for the Global Engagement and Research division with the International Fund for Agricultural Development (IFAD). He holds a MSc in Economics and Management of Government and International Organisations and a BSc in Economics from Bocconi University.

Rufaro Musvaire is a nutritionist with the World Food Programme based in the Regional Bureau for Southern Africa in Johannesburg. She specialises in nutrition in emergency contexts. Prior to this, Rufaro was with UNICEF Somalia where she supported nutrition monitoring and capacity strengthening for government and partners. She also has a background in development nutrition with a keen interest in nutrition-sensitive programming, specifically strengthening the response to malnutrition and food insecurity through proven, sustainable, home-grown solutions. She holds a MSc in Food Security from the University of KwaZulu-Natal, South Africa and a BSc Honours in Human Nutrition (with distinction) from Massey University, New Zealand. She is currently enrolled for a Masters in Public Health with the University of the Western Cape, South Africa.

Steven Were Omamo has been the World Food Programme (WFP) Country Representative for Ethiopia, since 1 July 2018. Prior to this, he held many crucial positions in WFP including being WFP Deputy Director for Policy and Programmes and Coordinator of Food Systems Strategy in Rome; WFP Representative to the African Union and UN Economic Commission for Africa in Addis Ababa; Chief of Food Security and Safety Nets; and Strategy Chief of Social Protection and Livelihoods. Omamo has also served (amongst other appointments) as IFAD Director of Global Engagement and Research; AGRA Director of Policy and Advocacy; Senior Research Fellow with IFPRI. He holds a PhD and MSc in Agricultural Economics, a MA in International Development Policy and a BSc in Agribusiness.

Hunadi Mapula Nkwana is a Senior Lecturer in the Department of Public Management and Administration at the University of Pretoria, South Africa. She teaches and supervises in Public Administration, Public Policy and Public Management. She completed a PhD in Public Administration in 2016 entitled: *A multisectoral public policy framework for food security in South Africa*. She is an active researcher in the areas of leadership development and food security. She has also been a facilitator and coach for the Young African Leadership Initiative (Public Management Track). She is an active peer reviewer for the *African Journal of Public Affairs* and *Administratio Publica*.

Nic J.J. Olivier is Professor Extraordinary at North West University and senior part-time consultant researcher at the Institute for Food, Nutrition and Well-being, University of Pretoria. He was visiting Professor at the Universities of Leiden and Fribourg (Switzerland), and EU Erasmus Mundus visiting Professor at Ghent. His fields of specialisation include sustainable development; international, human rights and constitutional law; governance; transformative policy, strategic and programme-level management; policy analysis; legal drafting and electronic databases of food security and nutrition documentation. He has completed various consultancies for various agencies including governments and the World Bank, UNDP, UNICEF, OHCHR and FAO.

Nico J.J. Olivier is a policy analyst based in the Garden Route, South Africa. He specialises in policy development, analysis and review within the broader rural development, land reform, agriculture and food security and nutrition sphere. In recent years he has been involved in several projects to establish electronic databases of sector-specific policy and legislative instruments, and to utilise technology to extract and analyse information from such databases.

Leila Oliveira works for the Food and Agriculture Organisation as the coordinator for the technical development of the Integrated Food Security Phase Classification (IPC). She chairs the multi-agency IPC Technical Advisory and Working Groups and leads the development of IPC protocols and technical manuals. Leila has been conducting food security analysis since 2001 in Southern Africa, Eastern and Central Africa, Latin America and Asia. She has worked with the World Food Programme, the Famine Early Warning System Network and various international non-governmental organisations, including Save the Children, Care and World Vision. Leila holds a Masters in International Development from Tulane University in the USA.

Beulah Pretorius is a Research Consultant at the Department of Animal and Wildlife Sciences and Extraordinary Lecturer at the School of Health Systems and Public Health at the University of Pretoria, South Africa. She holds a MSc in Biochemistry and PhD in Human Nutrition. She is a member of the South African Codex Committee on Nutrition and Foods for Special Dietary Uses, the South

xxvi List of contributors

African Consultative Working Group on Micronutrient Control Interventions and the Technical Working Group Food Based Dietary Guidelines. Her research interest is nutrient quantity, quality and bioavailability in human nutrition.

Danielle Resnick is a Senior Research Fellow and Governance Theme Leader with IFPRI, Washington, DC, USA. She focuses on the political economy of development, decentralisation and agricultural policy processes. She has published a number of books on these topics. She serves on the lead expert group of the Global Panel on Agricultural Food Systems and Nutrition (GloPan) and on the editorial boards of the journals Populism and Regional and Federal Studies. She previously held positions at the United Nations University-World Institute for Development Economics Research (UNU-WIDER), Finland and consulted for Oxford Analytica and the World Bank.

Luca Russo works at FAO as a Senior Food Crises Analyst and the Strategic Adviser in the Management Team tasked with overall implementation of the FAO Strategic Programme on Resilience, where he leads major food security and resilience related analytical works such as the Food Security Phase Classification (IPC), Early Warning for Early Action (EWEA) and the Resilience Index for Measurement and Analysis (RIMA) which are particularly relevant to evidence based policy making. Russo is an agricultural economist with extensive experience, particularly in Africa. His main area of expertise is food security and resilience in protracted crises and related policy and analytical frameworks. He has published extensively on the topic.

Hettie C. Schönfeldt is a Professor in the Department of Animal and Wildlife Sciences, Chair of the Department of Science and Technology and National Research Foundation of South Africa in Nutrition and Food Security and Director of the African Research Universities Alliance (ARUA) Centre of Excellence for Food Security led by the University of Pretoria, South Africa. Her research focuses on linking nutrient quantity and quality of foods to sustainable food systems for attaining nutrition and food security for all. Since the inception of her career she has published 83 scientific, peer-reviewed publications, 30 books or chapters in books and authored or co-authored 168 technical research reports.

Jeanette Sprinkhuizen is a Sector Expert for Rural Economy at the Department of Planning, Monitoring and Evaluation, in Pretoria, South Africa, managing and facilitating the implementation of the Delivery agreement on "Vibrant, Equitable and sustainable rural communities contributing towards food security for all". She has extensive experience in rural development, agricultural and land-related policies, and agricultural training and skills development, review of sector specific projects and processes, reports and policy analysis in enhancing of Government priorities.

Duncan Stewart was born into a farming family in the Valley of a Thousand Hills near Durban, South Africa. The farm boarded a large community settlement and soon realised that he was born into privilege and that his friends around him were relatively disadvantaged. This motivated his vision for more equal society. He completed an MSc in Agricultural Economics. He worked for the KwaZulu Department of Agriculture for a period of eight years starting off in small holder extension and ending up as Head of Agricultural Economics. In 1989 he founded the Lima Rural Development Foundation as an integrated community organisation. Lima leverages investor funding into poor rural communities and embeds qualified field workers in these communities on a long-term basis. Lima works across a wide range of disciplines and sectors and with 130 staff, is one of the largest rural development organisations in the country.

LIST OF ACRONYMS AND ABBREVIATIONS

AAAA	Addis Ababa Action Agenda
AGRA	A Green Revolution in Africa
AIDS	Acquired Immunodeficiency Disease Syndrome
AU	African Union
CCHIP	Community Childhood Hunger Index Programme
CFS	Committee on World Food Security
CGIAR	Consortium of International Agricultural Research Centres
COP 21	21st Conference of Parties of the United Nations Framework Convention on Climate Change
CSI	Coping Strategies Index
CSO	Civil Society Organisation
DFiD	United Kingdom Department for International Development
EBIA	Escala Brasileira de Insegurança Alimentar
EBPC	Evidence-based Policy Collaboration
EBSF	Evidence-based Food Security measures
ECOWAS	Economic Community of West African States
ELCSA	Escala Latinoamericana y Caribena de Seguridad Alimentaria
EMSA	Escala Mexicana de Seguridad Alimentaria
FAFS	Framework for African Food Security
FAO	Food and Agriculture Organisation of the United Nations
FBS	Food Balance Sheets
FEWS NET	Food Early Warning System Network
FHI360	Family Health International
FPIC	Free prior informed consent
GDP	Gross Domestic Product
GIEWS	Global Information and Early Warning Systems
GloPAN	Global Panel for Agriculture and Nutrition

HEA	Household Economy Approach
HFSSM	Household Food Security Survey Model
HHFIAS	Household Food Insecurity Access Scale
HHS	Household Hunger Scale
HIV	Human Immunodeficiency Virus
HLPE	High Level Panel on Food Security and Nutrition
IAASTD	International Assessment of Agricultural Knowledge, Science and Technology for Development
IFPRI	International Food Policy Research Institute
IOM	International Organisation for Migration
IPC	Integrated Food Security Phase Classification
ISECR	International Covenant on Economic, Social and Cultural Rights
ISPD4D	Integrated Sustainable Partnerships for Development
KM	Kaleidoscope Model
MDD-C	Minimum Dietary Diversity for Children
MDD-W	Minimum Dietary Diversity for Women
MDG	Millennium Development Goal
MTSF	Medium-term Strategic Framework
N.A.	Not applicable
NCDs	Non-communicable Diseases
NEPAD	New Partnership for Africa's Development
NGDSs	National Growth and Development Strategy
NGOs	Non-governmental Organisations
OECD	Organisation for Economic Cooperation and Development
PoU	Population Undernourished
PPP	Public Private Partmentship
rCSI	Reduced Coping strategies Index
ReSAKSS	Regional Strategic Analysis and Knowledge Support System
SDGs	Sustainable Development Goals
SEAGA	Socioeconomic and Gender Analysis
SUN	Scaling Up Nutrition
ToC	Theory of Change
UN	United Nations
UNCCD	United Nations Convention to Combat Desertification
UNCED	United Nations Conference on Environment and Development
UNDP	United Nations Development Programme
UNDRIP	United Nations Rights of Indigenous Peoples
UNDRO	United Nations Disaster Relief
UNECA	United Nations Economic Commission for Africa
UNESCO	United Nations Educational Scientific and Cultural Organisation
UNGA	United Nations General Assembly
UNHCR	United Nations High Commission for Refugees
UNHCR	United Nations Higher Commissioner on Refugees
UNISDR	United Nations Office for Disaster Risk Reduction

xxx List of acronyms and abbreviations

UNSC	United Nations Security Council
USA	United States of America
USAID	United States Agency for International Development
USDA	Unites States Department of Agriculture
VAM	Vulnerability Analysis and Mapping
WDDS	Women's Minimum Dietary Diversity Score
WEF	World Economic Forum
WFP	World Food Program
WHO	World Health Organisation
WTO	World Trade Organisation

FOREWORD

The effects of food and nutrition insecurity can be devastating, not just physically but, perhaps at least equally, psychologically. The struggle of a father or mother going to bed with the angst of not knowing how to react to the look of their children when they wake the next morning hoping to put some food into their stomachs. Or that of a woman who puts an empty pot of boiling water on a smoky pile of slowly burning wood to fake cooking a meal in order to distract the little ones while hoping for a miracle during the course of the day. This is the kind of life that can hardly be imagined by someone who has not gone through the same experience. But one does not have to go that far to reach the conviction that the current level of hunger and malnutrition in the world and the burden of suffering involved should not be acceptable to anyone. It is certainly not to the editor and contributing authors of this excellent volume.

African leaders in the agenda 2063 and, in particular, the Malabo Declaration on Agricultural Growth and Transformation for Shared Prosperity and Improved Livelihoods as well as the global community through the Sustainable Development Goals have signalled a shared determination to act. Current level of resources should allow for much better food and nutrition security outcomes globally, in particular in Africa which accounts for the largest share of food insecure but which, over the last two decades, has undergone the longest sustained period of rapid economic growth in its history.

Solutions are admittedly not simple, otherwise they would have been found. The root causes of food and nutrition insecurity can be complex: who is affected, when, where and why can vary significantly over time and across geographies. Success in the fight to confront hunger and malnutrition requires one to undertake the right action on many fronts. This includes the correct identification of the chronically vulnerable who may be one crisis away from descending into chaos. Equally important is having a solid grasp of: the factors underlying their vulnerability, the resources they depend on for their livelihoods, possible interventions to make them more productive on their journey towards self-sufficiency. While figuring all that out and taking the necessary action, one needs to deal with the short and medium-term challenge of providing effective safety net protection when crisis strikes and catch those before they get into a viscous cycle of shocks, asset depletion and worsening vulnerability.

The present volume is an impressive resource for anyone facing the above challenges. It offers extensive guidance for state as well as non-state actors and global and local organisations alike.

It has assembled in one place a vast body of evidence and experience in the fight for human dignity through freedom of hunger and malnutrition. It should be a reference guide on the desk, shelf or box of everyone working to turn into reality the dream of one day making food and nutrition security a reality for everyone.

Ousmane Badiane
Director for Africa
International Food Policy Research Institute

PART I

The fundamentals of food security policy assessment in the era of the SDGs

1

FOOD SECURITY POLICY ANALYSIS AS A KEY ELEMENT IN ATTAINING SGD2 AND ADDRESSING FOOD POLICY FAILURES OF THE PAST

Sheryl L. Hendriks

1.1 Food insecurity – a global challenge

Food insecurity is one of the greatest challenges of our time. It is a complex concept, describing the deprivation of people from vulnerable groups across the globe. It exists in every country – not only in developing and poor countries, but even in the wealthy nations of the world. Our understanding of its causes is generally well grounded in scores of assessments conducted across the globe since the 1940s when the concept first emerged. However, the complex tangle of direct and indirect causes confounds our efforts to propose solutions (Hendriks 2015). While some progress has been made on some aspects of food insecurity, we have yet to find appropriate comprehensive and sustainable solutions.

Past efforts to intervene through public policy and community level efforts have typically been sectoral approaches. The Sustainable Development Goal (SDGs) era offers some hope to driving integrated and sustainable solutions to problems such as food insecurity. Rather than focusing on developing countries alone, the SGDs are universal, applying to all countries and calling on us to ensure that 'no one is left behind' by development and progress. The SDGs come with a set of strong accountability principles for nations to work together to solving the critical issues of our time. Food insecurity is one of these issues.

Food security first emerged as a concept in the 1940s and is now is now widely used in designing, implementing and evaluating humanitarian emergency and development policies and programs. Food security is a central concern of every government – in the developed and developing world. Moreover, due to the nature of our globalized world, the actions of a single country or a region (such as Europe, Africa, South Asia, etc.) affect the food security of people in other countries, regions or the world. Disasters in one area affect food supply and demand in other geographical locations.

4 Sheryl L. Hendriks

Food security is defined as the situation where "all people, at all times, have physical and economic access to sufficient, safe and nutritious food to meet their dietary needs and food preferences for an active healthy life" (CFS 2012 as per the Food and Agricultural Organisation of the United Nations (FAO) 1996 definition). The concept includes four interrelated elements, namely availability, access, utilization (nutrition) and stability (resilience). The first three – availability, access and utilization – are hierarchical in nature: food availability is necessary but not sufficient for access, and access is necessary but not sufficient for utilization (Webb et al. 2006). However, all three dimensions depend on stable availability, access to food supplies and the resources to acquire adequate food to meet the nutritional needs of all household members throughout their life cycle (Hendriks 2015).

1.2 The SDGs give us an opportunity to act multisectorally

Overcoming food insecurity and improving nutrition requires comprehensive policies, legislation, programmes, service delivery and monitoring. Most countries have a plethora of policies, strategies and programmes broadly addressing food security. Some have specific food security policies. Others have sectoral food security policies (e.g. Nigeria's Agriculture Sector Food Security Policy). However, often a national vision for food security is lacking. Very few countries have comprehensive, consolidated, results-oriented action plans.

Yet, all 17 SGDs contain elements of food security-related indicators and principles. This offers an opportunity to integrate efforts to address the causes, mitigate the consequences and write food security impacts into the core accountability systems of national and global governance systems. This offers some promising opportunities to turn the tide of deprivation, break the cycle of undernourishment and tackle overweight issues. To take advantage of this moment, we need the human capacity for food security policy analysis, evaluation and impact assessment.

Currently, there is a lack of policy coherence. Fragmentation in the regulatory system and lack of harmonized policies, legislation and approaches of stakeholders (e.g. trade benefits vs health benefits) hinders implementation. No coordinating structure/body provides appropriate leadership and authority to reduce duplication and ensure efficient use of constrained resources. There is often lack of clarity on roles and responsibilities leading to a lack of accountability. Often there is no comprehensive national monitoring and evaluation framework and set of agreed upon indicators to determine if programmes are making an impact. Many countries do not have a single information system to provide comprehensive data for decision-making.

In addition, implementation capacity at all levels is often weak (especially with regard to community-based interventions and inter-sectoral coordination). There are leakages, bottlenecks and a lack of quality assurance in delivery. Coverage with regard to agricultural programmes, nutrition and social services is uneven and the neediest are often not able to access essential services and support. Human capacity is often lacking in many areas, especially with regard to community-based interventions. Referral systems across departments are lacking, resulting in mismanagement, leakages and duplication of services. This leads to inclusion and exclusion errors in targeting and in cases of severe undernutrition, contributes to increased mortality among infants.

Without comprehensive policies and strong institutions to coordinate and manage food security at the national and sub-national levels, governments and states are unlikely to make significant and rapid progress towards the SDGs (Hendriks and Covic 2016). As we know well, food security is a complex concept, requiring a comprehensive policy framework and leadership coordination that creates coherence in policy and actions across multiple sectors and levels (Hendriks and Covic 2016). While much can be done to improve food security through local initiatives and projects, it is most unlikely that a national-scale programme will succeed without strong leadership and visible signals of commitment from the highest levels in government (Malabo Montpellier Panel, 2017). Food security and nutrition need to be positioned as priorities at the highest level of governance within an integral element of funded comprehensive growth and development strategies (Hendriks and Covic 2016).

Recent increased interest in public policy influence and mutual accountability has given rise to the term 'evidence-based policymaking'. An increased availability of public data bases, renewed investments in policy research and a growing focus on results-based development (such as in the SGDs) enable the evaluation of whether public investments are achieving their intended outcomes (EBPC, 2016).

In sum, ensuring food security at the national level typically requires the following elements:

i Strong leadership at all levels of governance and society
ii Policy reform and alignment to ensure that food security is part of a prioritized policy agenda and framework that seeks to attain the state's various obligations and commitments while at the same time achieving national development objectives
iii Creating and strengthening institutional and policy environments that enable multi-sectoral support of food security as well as nutrition and health goals.
iv Establishment of strong institutional structures to coordinate efforts and ensure that existing resources in agriculture, social protection, education, water and sanitation are leveraged to deliver high impact interventions at scale. This is usually more effective when located at the highest level of government.
v Institutional arrangements for mutual accountability that bring together the various actors within government, the private sector and civil society.
vi Evidence to support the policymaking cycle, the identification of alternative policy options and the selection of the most appropriate choices among these alternatives.
vii Independent platforms for dialogue and engagement on emerging issues in the global, continental and national food security and nutrition domain.

6 Sheryl L. Hendriks

1.3 Do we have the capacity to face the challenge?

There is no traditional field of study for food security. Due to the complexity of the concept, food security policy, evaluation and analysis requires the collective thinking of professionals from a range of traditional disciplines: agriculture, agricultural economics, economics, geography, rural development, nutrition, public health and public administration. One of the major constraints to comprehensive agriculture, food security and nutrition policy making is that the different sectors speak past each other, struggling to connect and grappling with conceptualization of complexity. Where officials are not up to date with current developments in the field, this creates increased frustration. Getting professionals from such a range of disciplines to work together is challenging. Food security policy, evaluation and analysis requires a transdisciplinary approach.

Transdisciplinarity is an emerging science that offers innovative methodologies for high-impact science through understanding and taking action on complex societal problems that can no longer be approached and solved by mono-disciplinary approaches only (Regeer and Bunders 2008; Lang et al. 2012). It adopts the integration of theoretical and methodological perspectives of multiple disciplines to generate novel conceptual and empirical analysis that transcends discipline perspectives and moves between, across and beyond traditional disciplines (Holistic Education Network of Tasmania 2011). Transdisciplinarity produces new knowledge with, rather than for society.

Food security training, therefore, demands a radically different approach to teaching, learning and researching than traditionally happens in institutions of higher learning and research. It demands a sound grounding in traditional science and teamwork that includes pure, natural and social sciences working to solve critical and complex issues.

There is an urgent needed to scale up the capacity necessary to meet the increasing demand for food security policy, evaluation and analysis. This book seeks to provide a much-needed go-to resource to address a significant gap in rigorous policy analysis, equip future professionals and bring the current cadre of development practitioners up to speed with the tools to undertake rigorous policy analysis in the era of evidence-based and impact-driven planning demanded by the SDGs and the new era of mutual accountability. It is deliberately pitched at the graduate level to ensure that a sound undergraduate specialization is broadened to allow for transdisciplinary understandings of complexity.

1.4 Aim and purpose of the book

This book seeks to build a sound theoretical basis for evidence-based food security planning, monitoring and evaluation to strengthen university-level and professional development training on the fundamental understanding of food security policy analysis; essential elements to ensure sound policies and the appropriate measures to evaluate the impact of actions aimed at attaining SDG2 in particular. It attempts to address a significant gap in comprehensive policy analysis and seeks to build the capacity of a cadre of professionals equipped with the tools to undertake rigorous policy analysis in the era of evidence-based planning and impact-driven action through the SDGs in the new era of mutual accountability.

The content is relevant to a range of professionals including:

- Food security policy analysis professions
- Graduate student training and research in the disciplines of agriculture, agricultural economics, economics, geography, rural development, nutrition, public health and public administration
- Public sector professionals across the domains of agriculture, health, nutrition, social welfare and trade
- Multinational agency staff
- Humanitarian aid agency and NGOs staff
- Development planners and public administration units
- Monitoring and evaluation professionals.

1.5 Outline of the book

The book is presented in four parts. The chapters in Part 1 cover the core elements of food security policy, including elements related to improving the availability and access to food, malnutrition (under nutrition, micronutrients as well as overweight and obesity) and food system resilience. Each section will present the pressing contemporary issues, reasons for policy failure and imperatives for policy reform. Recent developments in the understanding of these policy issues will be provided including food systems, nutrition transitions, conflict, migration and resilience. Part 2 includes chapters related to the stages in food security policy analysis. Each of these chapters provides the theoretical underpinnings; offering practical guidance for qualitative and quantitative analysis, suggestions for tools, techniques and approaches to develop the know-how related to identify appropriate indicators for monitoring and evaluating the effectiveness of implementing food security programmes. Part 3 provides an indicator toolkit to improve monitoring and evaluation as well as mutual accountability. Part four presents an overview of institutional elements, including information system design and institutional arrangements for coordination and governance.

References

CFS (Committee on World Food Security) (2012) 'Coming to terms with terminology', Report of the 39th session of the Committee on World Food Security (CFS), 15–20 October, CFS at Rome.

Covic, N. and Hendriks, S.L. (2016). 'Introduction: The road to healthier diets and optimal nutrition', in: N. Covic and S. Hendriks (eds) *Achieving a nutrition revolution for Africa: The road to healthier diets and optimal nutrition*. ReSAKSS Annual Trends and

Outlook Report 2016, International Food Policy Research Institute (IFPRI), Washington DC, pp. 1–5.

Evidence-based Policymaking Collaboration (EBPC) (2016) 'Principles of evidence-based policymaking', http://www.evidencecollaborative.org/principles-evidence-based-policymaking

FAO (1996) 'Rome declaration on World Food Security and World Food Summit plan of action', World Food Summit 13–17 November 1996, FAO, Rome.

Hendriks, S. and Covic, N. (2016) 'Summary and policy recommendations: Toward a nutrition revolution for Africa', in: N. Covic and S. Hendriks (eds) *Achieving a nutrition revolution for Africa: The road to healthier diets and optimal nutrition*. ReSAKSS Annual Trends and Outlook Report 2016, International Food Policy Research Institute (IFPRI), Washington DC, pp. 179–184.

Hendriks, S.L. (2015) 'The food security continuum: A novel tool for understanding food insecurity as a range of experiences', *Food Security*, vol. 7, no. 3, pp. 609–619.

Holistic Education Network of Tasmania, Australia (2011) 'Transdisciplinary inquiry incorporating holistic principles', http://www.hent.org/transdisciplinary.

Lang, D.J., Wiek, A., Bergmann, M., Stauffacher, M., Martens, P., Moll, P., Swilling, M., and Thoms, C.J. (2012). 'Transdisciplinary research in sustainability science: practice, principles, and challenges', *Sustainability Science* 7(Suppl 1), pp. 25–43.

Malabo Montpellier Panel (2017). *Nourished: How Africa CAN BUILD A FUTURE FREE FROM HUNGER AND MALNUTRITION*. Malabo Montpellier Panel, Dakar.

Regeer, B. and Bunders, J. (2008) 'Knowledge co-creation: interaction between science and society', http://www.treccafrica.com/assets/Bunders%20and%20Regeer%20(2009)%20Knowledge%20Co-Creation.pdf.

Webb, P., Coates, J., Frongillo, E. A., Lorge Rogers, B., Swindale, A. and Bilinsky, P. (2006) 'Measuring household food insecurity: Why it's so important and yet so difficult to do', *Journal of Nutrition*, vol. 136, no. 5, pp. 1404–1408.

2

HOW THE UNDERSTANDING OF FOOD SECURITY AND NUTRITION SHAPES POLICY ANALYSIS

Sheryl L. Hendriks

2.1 Introduction

The current lack of consensus on the relationships between hunger, malnutrition and food insecurity frustrates efforts to design good policies and programs (Hendriks 2015) as well as the design of research programmes. Yet, how we understand and define food insecurity determines how we develop policies, establish targets for their assessment, measure progress and evaluate progress towards policy goals (Hendriks and Drimie 2011; Coates 2013; Candel 2014) as well as guiding research programme design.

Despite numerous attempts during the 1990s to develop definitive tools (see Hendriks 2005; Headey and Ecker 2013 for reviews of these), measuring food insecurity still evades simplification (Hendriks 2015). The complexity of the problem is understood through investigations of the causes, underlying determinants and experiences of those affected by international and localised crises.

These crises range from international food shortages, famines, price shocks and volatility, conflict and large-scale migration to climate change. These events have shaken the foundations of many widely accepted theories and assumptions related to food security causes and outcomes. For example, the global food price crisis of 2007/8 challenged the notion that the price of staple grains was inelastic. With inelastic commodities, consumers will only increase their consumption up to a point and then diversify consumption into other commodities or goods. In the case of staple grains, for example, human and animal consumption capacity was thought to impose a limit. However, the rapid development of biofuels produced from food stock, changed this in terms of foods such as maize, for which demand became infinitely elastic, driving up food prices (HLPE, 2013). The 2007/8 global crisis saw food and fuel prices moving upwards at the same pace, creating new complexity in our understanding food security when faced with changing market and price dynamics at a global scale. The crisis reached the most remote communities across the globe.

10 Sheryl L. Hendriks

A solid foundation of terminology is essential for a number of reasons. First, it is imperative that we know what we are measuring in food security analysis. Sound research requires a clear statement of purpose and objectives (Hendriks 2015). Second, it is important to know what aspect of food security we are dealing with or attempting to change as this informs the indicators, tools and analysis to be used. Third, it is important to understand the pathways and influences of policy. As food security is a broad and complex issue and only one part of national development policy, a plethora of other policies and programmes affect food security contexts, outcomes and impacts (Fan 2018, p. 8). Understanding these helps identify the possible reach of a particular policy or programme. Fourth, food security is a cross-cutting issue, requiring the engagement of various sectors in government and interaction of various academic disciplines (Hendriks 2018). Different government sectors and academic disciplines may differ in their understanding of the concept. Moreover, the plurality of our backgrounds (agronomy, economics, sociology, health, nutrition, among others) influences our understanding of what causes food insecurity and consequently of what we must do to deal with it. A policy analyst should be able to establish a common understanding among team members (Hendriks 2018).

2.2 Food security terminology

Food security is defined by the 1996 World Food Summit definition as existing "when all people at all times have physical, social and economic access to food, which is safe and consumed in sufficient quantity and quality to meet their dietary needs and food preferences allowing for a healthy and active life" (FAO 1996). The definition includes both food security and malnutrition, both forms of deprivation. While food insecurity is experienced at national, community and household level, malnutrition is experienced at an individual level as nutrient requirements are individually determined and depend on, among other things, the sex and age of each individual.

Often the terms food security and nutrition security are used in different combinations, including 'food security', 'nutrition security', 'food security and nutrition' and 'food and nutrition security'. Moreover, these terms are often used interchangeably. The term nutrition security emerged in the mid-1990s after the publication of the UNICEF's Conceptual Framework for Child Under Nutrition (UNICEF 1990). Often, this framework for child under nutrition is misinterpreted as a framework for food security. The framework defined nutrition security as adequate nutritional status in terms of protein, energy, vitamins and minerals for all household members at all times (UNICEF 1990).

While the broad definition of food security embodies key determinants of good nutrition, the term "*food security and nutrition*" is sometimes used as a way to combine the two concepts, emphasising the food availability, access and stability dimensions of food security. While

> *food and nutrition security* exists when all people at all times have physical, social and economic access to food, which is safe and consumed in sufficient quantity

and quality to meet their dietary needs and food preferences, *and is supported by an environment of adequate sanitation, health services and care,* allowing for a healthy and active life.

(CFS 2012, para 33)

However, much of the clarity of the definition is lost in the translation of the concept into different languages. In translations into vernacular, the concept may require an explanation rather than being translated directly into equivalent terms. This demands precision and clarity in the mind of the analyst or researcher at the point of translation.

Conflating food security and nutrition into 'food and nutrition security', has negative consequences for the design of essential comprehensive food security policies and programmes and the design of integrated monitoring and evaluation systems critical for the monitoring of SDG-related development progress. The SDGs are careful not to conflate food security and nutrition security. SDG two calls us to end hunger, achieve food security, improve nutrition and promote sustainable agriculture (UNGA 2016).

2.3 The four core elements of food security

For many policy makers, community members and survey respondents, these terms are still unclear. It is important for a food security analyst to understand the foundational elements of food security. Food security is achieved when households are able to access (through production or purchasing) enough food to meet their daily nutritional requirements. Food security includes four elements, namely: availability, access, nutrition (termed utilization in the original definition), and stability of supply (or resilience). The foundational definition from the 1996 World Food Summit encompasses four dimensions (FAO 1996):

- Availability of sufficient quantities of food of appropriate quality, supplied through domestic production or imports (including food aid).
- Access by individuals to adequate resources (also called entitlements) for acquiring appropriate foods for a nutritious diet.
- Utilization of food through an adequate diet, clean water, sanitation and health care to reach a state of nutritional well-being where all physiological needs are met.
- Stability in the availability of and access to food, regardless of sudden shocks (e.g. an economic or climatic crisis) or cyclical events (e.g. seasonal food scarcity).

The first component – availability – arose from the post-World War Two conceptualisation of food security that focused on increasing food supply. The inclusion of accessibility in the 1980s followed major famines in Africa in the 1980s and the ground-breaking work of Sen (1981).

The utilization component relates to the rise of attention to human rights (including the rights of children and their right to nutrition) in the early 1990s (Freeman 1994). The food price crisis of 2007/8 demonstrated the need to pay more attention to nutrition – especially among young children. Following the 2007/8 high food price crisis, there has been increasing attention to first under-nutrition. The second International Conference on Nutrition in 2014 further raised the profile of nutrition and its importance for development, drawing attention to malnutrition in all its forms (under nutrition, micronutrient deficiencies and over-weight and obesity) (FAO and the World Health Organisation (WHO) 2014).

While evidence in support of investment in nutrition has existed in health and nutrition circles for a very long time, the need to integrate nutrition objectives and deliberately consider nutrition in agriculture and development programmes has only become topical recently. Later, the stability element of food security was added. More recently in international circles resilience has been linked to effects of on-going con-flict and large-scale migration on local and global food security (Hendriks 2018).

The most recent conceptual development of food security and nutrition arises from an interest in food systems. Discussions and research on food systems embraces all four elements of food security, with a focus on sustainable supplies of a variety of nutritious foods and the reduction of waste (GloPAN 2014; Willett et al. 2019).

2.4 Conclusion

For many policy makers, community members and survey respondents, the clar-ification of the terminologies is unclear. For this reason, it is important for a food security analyst to understand the foundational elements of food security. Food security, in its current, widespread definition is proving to be and agile and enduring concept. As humanity confronts pressing global challenges presented by stressed human and natural systems, our ability to work collaboratively towards solutions depends on accurate, shared terms and concepts.

References

Candel, J.L. (2014) 'Food security governance: A systemic literature review', *Food Security*, vol. 6, no. 4, pp. 585–601.

CFS (Committee on World Food Security) (2012) 'Coming to terms with terminology', Report of the 39th session of the Committee on World Food Security (CFS), 15–20 October, CFS at Rome.

Coates, J. (2013) 'Build it back better: Deconstructing food security for improved measure-ment and action', *Global Food Security*, vol. 2, no. 3, pp. 188–194.

Fan, S. (2018) 'Food policy in 2017–2018: Progress, uncertainty, and rising antiglobalism', in IFPRI (ed.), *2018 Global Food Policy Report*. IFPRI, Washington DC.

FAO (1996) 'Rome declaration on world food security and world food summit plan of action', World Food Summit 13–17 November 1996, FAO, Rome.

FAO and WHO (2014) 'Rome declaration on nutrition', FAO, Rome.

Freeman, M. (1994) 'Whither children: Protection participation, autonomy?', *Manitoba Law Journal*, vol. 22, no. 3, pp. 307–320.

GloPan (Global Panel on Agriculture and Food Systems in Nutrition) (2016) 'Food systems and diets: Facing the challenges of the 21st century', Foresight report, GloPan, London, UK.

Headey, D. and Ecker, O. (2013) 'Rethinking the measurement of food security: From first principles to best practice', *Food Security*, vol. 5, no. 3, pp. 327–343.

Hendriks, S.L. (2005) 'The challenges facing empirical estimation of food (in) security in South Africa', *Development Southern Africa*, vol. 22, no. 1, pp. 103–123.

Hendriks, S.L., and Drimie, S. (2011) 'Global food crisis and African response: Lessons for emergency response planning', in D.S. Miller and J.S. Rivera (eds.), *Comparative Emergency Management: Examining global and regional responses to disasters*. CRC/Taylor & Francis, Boca Raton.

Hendriks, S.L. (2015) 'The food security continuum: A novel tool for understanding food insecurity as a range of experiences', *Food Security*, vol. 7, no. 3, pp. 609–619.

Hendriks, S.L. (2018) 'Food policy and nutrition economics in the SDG era', *Agrekon*, vol. 57, no. 3–4, pp. 167–180.

HLPE (2013) 'Biofuels and food security', Report no. 5, HLPE at Rome.

Sen, A. (1981) *Poverty and famines: An essay on entitlement and deprivation*. Oxford University Press, New York.

UNGA (United Nations General Assembly) (2016). *The Sustainable Development Goals*. UNGA, New York.

UNICEF (1990) *A UNICEF policy review: Strategy for improved nutrition of children and women in developing countries*. UNICEF, New York.

Willett, W., Rockström, J., Loken, B., Springman, M., Lang, T., Vermeulen, S. et al. (2019) 'Food in the Anthropocene: The EAT–Lancet Commission on healthy diets from sustainable food systems', The EAT Lancet Commissions, Oslo, Norway.

3

UNDERSTANDING THE DEPTH AND SEVERITY OF FOOD SECURITY AS A CONTINUUM OF EXPERIENCES

Sheryl L. Hendriks

3.1 Introduction

Over time and with more research, we have come to better understanding the ways that households experience food insecurity and the approaches they use in facing crises, shocks and stresses. These experiences and the ways households respond are relatively common.

Contrary to earlier periods of food security research that focused on famine and humanitarian crises, we now understand that these are extreme situations but are by no means the only context in which food security interventions are necessary. The Stockholm Resilience Centre's (2016) illustration (Figure 3.1) demonstrates how food connects all the other SDGs. The embeddedness of society and the economy in the biosphere reinforces the notion that food security is central to sustainable development. It underpins development efforts and offers the potential for individuals and households to participate in development efforts and to benefit from these.

The illustration also reinforces the fragility and vulnerability of households in all societies. All individuals and households have the potential to experience food insecurity – either in the short or long-run. Famine and production failures are not the only causes of food insecurity. People experience food insecurity when they are uncertain about their future supply of and access to food, when their intake (of energy as well as macro and micronutrients) is inadequate for a healthy life, when they are obliged to resort to socially unacceptable means of acquiring food or are unable to access adequate amounts of healthy food from the food system.

While hunger and undernutrition are likely outcomes of diets that are inadequate in terms of quantity and quality, hunger and undernutrition are not the only possible consequences of food insecurity. Poverty puts people at risk of poor quality, cheap diets can make a person obese (Caballero, 2005). While overweight

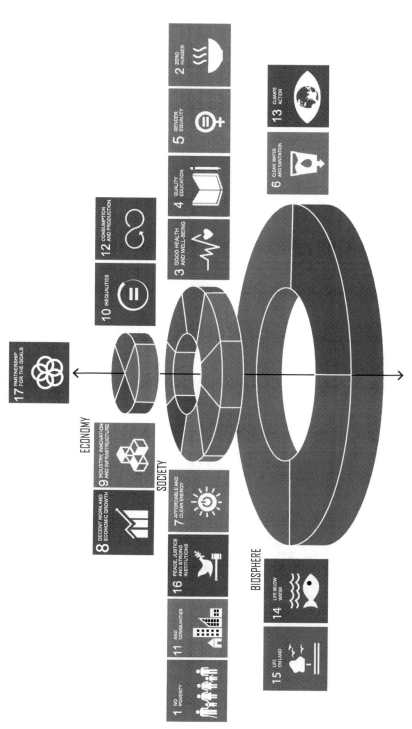

FIGURE 3.1 The SGDs and how they are all linked to food
Source: Stockholm Resilience Centre (2016)

is attributed to excessive food intake, the imbalance of diets consumed by poor people may well result in diets that may be high in fat and carbohydrates and yet micronutrient poor. This understanding leads us to the realisation that food insecurity exists as a continuum of experiences.

Food insecurity is not a single experience but a sequence of stages reflecting increasing deprivation of basic food needs, accompanied by a process of decision-making and behaviour in response to increasingly constrained household resources (Hendriks, 2015). Hendriks (2015) depicts food insecurity as a continuum of experiences ranging from the most severe form, starvation, to complete food security, defined as a state in which all the criteria of the FAO (1996) definition of food security are met, and there is no worry about future food supply to meet these criteria (Figure 3.2).

Moreover, the food (in) security status of an individual or household is not static and can change over time. These changes can be temporary, cyclical, medium-term or long-term (Figure 3.2). They may be sudden, seasonal or regular (over periods of a month); but may also be aperiodic, i.e., associated with temporary unemployment, episodes of ill health, or other recurring adverse events (Vaitla et al. 2009; Barrett 2010). The resultant shift can mean that individuals and households become more or less food secure.

The first sign of possible food insecurity is worry over future food supplies or the means to acquire food (Maxwell et al., 1999). At this stage, households find ways of reducing their food consumption (Maxwell, 1996; Maxwell et al., 1999). These changes usually start as subtle reductions in food quality, such as adding ingredients to "stretch" meals (such as bulking up meat dishes with legumes or other vegetables); using cheaper ingredients (such as bones instead of meat) or substituting with cheaper

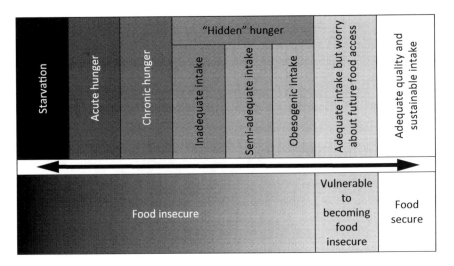

FIGURE 3.2 The food security continuum
Source: Hendriks (2015)

foods. While many of these strategies can compromise the nutritional value of meals, not all changes are necessarily detrimental to dietary quality. For example, substituting legumes for meat can lower cholesterol. Many changes have trade-off for households. For example, eating fewer processed foods may require more fuel and effort to cook meals, but may be healthier. Switching to the consumption of cheap, energy dense "fast foods" may have long-term detrimental health risks.

Subtle consumption reductions that compromise dietary quality may lead to micronutrient deficiencies or "hidden hunger" (Figure 3.3). Even small reductions can have devastating effects on the growth of the foetus and young children. Inadequate diets may further compromise the health and well-being of people whose health and nutritional needs are high (such as pregnant and breast-feeding mothers) and people whose health is already compromised (such as those who are underweight, malnourished, infirm or elderly).

If food shortages continue or worsen, households may continue limiting portion sizes and members of the household may be forced to skip meals. Households are likely to sell off non-productive assets to buy food, reducing the asset base – an essential element for recovery and resilience (Maxwell et al., 1999). Chronic food insecurity may set in. Continually inadequate intake leads to stunted growth and development in children and significant productivity losses for all household members (Hendriks, 2018). Underweight and stunting of children (being short for their age) are typical outcomes of chronic food insecurity. Not only is physical stature stunted, but development is affected in many ways, including cognitive and motor development that have life-long implications.

If households slip further into food insecurity, they face acute food insecurity – characterised by acute hunger, where hunger is a daily reality. Households may sell off productive assets to buy food, compromising their future livelihood opportunities and chances of recovery (Maxwell et al., 1999). Severe forms of under-nutrition characterise acute food insecurity, including wasting (marasmus or being severely underweight for age) and forms of protein-energy malnutrition (such as kwashiorkor). When faced with acute and enduring food insecurity, households may resort to reducing the household size by sending members to live with relatives (Maxwell et al. 1999). Mass migration can occur if the situation is widespread and long-term. Households need emergency assistance to ensure survival.

Starvation is the extreme experience of food insecurity. When severe hunger is widespread, a famine is declared. Death becomes a high possibility, especially for young children.

3.2 Differentiating between the severity and magnitude of food insecurity

Howe and Devereux define "severity" as the intensity of food insecurity at a particular point in time and "magnitude" to the aggregate impact of the crisis on the affected population. Food insecurity can, therefore, be severe and widespread or severe and individual. Classifying the severity of an experience of food insecurity by quantifying the

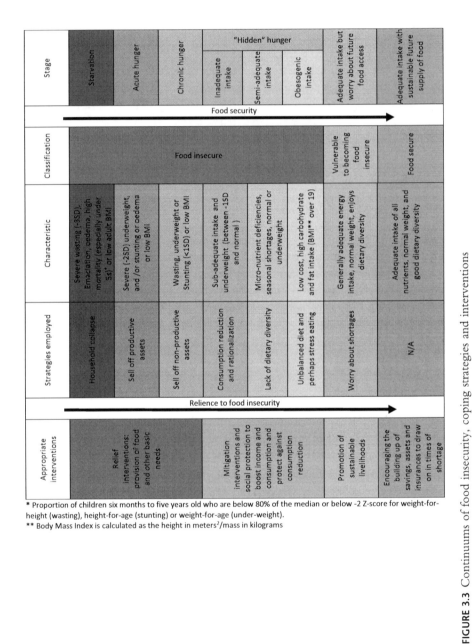

* Proportion of children six months to five years old who are below 80% of the median or below -2 Z-score for weight-for-height (wasting), height-for-age (stunting) or weight-for-age (under-weight).
** Body Mass Index is calculated as the height in meters^2/mass in kilograms

FIGURE 3.3 Continuums of food insecurity, coping strategies and interventions

Source: Hendriks (2015)

Food security as a continuum of experiences 19

intensity and magnitude of the deprivation is important for creating policies and designing emergency, mitigation and development programs (Howe and Devereux, 2004).

Figure 3.4 shows a variety of possible scenarios of varying severity and magnitude of experiences along the food security continuum. Interventions will differ according to the scale and nature of the problem and also according to the availability of the resources required to move individuals and households along the path towards food security.

The severity and magnitude of food insecurity determines the kind of help necessary: supplying food and ensuring that basic human needs are met, protecting access to food and the means to acquire food or promoting sustainable livelihoods (Hendriks, 2015). For households experiencing acute food insecurity or starvation, supplying food and attending to other basic needs such as for water and shelter is a priority to alleviate suffering. Once the situation has been stabilised, support is needed for the recovery of livelihoods to support in the (re)establishment of production systems or the capacity to earn income to purchase food. Interventions may take many forms, depending on the cause of food insecurity in the first place and the available options to recovery. They may simply be food provision to stave off hunger. They could include food or cash or a combination of these and other social protection measures that seek to fill consumption gaps by increasing the opportunity to acquire sufficient food to meet dietary needs (Zhou and Hendriks, 2017). The programs could take many forms, such as food fortification, supplementation, food parcel distribution and school feeding programs (HLPE, 2012).

Ultimately, these programmes seek to build capacities, assets and reserves to ensure that when households face hardship or shocks in future, they are more resilient. Resilient households are able to buffer or recover (bounce back) from shocks and stresses without detrimentally compromising their food security status.

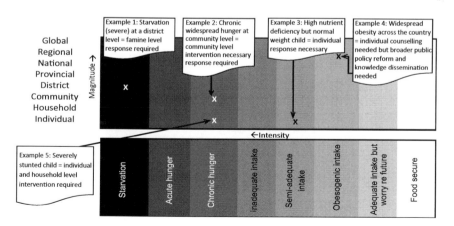

FIGURE 3.4 Continuums of magnitude and intensity of food insecurity
Source: Hendriks (2015)

Programmes such as the Catholic Relief Service's *Pathway to Prosperity Approach* illustrates how agriculture and livelihoods programming can be designed to "push" farmers recovering from shocks and stressors along this pathway by building and growing their assets, and to "pull" them by working and partnering with better-off farmers and other value chain actors.

References

Barrett, C.B. (2010) 'Measuring food insecurity', *Science*, vol. 327, no. 5967, pp. 825–828.

Caballero, B. (2005) 'A nutrition paradox: Underweight and obesity in developing countries', *New England Journal of Medicine*, vol. 352, no. 15, pp. 1515–1516.

Catholic Relief Services (CRS) (2017) *Understanding and assessing resilience: A sensemaker-based methodology*. CRS, Baltimore.

FAO (1996) 'Rome Declaration on World Food Security and World Food Summit Plan of Action', World Food Summit 13–17 November 1996, FAO, Rome.

Hendriks, S.L. (2015) 'The food security continuum: A novel tool for understanding food insecurity as a range of experiences', *Food Security*, vol. 7, no. 3, pp. 609–619.

Hendriks, S.L. (2018) 'Food policy and nutrition economics in the SDG era', *Agrekon*, vol. 57, no. 3–4, pp. 167–180.

HLPE (2012) 'Social protection for food security', Report no. 4, Committee on World Food Security (CFS), Rome.

Howe, P. and Devereux, S. (2004) 'Famine intensity and magnitude scales: A proposal for an instrumental definition of famine', *Disasters*, vol. 28, no. 4, pp. 353–373.

Maxwell, D.G. (1996) 'Measuring food insecurity: The frequency and severity of coping strategies', *Food Policy*, vol. 21, no. 3, pp. 291–303.

Maxwell, D., Ahiadeke, C., Levin, C., Armar-Klemesu, M., Zakariah, S., and Lamptey, G.M. (1999) 'Alternative food-security indicators: Revisiting the frequency and severity of 'coping strategies'. *Food Policy*, vol. 24, no. 4, pp. 411–429.

Stockholm Resilience Centre (2016) 'How food connects all the SDGs', https://www.stockholmresilience.org/images/18.36c25848153d54bdba33ec9b/1465905797608/sdgs-food-azote.jpg.

Vaitla, B., Devereux, S., and Swan, S.H. (2009) 'Seasonal hunger: A neglected problem with proven solutions', *PLoS Medicine*, vol. 6, no. 6, e1000101.

Zhou, A.C. and Hendriks, S.L. (2017) 'Does food assistance improve recipient's dietary diversity and food quality in Mozambique?', *Agrekon*, vol. 56, no. 3, pp. 248–262.

4

CONTEMPORARY POLICY ISSUES RELATED TO FOOD AVAILABILITY

Sheryl L. Hendriks

4.1 Introduction

A number of food security-related incidences over the past decade have challenged our thinking about food security causes and the impact of shocks and stresses on food supply and household consumption. The current discourse and future concerns around these issues are introduced to inform research and update practitioners about these matters. Each issue has a body of scientific literature and a toolkit of empirical methods for analysis and estimation that are specific to the core discipline. While each topic could lend itself to a full volume on the issues and their complexities, the topics can only be briefly introduced here to raise awareness of the need to consider them within the boarder context of food security analysis and policymaking.

A considerable body of detailed literature exists on the topics introduced here. The UN Committee on World Food Security's High Level Panel of Experts on Food Security and Nutrition (the HLPE) has, since 2011, produced a set of reports that provide overviews of many of these issues. The annual State of Food Insecurity reports published by FAO focus on contemporary issues of relevance to food insecurity, with detailed accounts of the impacts and interlinkages. The reports prepared for the AGRA annual conference (A Green Revolution in Africa) focus on agriculture-related topics. The recently established Malabo Montpellier Panel (established in 2016) provides evidence-based assessments of pertinent topics for Africa, presenting successes and failures for other countries to learn from. The recently published set of regional reports and a global summary reports prepared by the Inter-Academy Partnership (IAP) provides a useful science-based focus on the issues along with technical solutions.

This chapter deliberately takes a food systems approach, demonstrating the central role of food environments and food systems in food security analysis. This moves beyond traditional approaches of supply and demand. For further analysis of the constraints of earlier approaches to food security analysis that focussed on supply and demand, see Hendriks (2018).

4.2 Food environments and food systems

The desired outcome for food security is access for all to a healthy and affordable diet that is environmentally and culturally sustainable (InterAcademy Partnership (IAP), 2018). The challenge for contemporary agriculture and food systems is how to meet the increasing and evolving dietary needs of a growing population in a sustainable way, within the context of climate change and increased pressure on natural resources, paying specific attention to the rights and needs of the more vulnerable groups (HLPE, 2016; 2017a). A food system includes "all the elements (environment, people, inputs, processes, infrastructures, institutions, etc.) and activities that relate to the production, processing, distribution, preparation and consumption of food and the output of these activities, including socio-economic and environmental outcomes" (HLPE, 2014a). Therefore, a sustainable food system "ensures food security and nutrition for all in such a way that the economic, social and environmental bases to generate food security and nutrition of future generations are not compromised" (HLPE, 2017a). Figure 4.1 illustrates the food system and its components.

The IAP (2018) explains that "it is vital to take an integrative food systems perspective and to identify the inter-related issues for resource efficiency, environmental sustainability, resilience and the public health agenda, while also taking account of the local–global interconnectedness of systems". Taking a food systems approach to food security policy, evaluation and impact assessment requires the consideration of the elements of the food system as a whole, rather than a sectoral (single sector) approach or seeing food security systems as simple outcomes of supply and demand. Central to the idea of ensuring food security in terms of the four key dimensions (availability, access, nutrition and resilience) is the food environment.

A food environment refers to the physical, economic, political and socio-cultural context in which consumers engage with the food system to make their decisions about acquiring, preparing and consuming food (HLPE, 2017a). The food environment consists of:

- The physical spaces where food is purchased or obtained
- Features and infrastructures of the built environment that allow consumers to access these spaces
- Personal determinants of consumer food choices (including income, education, values, skills etc.) and
- The political, social and cultural norms that underlie these interactions (HLPE, 2017a).

The HLPE (2017a) identifies three broad types of food systems:

- Traditional food systems in which consumers rely on minimally processed seasonal foods (when available), collected or produced for self-consumption or sold mainly through informal markets where supply chains are often short and local.

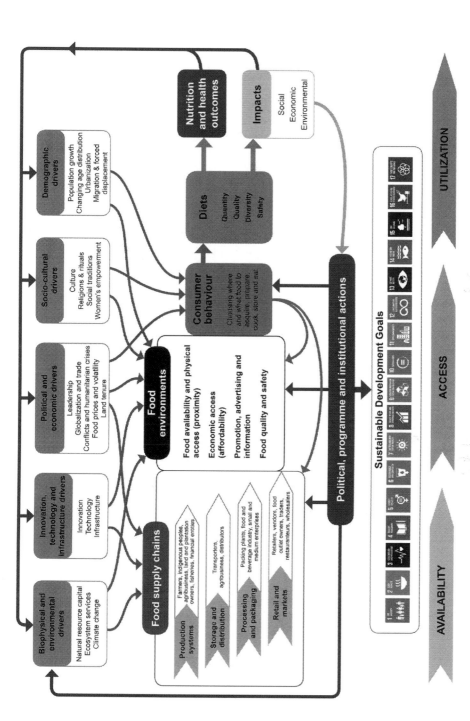

FIGURE 4.1 Conceptual framework of the food system
Source: HLPE (2017a)

- Mixed food systems where food producers rely on formal and informal markets to sell their produce. Highly processed and packaged foods are offered.
- Modern food systems characterised by the availability of more diverse food options all year round through processing and packaging to extend the shelf life of foods.

The need to feed a growing global population, and to address a growing demand for food, puts pressure on natural resources and challenges the sustainability of all food systems – crops, livestock, marine and inland fisheries and of aquaculture development. It also raises several issues relating to the management of value chains to realise the right to food of communities and to make food available for all.

4.3 Demographic drivers of food system changes

The pressures of the growing population and urbanisation (IAP, 2018) compound major global challenges for delivering food security objectives and achieving SDG2. Population growth and changing age distributions (more youth and older people), urbanisation, migration and forced displacement have driven radical changes in food systems and diets in the past decades and will remain major drivers in the future (HLPE, 2017a). A large share of the youth lives in rural areas, where the demand for rural labour services will be essential to absorbing these new entrants and stemming the tide of urban migration. A shift to higher-value agriculture, more rural-based non-farm economic activity and assistance to people transitioning out of agriculture are needed to drive transformation of these economies (World Bank, 2016).

Urbanisation is also likely to put additional stress on food systems through increased demand for a greater diversity of foods and for affordable nutritious foods. The HLPE (2017a) postulates that urban demand will increasingly dictate what foods are grown by rural producers and how these foods are processed, distributed and marketed. This will place greater stress on land, water and other resources.

Greater consideration of the planetary boundaries and sustainability of the food system with regard to feeding a growing population will also drive changes in the food system. This may well shift the dynamics of land, water and other resources in both positive and negative ways.

4.4 The changing nature of what affects food availability

Figure 4.2 demonstrates the increasing number of extreme weather-related crises between 1996 and 2016. The 2018 annual *State of Food Insecurity: Building climate resilience for food security and nutrition* (FAO et al., 2018) provides a sobering and detailed discussion of the effects of weather-related shocks on food security, including the interlinkages of the outcome on the four dimensions of food security (availability, access, nutrition and resilience) as well as the related health effects. Climate change and variability, as well as more severe and frequent floods and droughts, will have an impact on food prices, health, productivity, and resilience of ecosystems, communities and households, particularly for the most vulnerable (HLPE, 2016). The effect of

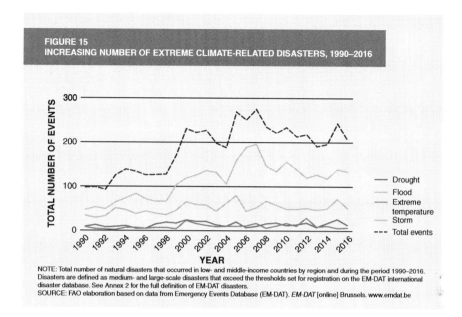

FIGURE 4.2 The increasing number of extreme weather-related crises between 1996 and 2016
Source: FAO et al. (2018)

multiple crises on food production can push countries into becoming food import-dependent. This will increase vulnerability to price shocks.

FAO et al. (2018) have reported that of the 51 countries identified as experiencing high exposure to climate extremes in 2011–2016, 23.5% were low-income countries and 76.5% are middle-income. Most (76%) of these countries were in Africa and Asia (39 and 37%, respectively), 15.5% in Latin America and the Caribbean; and the rest in Oceania and Europe. The vulnerability to these events is an important risk factor for food security and nutrition that merits more study, especially with regard to conditions that raise the probability that extreme climate will negatively affect food security (FAO et al., 2018).

The risk of increased food insecurity with regard to climate change exists where cereal production and/or yields are sensitive to climate variability and extremes and where livelihoods are sensitive to climate (FAO et al., 2018). Risks also exist where a high proportion of the population already suffers from undernourishment – these countries are often highly dependent on agriculture for livelihoods (FAO et al., 2018). Together, conflict and climate shocks exacerbate acute food insecurity (FAO et al., 2018).

4.5 Biophysical and environmental drivers of food system changes

Predicted challenges in feeding humanity point to the need to pay greater attention to the sustainable use of natural resources and to limit damage to the environment. At a global scale, attention must be given to the increasing scarcity of fossil fuels, water, soil fertility and biomass (HLPE, 2013). "Historically, both markets and policy have focused on driving agricultural efficiency (yield per unit inputs), partly in the assumption that this becomes a proxy for the efficiency of the food system" (IAP, 2018). The IAP (2018) warns that: "Excessively promoting agricultural efficiency risks incentivising the externalisation of costs onto the environment and the over-production of food that may lead to higher levels of waste, reducing the efficiency of the food system to feed people healthily and sustainably".

All regions of the world face environmental degradation, including loss of essential land and water resources (IAP, 2018). Agriculture is dependent on energy, water resources (particularly ground water), soil quality and infrastructure investments, ranging from transport to research and education. Innovation is crucial in tackling these challenges but the pace of technological advance may be slowing owing to static public investment in some countries (IAP, 2018).

Food production is also dependent on biodiversity and ecosystems, including forests, aquatic ecosystems and mosaic landscapes (HLPE, 2016). Agricultural practices are increasingly moving towards intensified monoculture, which may improve grain yields in the short term but threaten the biological diversity necessary for high quality diets (HLPE, 2016) and threaten resilience of food systems (Bullock et al., 2017), as well as the interdependence among countries in their food supplies (IAP, 2018). These concerns focused on the possible negative impact of agricultural development on water availability and quality, soil degradation, air quality, greenhouse gas emissions and climate change and on ecosystems and biodiversity and diets (HLPE, 2016). These concerns over externalities question the roles and contributions of various actors (communities, smallholders and international companies, etc.) in a world prone to significant inequalities (HLPE 2014a).

The influence of food systems on inequalities and the role of inequality on access to food is illustrated through the following examples drawn from the HLPE (2014a) report *Sustainable fisheries and aquaculture for food security and nutrition*. This example is used deliberately as limited attention has been given so far to fish as a key element in food security and nutrition strategies at national level and in wider development discussions and interventions but there is growing recognition of the nutritional and health-promoting qualities of fish (HLPE, 2014a). Fish is a primary source of protein and essential nutrients whether produced through fish farming (or aquaculture) or caught from wild marine or freshwater stocks. Fish are one of the most efficient converters of feed into high quality food, providing income and livelihoods.

As with other sectors (crops, forests, horticulture and livestock), the capacities of the fish sector to deliver food security and nutrition are limited or reduced when the environment, production ecosystems and/or the resource bases (for example fish stocks) are degraded or overexploited (HLPE, 2014a). Activities such as oil drilling, energy installations, coastal development and construction of ports and other coastal infrastructures, dams and water flow management (especially for inland fisheries), among others, impact on aquatic productivity. Conservation activities and the establishment of Marine Protected Areas can also impact on the livelihoods of local fishing communities, limiting access to resources for livelihoods and social and cultural values through the denial of access to fishing grounds or displacement from coastal settlements (HLPE, 2014a). Sustainability of these systems does not only depend on stock recovery but also on access to, and distribution of the harvest (HLPE, 2014a).

Climate change impacts on fish-dependent populations will depend on the evolution of fishing opportunities (evolution of resources available, entitlements and capacities to fish, evolution of operational costs in production and marketing) and the evolution of prices (HLPE, 2014a). Climate change impacts are already visible in the fisheries sector, with changes in the geographic distribution of species and warmer water species moving towards the poles, ocean acidification and changes in coastal conditions that affect habitat (HLPE, 2014a). Inland fisheries and aquaculture may face higher mortality due to heat waves, water scarcity and competition for water. Extreme events are increasing, with greater risk of damage or loss of infrastructure and housing. In addition, sea level rise might lead to the relocation of communities. Pollution renders water unfit for use and undermines ecosystem health (HLPE, 2015). Fisheries also contribute to food waste. Fish caught can end-up being dumped overboard (discarded) – either due to accidental by-catch of non-targeted species or legally undersized fish, or due to low quality, partial damage or spoilage (HLPE, 2014a).

Ecosystems and landscapes sustain water resources, ensuring quantity, quality and stability of water for human use (HLPE, 2015). Unsustainable water use and management reduce the ecosystems functions of land, fisheries, forests and water bodies, including their ability to provide food and nutrition. The growing demand for food, feed, wood and energy also drive deforestation (HLPE, 2017b). Deforestation and forest degradation threaten the income, livelihoods and ways of life of forest-dependent populations, compromising the provision of ecosystem services that are essential to food security and sustainable development (HLPE, 2017b).

Climate change will affect precipitation, runoff, hydrological flows, water quality, water temperature and groundwater recharge (HLPE, 2015). It will impact both rainfed systems through changes in precipitation patterns and on irrigated systems through the availability of water at basin level (HLPE, 2015). Droughts may intensify in some seasons and areas, due to reduced precipitation and/or increased evapotranspiration. Climate change will also significantly impact sea level, with impacts on freshwater resources in coastal areas (HLPE, 2015).

Food-borne diseases resulting either from biological contamination (pathogens, microbes) or chemicals are still a significant cause of human health problems related mainly to fresh food products such as animal-sourced foods, fruits and vegetables (HLPE, 2016). New and resurgent zoonotic diseases are also a concern. Zoonotic diseases are transferred from animals to humans, often in systems where there is close proximity of humans to animals, including in urban livestock farms. These include outbreaks of avian and swine influenza, and severe acute respiratory syndroms that result in deaths, serious illness and significant costs for their containment and eradication. There is also growing concern about antimicrobial resistance in human health linked to the use of antibiotics for farmed animals, mainly in intensive systems (HLPE 2016).

28 Sheryl L. Hendriks

4.6 Political, economic and social drivers of food system changes

Due to market liberalisation over the past 20 years, in many countries domestic prices are more connected to international prices than in earlier periods of high volatility (such as in the 1990s). For some developing countries, liberalisation has led to greater reliance on food imports, making international food price volatility even more a concern than it would have been in the 1970s (HLPE, 2011a). Since 2007, the degree of price volatility has been extraordinary and the number of countries affected has been very high (HLPE, 2011a).

An HLPE (2011a) report attributes the volatility three possible causes of international food price volatility: demand elasticity, trade policies and speculation. The report explains that:

> Of these three, the role of speculation in the futures market is clearly the most controversial. Nobody contests the dramatic increase in the volume of non-commercial transactions on the futures market. However, conclusions diverge widely as to whether increased non-commercial transactions led to the formation of price bubbles. By contrast, the effects of both the demand from the biofuel industry and the use of restrictive trade measures (mostly export bans) on prices are far less controversial.

Both issues are politically sensitive. Biofuel support policies created a demand shock while restrictive trade measures adopted by many countries to protect consumers during that time may have accelerated price increases (HLPE, 2011a).

Second, higher levels of volatility could be attributed to decreased price elasticity of demand as a result of increased income given the overall growth in world incomes (HLPE, 2011a). As consumers in poor countries are more sensitive to price changes, a spike in food prices forces poorer consumers to reduce their consumption, while wealthier consumers can maintain roughly the same level of consumption. This increases inequity in the overall distribution of food.

Inequality is also evident in the transmission of international food price spike to domestic economies. Domestic food price inflation and volatility determine the local poverty and food security impacts of international food crises. The 2007/08 international food price rise was transmitted to domestic prices in most developing counties, although not evenly and in some cases with significant delays (HLPE, 2011a). However, the subsequent drop in international prices was only partially transmitted (HLPE, 2011a).

The HLPE's (2011a) third explanation posits price increases as an early signal of a long-lasting scarcity in agricultural markets.

> According to this explanation, the world could be facing the end of a long period of structural overproduction in international agricultural markets, made possible by the extensive use of cheap natural resources (e.g. oil, water, biodiversity, phosphate, land) backed by farm subsidies in OECD countries. In

Contemporary policy issues **29**

other words, we might be at the end of a period of historically unprecedented growth in agricultural production that relied on a strategy akin to mining.

There has been an increase in large-scale land acquisitions in developing countries after the 2007/8 food price crisis for the purpose of agricultural production (food or agro-fuel production), timber extraction, carbon trading, mineral extraction, conservation or tourism. Ecological stress, such as water shortages and drought, combined with environmental policy, such as nature conservation, and carbon sequestration are also prompting increased international investment in land. For a significant part of the world population, including smallholders, pastoralists, agricultural workers, artisanal fisher folk and indigenous peoples, access to land and security of tenure stand as crucial elements in the achievement of the right to food (HLPE, 2016). Although emotively debated and written about, there is currently little empirical evidence that these large-scale acquisitions positively or negatively affect household food security and rural livelihoods. However, it is clear that these investments will affect the access to land, livelihoods and incomes. The effects probably depend on the nature of the business conducted, the organisational model (employment opportunities or contracting) and the overall effect the new occupant has on the availability of and access to food and the means with which to access food. A great deal more research is need with respect to the impact of large-scale plantations on small-scale farming, including economic, social, gender and environmental impacts (HLPE, 2011b).

4.7 Waste and losses in the food system

The issue of global food losses and waste has recently received much attention (IAP, 2018). Food losses occur before consumption regardless of the cause, while food waste occurs at consumption level regardless of the cause (HLPE, 2014b). Food losses and waste impact food security and nutrition by three main ways:

- A reduction of global and local availability of food
- A negative impact on food access for those involved in harvest and post-harvest operations, those who face food waste and loss-related economic and income losses and for consumers due to the contribution of these losses to raising prices of food.
- A longer-term effect on food security results from the unsustainable use of natural resources on which the future production of food depends (HLPE, 2014b).

Reducing waste along the entire food chain is essential to improve food security and to reduce the environmental footprint of food systems (HLPE, 2014b). Reducing food loss and waste will also help to relieve pressure on land and other natural resources. Modifying overconsumption will also help, not least in mitigating climate change (IAP, 2018).

Topics that have recently emerged with promise for reducing food loss and food waste are the circular economy objectives and opportunities at the intersection of the circular economy and bioeconomy (IAP, 2018). The circular economy is a model of reducing, re-using and recycling in production that could promote environmental and economic sustainability and encourage value addition for processed foodstuffs and other important products. The bioeconomy is based on intensive use of knowledge of biological resources, processes and principles for the sustainable production and conversion of biomass into products and services, enabling substitution of non-renewables by renewables – from both land and sea (IAP, 2018).

4.8 Conclusion

Innovation has been a major engine for food system transformation in the past decades and will be critical to address the needs of a rapidly growing population in a context of climate change and natural resource scarcity (IAP, 2018).

> Building more sustainable food systems to enhance food security will require not only new research and new technologies, but also better access to and use of existing technologies, developing context specific solutions for local ecosystems, adapted to local socio-economic and socio-cultural conditions. More investment is needed in research and development of nutritious food crops (such as fruits, vegetables and pulses, as well as neglected and orphan crops) as opposed to major staple commodities.

References

Bullock, J.M, Dhanjal-Adams, K.L., Milne, A., Oliver, T.H., Todman, L.C, Whitmore, L. P., and Pywell, R.F. (2017). 'Resilience and food security: Rethinking an ecological concept', *Journal of Ecology*, vol 105, pp. 880–884.

FAO, IFAD, UNICEF, WFP and WHO. (2018). 'The state of food security and nutrition in the world 2018: Building climate resilience for food security and nutrition'. FAO, Rome.

Hendriks, S.L. (2018) 'Food policy and nutrition economics in the SDG era', *Agrekon*, vol. 57, no .3–4, pp. 167–180.

HLPE. (2011a). 'Price volatility and food security'. Report no. 1, HLPE, Rome.

HLPE. (2011b). 'Land tenure and international investments in agriculture'. Report no 2, HLPE, Rome.

HLPE. (2013). 'Biofuels and food security'. Report no. 5, HLPE, Rome 2013.

HLPE. (2014a). 'Sustainable fisheries and aquaculture for food security and nutrition'. Report no 7, HLPE, Rome.

HLPE. (2014b). 'Food losses and waste in the context of sustainable food systems'. Report no 8, HLPE, Rome.

HLPE. (2015). 'Water for food security and nutrition'. Report no. 9, HLPE, Rome.

HLPE. (2016). 'Sustainable agricultural development for food security and nutrition: What roles for livestock?' Report no 10, HLPE, Rome.

HLPE. (2017a). 'Nutrition and food systems'. Report no. 12, HLPE, Rome.

HLPE. (2017b). 'Sustainable forestry for food security and nutrition'. Report no. 11, HLPE, Rome.

IAP. (2018). 'Opportunities for future research and innovation on food and nutrition security and agriculture: The InterAcademy Partnership's global perspective'. IAP, Halle.

World Bank. (2016). 'The world development report'. World Bank, Washington DC.

5

CONTEMPORARY POLICY ISSUES RELATED TO POVERTY AND INEQUALITY AND THE IMPERATIVES TO IMPROVE ACCESS TO FOOD

Nic J.J. Olivier, Francette Gouws and Nico J.J. Olivier

5.1. Introduction

While food security started out as a concept focusing on food availability nested in macroeconomic theories of food supply and demand, the 1974 global food crisis shifted research in food security to understanding the influence and impact at the micro-level (Burchi and De Muro, 2016). This approach drew food security research closer to poverty assessment (Josling, 1975), and observed that a large proportion of the world's population is born into poverty. Malnutrition and hunger are concentrated among the poor. Josling (1975) has noted that: "… the poor are, almost by definition, outside the mainstream of economic activity. This fact alone presents a major difficulty in finding solutions".

Sen's work in the 1980s brought about awareness that people experience food deprivation because they have difficulty accessing it. Poverty constrains access to income and other resources (such as transfers and gifts), affecting household purchasing power (Sen 1981). Consequently, during the 1990s, food security research and interventions focused on poverty reduction, food price stabilization and social protection policies (Webb et al. 2006; Barrett 2010).

De Schutter (2011) claimed that too much attention had been paid to addressing the mismatch between supply and demand on the international markets, "while comparatively too little attention has been paid both to the imbalances of power in the food systems", and to the failure to support the ability of small-scale farmers to feed themselves, their families and their communities and for food consumers to gain access to sufficient healthy food to feed themselves and their families. Not only does the food system leave many poor people inadequately fed; the same system also determines the employment and income opportunities for poor people; the prices they pay for food and other goods and services and their ability to migrate in search of better opportunities (Hendriks, 2018).

A number of failures in the economic and social structure of societies led to inequalities that pose significant barriers and challenges to development. While poverty is a cause of food insecurity, food insecurity prevents individuals escaping poverty, creating intergenerational cycles of poverty. Further constraints to escaping both poverty and food insecurity are deeply rooted in structural inequalities that enforce and perpetuate deprivation. These include class, gender, nationality and religious inequalities. Inequalities directly affect food access.

The SDG agenda itself prioritises inclusion. The SGDs recognise that growth and prosperity for all is only possible if inequality is reduced or eliminated (UN DESA, 2015). SDGs 1–9 include various elements of inequality. SDG 10 specifically focuses on reducing inequalities both within and between countries.

5.2 The right to food

A number of international instruments contain provisions relating to the right to food. Some of these instruments (conventions, treaties, protocols, etc.) are legally binding on countries that have ratified such instruments, creating legally enforceable obligations. In addition, there are a number of instruments (declarations, etc.) that, although not legally binding, create commitments that have a strong persuasive force (e.g. the SDGs).

The right to food (set out in the Universal Declaration of Human Rights in 1948 and the International Covenant on Economic, Social and Cultural Rights (ICESCR) in 1966) has the following two dimensions (Moyo, 2016; Brand, 2013, p. 56C–4):

- The immediate realisation of the right to food: Each State party (country) is obliged to, without any delay, take all necessary and appropriate steps to comply with the obligation to ensure the provision of adequate food
- The progressive realisation of the right to food: Each State party (country) must in a progressive manner, within the framework of both (a) the priority it affords to the realisation of the right to food within the context of all its national priorities, and (b) its available resources, take all appropriate steps to ensure the right to food is increasingly realised in the course of time.

Article 25 of the 1948 Universal Declaration of Human Rights states that: "Everyone has the right to a standard of living adequate for the health and well-being of himself and of his family, including food, clothing, housing, medical care and social services."

Article 11.1 and 11.2 of the ICESCR recognises the right to food and the right of everyone to be free from hunger, and obliges states to implement the necessary measures to give effect to the right to food. The Covenant is legally binding on State parties that have ratified it (160 States parties by 1 June 2012). Article 11.1 of the ICESCR states that State parties recognise the right to food as part of the right of everyone to an adequate standard of living for himself and his family, "including adequate food, clothing and housing, and to the continuous improvement of living conditions". It commits State parties to take "appropriate steps to ensure the realisation of this right" and "individually and through international cooperation, the measures, including specific programmes, which are needed". The State parties are obliged to ensure adequate (access to) food and freedom from hunger (Brand, 2013:56C-6).

The ICESCR (article 11(1)) refers to the "right to an adequate standard of living for himself and he's family, including adequate food, housing and clothing...". Article 11(2) recognises the "fundamental right of everyone to be free from hunger". It is important to note that the right to freedom from hunger is the only right in the ICESCR that is characterised as "fundamental".

The 1996 World Food Summit reaffirmed "the right of everyone to have access to safe and nutritious food, consistent with the right to adequate food and the fundamental right to be free from hunger", and requested the United Nations High Commissioner for Human Rights (OHCHR) in consultation with FAO to clarify these rights (HLPE, 2013). This was achieved in 1999 through the UN Committee on Economic, Social and Cultural Rights' (UN CESCR) General Comment No. 12 on the right to adequate food. This is the most comprehensive and authoritative interpretation of the normative content of the right to food. General Comment No. 12 states that governments are obliged to, amongst others:

- Respect existing access to adequate food and requires that Parties do not adopt measures that could prevent such access
- Protect access to adequate food
- Fulfil (facilitate) access to and use of resources and means to ensure sustainable livelihoods (of which food security is an outcome).
- Fulfil (provide) that right directly whenever an individual or group is unable to enjoy the right to adequate food (OHCHR, 1999).

Paragraph 6 states that:

> The right to adequate food is realised when every man, woman and child, alone or in community with others, has physical and economic access at all times to adequate food or means for its procurement. The right to adequate food shall, therefore, not be interpreted in a narrow or restrictive sense that equates it with a minimum package of calories, proteins and other specific nutrients.
>
> *(UN CESCR 1999, paragraph 6)*

A number of other UN conventions specifically mentions the right to food for specific groups of people. For example, the binding 1981 UN Convention on the Elimination of All Forms of Discrimination against Women (CEDAW) obliges governments to put measures in place that will ensure that poverty-stricken women have access to food. In similar vein, the binding 1989 UN Convention on the Rights of the Child contains key provisions (and impose related

34 Nic J.J. Olivier et al.

obligations on national governments) in respect of, amongst others, healthcare which includes the provision of "adequate nutritious foods and clean drinking-water" and additional support programmes (art. 24).

In its General Comment No. 19, adopted in 2007, the OHCHR provided its interpretation and elaboration of the human right to social security, as set out in Article 9 of the ICESCR. The Committee states that:

> The right to social security includes the right not to be subject to arbitrary and unreasonable restrictions of existing social security coverage, whether obtained publicly or privately, as well as the right to equal enjoyment of adequate protection from social risks and contingencies.
>
> *(UN CESCR 2008, paragraph 9)*

An optional protocol to the ICESCR (OP – ICESCR) was adopted by the UN General Assembly in 2009 that states that State parties to the ICESCR may, in their discretion, decide to provide a framework in their domestic law for their citizens to access international forums in respect of the manner in which the State party concerned has complied with its ICESCR obligations.

The 2004 FAO Voluntary Guidelines to Support the Progressive Realisation to Adequate Food in the Context of National Food Security proposes a number of mechanisms that should be implemented by individual governments. The Voluntary Guidelines relate specifically to the rights of specific groups, such as:

- The Voluntary Guidelines for Securing Sustainable Small-Scale Fisheries in the Context of Food Security and Poverty Eradication (FAO, 2015)
- The Voluntary Guidelines on the Responsible Governance of Tenure of Land, Fisheries and Forests in the Context of National Food Security (FAO, 2012)

As regards non-binding declarations and commitments, various instruments have been approved by a range of international institutions and a number of member states. These instruments do not establish legal obligations (and are thus not legally enforceable), but create commitments with a strong persuasive nature. Key examples within the context of the right to food include, but are not limited to, the 1974 Universal Declaration on the Eradication of Hunger and Malnutrition; the 2012 UN General Assembly Resolution 67/174 reaffirming countries' undertaking to realise the right to food; the 2000 UN General Assembly's Millennium Declaration and the 2015 SDGs.

5.3 Access and food insecurity

Amartya Sen's work did not explicitly mention food insecurity, but focussed on hunger and entitlements (Burchi and De Muro, 2016). However, the inclusion of access to food in food security definitions is widely attributed to his 1981 work entitled *Poverty and Famine: An Essay on Entitlement and Deprivation*. Sen's entitlement approach challenged the Malthusian view of famine and hunger, and shifted the focus from national food availability to people's access to food within the context of entitlements and how these affect access to a bundle of commodities, including food (Sen, 1981; Burchi and De Muro, 2016). Sen explained that entitlements depend on (i) personal endowments (resources a person legally owns) and non-tangible goods and (ii) a set of commodities a person has access to through trade and production. Sen further asserted that hunger is a consequence of the failure of the production and trade system that results in "entitlement failures". "Starvation is a matter of some people not having enough food to eat, and not a matter of there being not enough food to eat" (Sen, 1981: 434). *Hunger and Public Action* (Drèze and Sen, 1989), expanded on Sen's entitlement theory, drawing attention to a broader set of entitlements that affect hunger, i.e. the set alternative bundles of commodities (e.g. drinkable water) or services (e.g. sanitation and health care) that affect not only hunger, but also nutrition (Burchi and De Muro, 2016). Drèze and Sen (1989: 13) explained why access is not sufficient and utilization is crucial, recognising that "the relationship between food intake and nutritional achievement can vary greatly depending not only on features such as age, sex, pregnancy, metabolic rates, climatic conditions, and activities, but also access to complementary inputs".

In drawing attention to food intake and nutrition, Drèze and Sen (1989), introduced a new focus on nutrition into food insecurity. *Hunger and Public Action* (Drèze and Sen, 1989) emphasised the capability to avoid undernourishment and escape deprivations associated with hunger (Drèze and Sen, 1989: 13), i.e. the capability to be free from hunger. Such capabilities include health, being educated and being able to take part in household decision making and community life (Burchi and De Muro, 2016).

The Fabian Commission (2015: 9) states that:

> Because food is the most flexible part of the household budget, it becomes the most likely to be squeezed.

This deprivation does not only lead to under nutrition and not only people in developed countries are adversely affected by food insecurity. The Fabian Commission (2015: 9) found that in the United Kingdom "[t]he evidence shows that calorie for calorie, healthier food tends to be more expensive than unhealthy food and the struggle to afford other key living costs means many households have to prioritise calories over nutrients". Moreover, people on low incomes are one-and-a-half times more likely to develop diabetes than those on an average income, and children growing up in low-income households are three times more likely to be obese than those in high-income households.

Poverty affects health outcomes, reduces levels of participation in society and ultimately the quantity and quality of food. Poverty affects many groups of people, such as:

- Rural and isolated communities – the costs of transportation can increase the price of fresh fruit and vegetables
- Low income and unemployed people
- Homeless people
- Alcohol and drug users – not only does addiction mean making choices between food and substances, but alcohol and substance abuse can cause malnutrition and addiction may affect one's ability to take care of oneself
- Women and children – children are completely reliant on their parents' care and support, while maternal health affects children's nutrition
- Indigenous people – in addition to continued marginalisation and discrimination, many live in isolated and remote areas
- Elderly people are more prone to diseases and have special nutritional and care needs
- Chronically ill people.

5.4 The impact of inequality on food insecurity

Unequal access to entitlements severely affects the capabilities necessary to be free from hunger. Inequality is the outcome of unequal access. We illustrate this with examples extracted from HLPE reports on a range of topics:

- Rising incomes are important for food security. However, income disparities can skew the distribution system to cater to the demands of higher-income consumers at the expense of the availability of more affordable food. Trade openness can disadvantage vulnerable groups if they do not have adequate purchasing power (HLPE, 2011).
- Deeply rooted traditional or historical inequalities can limit women's and other vulnerable groups' access to land and water for agricultural uses, hampering livelihood strategies and negatively impacting on food security (HLPE, 2015).
- Small-scale farmers and landless labourers, with limited resources and also likely underserved by public and private activities, are particularly susceptible to the socioeconomic effects of climate change (HLPE, 2013).
- Climate change will affect precipitation, runoff, water quality, water temperature and groundwater recharge (HLPE, 2015) and may worsen water scarcities (HLPE, 2015). Changes in precipitations and snow/ice melt are changing hydrological systems and will likely impact the sea level. These changes will particularly affect poorer households and may disproportionately affect women (HLPE, 2015).
- Lack of access to land is typically a problem for smallholders (HLPE, 2013).
- Much fish sector work has become feminized and casualised. In the process, women may lose their access to fish for trading while unpaid and uncounted (often migrant) female labour is likely to increase (HLPE, 2014).
- Water availability, access and use depend on context-specific socioeconomic, cultural and political factors as well. Water shortages increase competition within and across sectors, disproportionately affecting poor and marginalized

women, men and children, because of existing power imbalances, skewed access to resources, structural discrimination and gender inequalities. Some groups suffer from lack of water even when there is more than sufficient water available in a region (HLPE, 2015).

- The vast majority of those without sanitation live in rural areas and progress in rural areas lags behind progress in urban areas (HLPE, 2015).
- Cultural norms can dictate that women and girls are responsible for water collection, and they may spend several hours per day collecting water. "Unequal power relationships within the household, and women's minimal control over household finances or spending, can force women into a daily trudge (taking precious time) for fetching cheaper or free untreated water, which may result in health problems and increased poverty and destitution" (HLPE, 2015, p. 40).

5.5 Social protection as a means of addressing food access

The HLPE (2012a, p. 30) explains that the interpretation of General Comment 12 (see above) notes "that social security should be treated as a social good, and not primarily as a mere instrument of economic or financial policy" (paragraph 10). Drawing on ILO instruments, the UN CESCR lists nine elements of a legally established, publicly administered or supervised and sustainable social security system (paragraph 12):

- Adequate access to health care for all
- Cash transfers to those incapable of working due to ill-health
- Non-contributory pensions for all older persons who have no other means of support
- Unemployment benefits
- Compensation for employment-related injury
- Family and child benefits (sufficient to cover food, clothing, housing, water and sanitation)
- Paid maternity leave
- Disability benefits
- Survivor and orphan benefits.

The Comment also draws attention to the social protection needs of groups not normally covered by a contributory social security system (HLPE, 2012a). "State parties should also consider schemes that provide social protection to individuals belonging to disadvantaged and marginalized groups, for example crop or natural disaster insurance for small farmers or livelihood protection for self-employed persons in the informal economy" (paragraph 28). In addition, the Comment recognised that "[s]ocially vulnerable groups such as landless persons and other particularly impoverished segments of the population may need attention through special programmes" (paragraph 12.1) (HLPE, 2012a).

38 Nic J.J. Olivier et al.

A wide range of social protection measures are available. A detailed discussion of these is presented in the 2012 HLPE report entitled *Social protection for food security*. The report demonstrates how Sen's food entitlement failures can be counteracted with social protection measures. A summary of some of these measures is presented in Table 5.1.

5.6. Gender bias and inequality

Issues related to inequality do not only relate to the daily experiences of those marginalized and excluded by entrenched inequalities, but the bias also permeates into the research and policy system. Doss et al. (2013) explain that the lack of gendered data, accompanied by a lack of proper conceptualisation for statistics to embark on gender aspects is a challenge, with gender inequalities often poorly quantitatively documented. A concrete example is provided by the HLPE (2014) that states that a consequence of gender-blindness in the fish sector is that little has been invested in research to help understand the problems of gender inequality and how to address them (HLPE, 2014).

As a result, development projects incorporating gender have tended to focus on narrow economic approaches for women's empowerment. Often programmes are directed at giving women income-earning opportunities, often only at the welfare level, and ignoring deeper social and cultural factors. Some merely overburden women rather than relieving the burden. Gender research mainly focuses on women, with very few studies examining the relevance of masculine behaviour, gender relations and their impacts on food security and nutrition (HLPE, 2014).

TABLE 5.1 Food entitlement failures and social protection responses

Entitlement category	Social protection instruments	Food security objectives
Production	2.1 Input subsidies 2.2 Crop and livestock insurance	– promote food production – protect against harvest failure or livestock mortality
Labour	2.3 Public works programmes	– provide temporary employment – create useful infrastructure – promote agricultural production
Trade	2.4 Food price stabilisation 2.5 Food subsidies 2.6 Grain reserves	– maintain market access to food – keep food affordable for the poor – ensure adequate market food supplies
Transfers	2.7 School feeding 2.8 Supplementary feeding 2.9 Conditional cash transfers 2.10 Unconditional cash transfers	– reduce hunger – promote access to education Promote local food production – Enhance food consumption – reduce hunger or poverty – promote children's access to education and healthcare – reduce hunger or poverty

Source: HLPE, 2012a, p. 31

Moreover, existing data are often not sufficiently disaggregated to allow for monitoring of intra-household inequalities in access based on gender, age or disability, as well as in religious and other types of minority communities.

5.7 Conclusion

Structural and systemic inequalities often impact negatively on programmes aimed at eradicating poverty and food insecurity. Internationally, individual states are legally obliged to the progressive adherence to, and implementation of, the right to food, subject to the dual proviso of availability of state resources and its relative importance and focus within a given state's priorities. In addition, many countries have made non-binding commitments that are not legally enforceable to ensure the implementation of measures aimed at eradicating food insecurity. A key mechanism aimed at addressing food insecurity, and specifically (but not limited to) at improving access to food, that recently have found favour in a number of countries is the establishment, enhancement and operationalisation of an all-encompassing social protection system and related structures. Within this context however, a gender bias is often prevalent, with a skewed focus which marginalizes women, the aged, people living with disabilities, as well as religious and other types of minority communities.

References

Barrett, C.B. (2010) 'Measuring food insecurity', *Science*, vol. 327, pp. 825–828.

Brand, D. (2013) 'Food', in S. Bishop and M. Woolman, (eds) *Constitutional law of South Africa*. Juta, Cape Town.

Burchi, F. and De Muro, P. (2016) 'From food availability to nutritional capabilities: Advancing food security analysis', *Food Policy*, vol. 60, pp. 10–19.

De Schutter, O. (2011) 'New mandate of the special rapporteur on the right to food', Report, Global Policy Forum UN General Assembly (UNGA), New York. https://www.globalpolicy.org/global-taxes/50191-new-mandate-of-the-special-rapporteur-on-the-right-to-food-.html.

Doss, C.R., Kovarik, C., Peterman, A., Quisumbing, A.R. and van den Bold, M. (2013) 'Gender inequalities in ownership and control of land in Africa: Myths versus reality', Discussion paper 01308, IFPRI, Washington DC.

Drèze, J. and Sen, A. (1989) *Hunger and public action*. Oxford University Press on Demand, Oxford.

Fabian Commission (2015) 'Hungry for change', the final report of the Fabian Commission on food and poverty, The Fabian Society, London, UK.

FAO (2015) *The voluntary guidelines for securing sustainable small-scale fisheries in the context of food security and poverty eradication*. FAO, Rome.

FAO (2012) *The voluntary guidelines on the responsible governance of tenure of land, fisheries and forests in the context of national food security*. FAO, Rome.

FAO (2012) *Voluntary guidelines to support the progressive realization of the right to adequate food in the context of the national food Security*. FAO, Rome.

Hendriks, S.L. (2018) 'Food policy and nutrition economics in the SDG era', *Agrekon*, vol. 57, no .3–4, pp. 167–180.

HLPE (2011) 'Price volatility and food security', Report no. 1, HLPE, Rome.

HLPE (2012a) 'Social protection for food security', Report no. 4, HLPE, Rome.

HLPE (2012b) 'Food security and climate change', Report no. 3, HLPE, Rome.

HLPE (2013) 'Investing in smallholder agriculture for food security', Report no. 6, HLPE, Rome.

HLPE (2014) 'Sustainable fisheries and aquaculture for food security and nutrition', Report no. 7, HLPE, Rome.

HLPE (2015) 'Water for food security and nutrition', Report no. 9, HLPE, Rome.

Josling, T. (1975) 'The world food problem: National and international aspects', *Food Policy*, vol. 1, no. 1, pp. 3–14.

Moyo, K. (2016) 'The jurisprudence of the South African Constitutional Court on socio-economic rights', in Foundation for Human Rights (ed.) *Socio-economic rights: Progressive realisation*. Foundation for Human Rights, Houghton Estate.

Office of the High Commissioner for Human Rights (OHCHR) (1999) The right to adequate food (Art. 11) adopted at the twentieth session of the Committee on Economic, Social and Cultural Rights, CESCR General Comment No. 12, OHCHR, Geneva, Switzerland.

Sen, A. (1981) 'Ingredients of famine analysis: Availability and entitlements', *The Quarterly Journal of Economics*, vol. 96, no. 3, pp. 433–464.

UN CESCR (1999) General comment No. 12: The right to adequate food (Art. 11). Available at: https://www.refworld.org/pdfid/4538838c11.pdf.

UN CESCR (2008) General comment No. 19: The right to social security (Art. 9). Available at: http://docstore.ohchr.org/SelfServices/FilesHandler.ashx?enc=4slQ6QSmlBEDzFEovLCu W1a0Szab0oXTdImnsJZZVQdrCvvLm0yy7YCiVA9YY61Z8YHJWla0qOfZ9fbBAjHL% 2fISC4lbLC8mquOIR6C2grPnTYKTk7TbHf5LmpV4xK%2fEs.

UN DESA (Development Strategy and Policy Analysis Unit) (2015) 'Inequality and the 2030 agenda for sustainable development', *Development Issues*, no. 4, pp. 1–10. Available at: https://www.un.org/en/development/desa/policy/wess/wess_dev_issues/dsp_policy_04.pdf.

Webb, P., Coates, J., Frongillo, E.A., Rogers, B. L., Swindale, A. and Bilinsky, P. (2006) 'Measuring household food insecurity: Why it's so important and yet so difficult to do', *The Journal of Nutrition*, vol. 136, no .5, pp. 1404–1408.

6

CONTEMPORARY POLICY ISSUES AND THE IMPERATIVES TO REDUCE MALNUTRITION

Beulah Pretorius, Suresh C. Babu, Angela M. McIntyre and Hettie C. Schönfeldt

6.1 Introduction

Malnutrition affects the sustainable development of nations in different ways. At the individual level malnutrition manifests as undernutrition, over-weight and obesity, unbalanced dietary intake and hidden hunger in the form of micronutrient deficiencies. These conditions have high costs in both the short and the long run. In the short run, reduced productivity of the workforce results in low levels of outputs, and in the long run, it increases the cost of health care due to the disease burden associated with poor nutrition. Malnutrition results in the loss of return to human capital resulting from the reduced ability to fight disease and the reduced human potential of growing children (Headey et al., 2016). Continued high levels of malnutrition in different forms result in high costs, and the recent technical brief of the Global Panel on Agriculture and Food Systems for Nutrition estimates that malnutrition costs up to the US $3.5 trillion per year to the global economy (GloPan, 2016).

The WHO's Member States have endorsed global targets for improving maternal, infant and young child nutrition by 2025 and are committed to monitoring progress. The targets are vital for identifying priority areas for action and catalysing global change. These targets include:

- A 40% reduction in the number of children under five years of age who are stunted
- A 50% reduction of anaemia in women of reproductive age
- A 30% reduction in low birth weight
- No increase in child overweight
- An increase (50%) in the rate of exclusive breastfeeding in the first six months of a child's life
- Reduce and maintain childhood wasting at less than 5% *(WHO, 2018).*

These indicators form the basis of the SDG indicators for nutrition, although nutrition indicators are found in at least 12 of the 17 SDGs.

The majority of the food policies in developing countries focus on the consumption of adequate calories only (Suryanarayana, 2013). Along with consuming adequate calories, consumption of micronutrients is also important to eliminate under nutrition. Rising income does increase intake of quality food; however, income alone does not improve the quality of people's diets. As income increases, food scarcity diminishes but the cost of many nutritious foods remains high and the ability to purchase food that do not support high-quality diets increases. Income growth is a double sword when it comes to improving diets (GloPan, 2016).

Agriculture has traditionally comprised a significant share of national economies. It holds an especially critical role in low-income countries: in 2017, it accounted on average for 25% of low-income countries' gross domestic product (GDP) and employed a large portion of their population (World Bank, 2018). The lack of dietary diversity is strongly associated with inadequate intake and risks of micronutrient deficiencies. Increasing diversity in agricultural production can improve diversity in diets, but the relationship is not necessarily straightforward (Ruel, 2013; IFPRI, 2016).

Agriculture can play three interlinked roles to improve nutrition outcomes by providing nutritious food, being a source of income for people to buy nutritious food and health care, and empowering women, if agriculture interventions are undertaken in a gender-sensitive fashion (Babu, 2019; Hoddinott, 2016). Although with the advancement in science and technology, food production has substantially increased in many developing countries and globalisation has made the transportation of food easier, the challenge of malnutrition remains a major development concern and is critical for both economic and human development (Shekar et al. 2017).

6.2 A universal problem

Malnutrition and severe food insecurity appear to be increasing in almost all sub-regions of Africa, South America and Southeast Asia. Under nutrition contributes to around 45% of deaths among children under five, mostly in low- and middle-income countries (LMICs) (HLPE, 2017). The State of Food Security and Nutrition Report (FAO et al., 2018) reported that, after a prolonged decline, recent estimates showed global hunger had increased in 2016 and again in 2017. In 2017, the number of undernourished people was estimated to have reached 821 million.

All countries in the world experience malnutrition in at least one of its forms: under nutrition, micronutrient deficiencies and overweight and obesity. The developmental and economic impacts of malnutrition, are borne largely by low and middle income countries. Changes in lifestyle and dietary patterns, having impacts on nutrition and health outcomes is described as the 'nutrition transition'. These changes are driven by urbanisation, globalisation and economic growth (HLPE, 2017). Overweight and obesity rates have risen sharply in low and middle-income countries, with high relative changes in low-income, rural populations

(Popkin et al., 2011). A person is considered overweight when their Body Mass Index (BMI) is over ≥ 25 and obese when the BMI is over ≥ 30. BMI is calculated as the ratio of height in metres squared over weight in kilograms (m^2/kg).

Optimal nutritional status is more than the absence of disease or infirmity; it contributes to a state of complete physical, mental and social well-being. Signs of malnutrition include wasting (underweight for age), stunting (short for age) and underweight, as well as overweight and obesity and are caused by imbalances in macronutrient or micronutrient intake, or both. Under nutrition includes energy, macronutrient (protein, fat and carbohydrates contributing to total energy intake) and micronutrient (vitamin and mineral) deficiencies. The body adapts to inadequate food intake to maintain vital functions, involving a decline in metabolic rate and the slowing of cell growth. If prolonged, this leads to decreased physical and mental development, a compromised immune system and increased susceptibility to infectious diseases. Overweight and obesity result when energy intake chronically exceeds requirements and is associated with an increase in diet-related chronic non-communicable diseases (NCDs), such as hypertension, cardiovascular diseases, type 2 diabetes and cancer.

In 2017 it was estimated that one fifth of the global under-five population, over 150 million children, had stunted growth (Development Initiative, 2017). Stunting disrupts critical brain development that can limit life opportunities and impede socio-economic development. Investing in nutrition supports human development throughout life and enhances mental and productive capacity, offering a \$16 return for every \$1 invested (Development Initiative, 2017). More than 7% (51 million) of the global population of children younger than 5 years of age are wasted and 2.4% (16 million) are severely wasted. Globally, the prevalence of underweight children is decreasing, but in Africa, there has been a relative increase in the number of underweight children due to population growth and persistent poverty (FAO et al., 2017).

The relationship between the causes and consequences of malnutrition is complex (Kimani-Murage et al., 2010). Poverty and high food prices reduce consumer purchasing power, exacerbating nutritional vulnerability. Malnutrition adversely affects both mental and physical development and significantly reduces the productivity and economic potential of an individual (Lanigan and Singhal, 2009). A vicious cycle of poor health, impaired ability to concentrate and learn and depressed productivity traps families in poverty and erodes economic security. Poverty contributes to poor childcare, maternal under nutrition and unhealthy environments, frequent infections and poor health care.

6.3 Nutrition transitions

Energy-rich, nutrient-poor diets are one of the five highest risk factors in the global burden of disease (GBD, 2016). Approximately three billion people across the world's 193 countries have low-quality diets (GloPan, 2016). Monotonous diets of inexpensive, energy-dense, but nutrient-poor (staple) foods aggravate the epidemic of obesity and chronic diseases. Often poor households can only afford low cost staple foods, sacrificing more nutritious foods with the associated vitamins and minerals needed for good health (Fanzo et al., 2014). Rising prices mean people remove fruits and vegetables from their grocery lists. Accessing enough "cheap" food to maintain satiety can leave families with micronutrient deficiencies and "hidden hunger", which are a persistent health concern. Ready access to sugary drinks and a rising proportion of food obtained away from home with added fats, sugar and salt, have steadily increased per capita caloric consumption (Popkin, 1993).

Global food systems are failing to keep everyone fed, let alone healthy. Supply chains encompass the ways in which food is grown, distributed, processed, marketed and sold determines which foods are available, affordable and desirable. In the next few decades, food systems will be under further stresses from population and income growth, urbanisation, globalisation, climate change and increasingly scarce natural resources (Haddad, 2013).

6.4 A life course approach

In-utero and early life nutrition and growth have profound impacts on health later in life, including the susceptibility to chronic diseases and what is known as metabolic syndrome. Nutrition prior to conception is critical and is influenced by the age and the lifestyle of parents (Figure 6.1). Development in a suboptimal uterine environment increases the likelihood of disease later in life

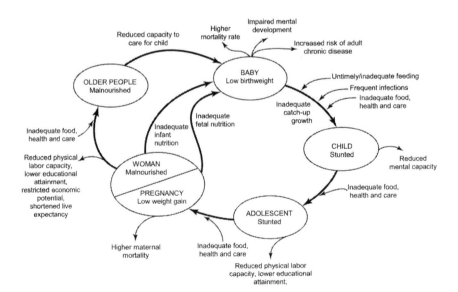

FIGURE 6.1 Impacts of malnutrition over the life course
Source: Adapted from ACC/SCN (2000)

(Aiken and Ozanne, 2013). The first 1000 days of life (from conception to the child's second birthday) present an important window of opportunity to improve a child's nutritional status (Demaio and Branca, 2018).

Maternal age is also known to influence the uterine environment, and is a risk factor for adverse outcomes in pregnancy, including low birth weight and intrauterine growth restriction (Aiken and Ozanne, 2013). Family planning can have a greater effect on nutrition outcomes than interventions such as vitamin A and iron supplementation. Adolescent girls should be at the heart of a life cycle approach. In addition to actions to prevent adolescent pregnancy and encourage pregnancy spacing, efforts are required to ensure that adolescent girls are adequately nourished. Moreover, lifestyle choices such as tobacco and alcohol use and inactivity put young people at risk of developing NCDs (Saksena and Kariotis, 2018).

The life course approach can inform nutrition interventions and programs. Dietary guidelines, for example, can be directed specifically at pregnant and reproductive-age women, or infants and young children, or pre-school and school-age children. Similarly, vitamin and mineral supplementation programs, feeding programs, deworming, and interventions to manage moderate or acute malnutrition are tailored to the needs of these groups, delivered through health, community and school programs (WHO, 2018).

Nutrition-sensitive actions in agriculture, social protection, early childhood development and education address the immediate determinants of malnutrition and adequate food and nutrient intake. Among these are food security, adequate caregiving resources at the maternal, household and community levels and access to health services and a safe and hygienic environment (Ruel and Alderman, 2013). The importance of agriculture for food security and nutrition is increasingly recognised. However, the links between agriculture, nutrition and health policies and programmes have tended to be weak. Agriculture policies are not always aligned with the goals of accessible nutritious foods and dietary diversity needed to combat micronutrient deficiencies and hidden hunger.

Education sector policies influence nutrition along several pathways. Parental education is an important predictor of nutritional improvement in most countries (Islam et al., 2015; Branca et al., 2015).

6.5 Keeping up to date with nutrition policy change

There is no shortage of nutrition policy documents and high-level pledges, and while these have become better-informed by evidence and increased in scope over the years, delivering on commitments is still a challenge (WHO 2018). The WHO's second Global Nutrition Policy review (2018) found that slow buy-in from senior officials outside the health sector impedes progress. Food security and agriculture policies do not always include diet and nutrition targets and nutrition does not always appear in national development plans (WHO, 2018). Sectoral commitments from the finance and budgeting, social welfare and environment sectors were universally low (WHO, 2018). Table 6.1 attempts to summarise the shift in attention and focus in international policy discourses that has influences policy change over the decades.

The relevance of agricultural policies to nutrition was more explicitly recognised with the appearance of the term "nutrition-sensitive agriculture" and the role of food production and food systems in ensuring the availability and accessibility of nutritious diets (Ruel and Alderman, 2013). Until the 2010s, many policies and programs concentrated on the availability, accessibility and utilization dimensions of food security. However, rising poverty and hunger attributed to climate change, conflict and the financial crises began to shift policy focus to these more distal drivers of malnutrition, including concerns about the environmental impacts of food production, food safety and equity. The term "sustainable diets" refers to:

> "diets with low environmental impacts which contribute to food and nutrition security and to healthy life for present and future generations. Sustainable diets are protective and respectful of biodiversity and ecosystems, culturally acceptable, accessible, economically fair and affordable; nutritionally adequate, safe and healthy; while optimizing natural and human resources."
>
> *(Burlingame, 2010)*

Where national development policies incorporate nutrition goals and objectives, these have tended to focus on infant and young child nutrition, with a persistent policy gap in obesity and diet related non-communicable diseases (WHO, 2018). Transformation in this policy area is proving to be challenging. Measures to create healthier food environments need to reach beyond the traditional field of behaviour change and into food environments and food systems. Regulatory reforms, taxation, marketing and food labelling are all areas that expand the stakeholder field well beyond the traditional boundaries of nutrition policy and into wider food systems.

6.6 Nutrition economics – an emerging field of study

Studying the economics of nutrition can be helpful in addressing a wide range of policy questions that the policy makers are grappling with to attaining food and nutrition security for their populations. This emerging field of policy and econometrics pioneered by Babu, Gajanan and Hallam (2017) shifts the focus of agriculture and food security policy analysis beyond food intake and its nutrient content to a broader consideration of nutrition as an outcome of a complex process that includes effective use of food and nutrients along with clean water, sanitation, care, health services, and safe food sources.

TABLE 6.1 Summary of policy discourse and policy change related to nutrition over the decades

	WWII to 1970s	*1980s*	*1990s*	*2000s*	*2010s*
Global malnutrition and hunger	960 million hungry in 1970	Over 900 million hungry	Diabetes, hypertension and obesity dominate (Popkin, 1993)	820 million hungry (CFS 2001, FAO 2006) Increases with global food crisis (2017/8) to 963 million (FAO, 2008) In 2009 hunger reaches historic level at 1020 million people	Evidence continues to signal that the number of hungry people in the world is growing, reaching 821 million in 2017
Science and malnutrition	High income countries: fat, not sugar, becomes the "culprit" in NCDs Scientists debate the importance of protein and calories; protein enrichment of baby formulas and foods in Low income countries.	HIC: dietary guidelines begin to address NCDs	LICs: focus on hunger and micronutrient deficiencies HICs: debating supplementation versus dietary patterns	LICs: the "triple burden" appears in policy and research HIC: food safety concerns around agricultural chemicals, processing and additives *Lancet* series on maternal and child nutrition	Focus on food systems HICs: attention to diet-micro biomes-hosts; personalised nutrition; influence of social status and place LICs: new focus on dietary diversity pathways Nutrition transition: Increased reliance on processed foods, away from home food, edible oils and sugar-sweetened beverages; reduced physical activity and increased sedentary time (Popkin, 1993) Globalising supply chains and market integration have different effects on dietary patterns Local food systems, biodiversity affected by climate change

	2010s	2000s	1990s	1980s	WWII to 1970s
Global commitments	Monitoring period for the Millennium Development Goal targets ends in 2015. Undernourished people in the total population in developing regions has decreased from 23.3% in 1990–92 to 12.9% (FAO, 2014) SDGs–September 2015, 193 countries agreed to SDG 2: Achieving zero hunger by 2030 UNGA Declaration on the Prevention and Control of NCDs; UN appoints Special Rapporteur on the Right to Food	Millennium Development Goals; WHO resolutions on Integrated Chronic Disease Prevention; 2018–2013 Action Plan for the Global Strategy for Prevention and Control of NCDs, Global Strategy on Diet, Physical Activity and Health; WHO Commission Report on Social Determinants of Health; Scaling up Nutrition (SUN)	World Summit on Children; International Conference on Nutrition; African Charter on the Rights and Welfare of the Child	International Convention on the Rights of the Child	Alma Ata declaration: health for all by the year 2000; 1979 is the UN Year of the Child; Universal Declaration on Eradication of Hunger and Malnutrition; International Covenant on Economic, Social and Cultural Rights
Major global food and agricultural developments (FAO, 2000)	2015 UN Climate Change Conference (COP21); climate: change mitigation	Global food crisis caused by food price volatility and price shocks	Emergence of a new political, economic and trade order Liberalisation, globalisation and financial upheavals Food security – the World Food Summit UNCED – sustainable agricultural and rural development Trade – conclusion of the Uruguay Round	A "lost decade" for many countries in Latin America and Africa Economic stabilisation and structural adjustment Famine in Africa, Environment and sustainable development Trade tensions and the launching of the Uruguay Round; Intergovernmental Panel on Climate Change established (1988)	Food and energy crises and a less stable development environment, the World Food Conference, Famines in Africa the World Conference on Agrarian Reform and Rural Development Environmental concerns, Trade issues Fisheries and the Law of the Sea

Studying nutrition economics from a policy perspective requires understanding, among other things, the changes in food and nutrition intake patterns in various societies. The pattern of food and nutrient intake changes as the countries transform their economies in general, and their rural and agricultural sector in particular. Further, as the income of households increases, the intake of high quality foods increases, along with foods that contain high levels of saturated and trans fats, sugar, and salt contributing to the incidence of overweight and obesity, and to the development of noncommunicable diseases. Moreover, members of households with higher income levels and urban households tend to have sedentary lifestyles and increasingly eat processed foods. Households in the lower income strata also add more oil and sugar to their already high energy diet when incomes increase (Popkin et al., 2012; Hawkes et al., 2007). Thus, studying changes in the pattern of food and nutrient intake is key for designing policies and programs that can help attain optimal nutrition and health for any society (Ruel and Alderman, 2013; Reardon et al., 2012).

A broad set of factors affect nutritional outcomes, although the causes of malnutrition are wide-ranging and complex to tie down. Among the major contributors are food security, clean water, health, sanitation, care, gender relations, and the availability of nutritional and health interventions (Smith and Haddad, 2015). Several technological, environmental, political, cultural, and socioeconomic factors affect determinants of nutrition at the community level. Consequently, the factors that affect these determinants will have a second-round effect on nutritional status. For example, to the extent that climate change affects food security and environmental conditions, it will have a profound effect on the nutritional status of the affected population (Springmann et al., 2016). Similarly, food safety could influence nutritional status by affecting the quality of food and health-related outcomes. Analysing the determinants of nutritional outcomes can help generate evidence for designing policy and program interventions.

Babu et al. (2017) provide a set of analytical methods for policy analysis of nutrition challenges facing the world population in this new field of study in a recently published book on nutrition economics.

6.7 Conclusion

Recent policy developments bring greater focus to nutrition and unique opportunities for countries to implement coherent and intensified efforts to scale up evidence-based inter-sectoral solutions to address all forms of malnutrition, to accelerate the achievement of global nutrition targets, to attain the SDGs.

A policy environment conducive to alleviating malnutrition takes commitment from multiple stakeholders sharing responsibility with governments. Governments need support from research institutions, indigenous knowledge holders and industry and science organisations. Working across institutions producing high quality research

50 Beulah Pretorius et al.

is imperative. Critically assessing best practices and strong evidence to improve health and well-being outcomes and to inform policy are essential. Understanding the dynamics of nutrition policy and its effect on development outcomes is essential in development planning, policy assessment, evaluation and impact assessment.

References

ACC/SCN (Administrative Committee on Coordination/Subcommittee on Nutrition) (2000) 'Fourth report on the world nutrition situation', Report, ACC/SCN in collaboration with IFPRI, Geneva.

Aiken, C.E. and Ozanne, S.E. (2013) 'Transgenerational developmental programming', *Human Reproduction Update*, vol. 20, no. 1, pp. 63–75.

Babu, S.C. (2019) 'Building capacity to link agriculture and nutrition', in S. Fan, S. Yosef and R. Pandya-Lorch (eds) *Agriculture for Improved Nutrition: Seizing the Momentum*. CABI International, Oxfordshire.

Babu, S.C., Gajanan, S.N., and Hallam, J.A. (2017) *Nutrition Economics: Principles and Policy Applications* . Elsevier, Amsterdam.

Branca, F., Piwoz, E., Schultink, W. and Sullivan, L.M. (2015) 'Nutrition and health in women, children, and adolescent girls', *BMJ*, vol. 14, no. 351, pp. 27–31.

Burlingame, B. 2010. 'Preface' in B. Burlingame, S. Derini and FAO (eds) *Sustainable Diets and Biodiversity Sustainable Diets and Biodiversity*. FAO, Rome.

Champroux, A., Cocquet, J., Henry-Berger, J., Drevet, J. and Kocer, A. (2018) 'A decade of exploring the mammalian sperm epigenome: Paternal epigenetic and transgenerational inheritance', *Frontiers in Cell and Developmental Biology*, vol. 6, no. 50, pp. 1–19.

Demaio, A.R. and Branca, F. (2018) 'Decade of action on nutrition: Our window to act on the double burden of malnutrition', *BMJ Global Health*, vol. 3, no. 1, pp. 1–3.

Development Initiatives (2017) *Global nutrition report 2017: Nourishing the SDGs*. Development Initiatives, Bristol, UK.

Fanzo, J., Cohen, M., Sparling, T., Olds, T. and Cassidy, M. (2014) *The Nutrition Sensitivity of Agriculture and Food Policies: A Synthesis of Eight Country Case Studies*. United Nations, New York.

FAO (2000). 'The State of Food and Agriculture 2000: Lessons from the past 50 years', FAO Agriculture Series no. 32, FAO, Rome.

FAO (2006) *The State of Food Insecurity in the World: Eradicating World Hunger – Taking Stock Ten Years after the World Food Summit*. FAO, Rome.

FAO (2008) 'Number of hungry people rises to 963 million', http://www.fao.org/news/story/en/item/8836/icode/

FAO (2014) *Second International Conference on Nutrition (ICN2). Rome declaration on nutrition*. FAO, Rome.

FAO, IFAD, UNICEF, WFP and WHO (2017) *The State of Food Security and Nutrition in the World 2017: Building resilience for peace and food security*. FAO, Rome.

FAO, IFAD, UNICEF, WFP and WHO (2018) *The State of Food Security and Nutrition in the World 2018. Building climate resilience for food security and nutrition*. FAO, Rome.

GBD (Global Burden of Diseases) (2015) 'Risk factors collaborators', *Lancet*, vol. 386, pp. 2287–2323.

GloPan (Global Panel on Agriculture and Food Systems in Nutrition) (2016) 'Food systems and diets: Facing the challenges of the 21st century', Foresight report, GloPan, London, UK.

Gomez, M., Barret, C.B., Raney, T., Pinstrup-Andersen, P., Meerman, J.Croppenstedt, A., Carisma, B. and Thompson, B. 'Post-green revolution food systems and the triple burden of malnutrition', *Food Policy*, vol. 42, pp. 129–138.

Haddad, L. (2013) 'From nutrition plus to nutrition driven: How to realise the elusive potential of agriculture for nutrition?', *Food and Nutrition Bulletin*, vol. 34, no. 1, pp. 39–44.

Hawkes, C., Ruel, M. and Babu, S. (2007) 'Agriculture and health: Overview, themes, and moving forward', *Food Nutrition Bulletin*, vol. 28, no. 2, pp. 221–226.

HLPE (2017) 'Nutrition and food systems' Report no 12, HLPE, CFS, Rome.

Headey, D., Hoddinott, J., and Park, S. (2016) Drivers of nutritional change in four South Asian countries: A dynamic observational analysis. *Maternal and Child Nutrition*, vol. 12, 210–218. doi: doi:10.1111/mcn.12274

IFPRI (2016) *Global Food Policy Report*. IFPRI, Washington DC.

Islam, M.S., Rahman, S.S., Kamruzzaman, M., Raza, M.S., Saifuzzaman, M., Aktar, M.J. and Hossain, M.S. (2015) 'Impact of nutrition education on nutritional status of adolescent girls in south-west region of Bangladesh', *American Journal of Nutrition and Food Science*, vol. 1, no. 6, pp. 1–6.

Kimani-Murage, E.W., Kahn, K., Pettifor, J.M., Tollman, S.M., Dunger, D.B., Xavier, F., Gómez-Olivé, X.F. and Norris, S.A. (2010) 'The prevalence of stunting, overweight and obesity, and metabolic disease risk in rural South African Children', *BMC Public Health*, vol. 10, no. 158, pp. 1–13.

Lanigan, J. and Singhal, A. (2009) 'Early nutrition and long-term health: A practical approach', *Proceedings of the Nutrition Society*, vol. 61, no. 4, pp. 422–429.

Popkin, B.M. (1993). 'Nutritional patterns and transitions', *Population and Development Review*, vol. 19, no. 1, pp. 138–157.

Popkin, B.M., Adair, L.S. and Ng, S.W. (2011) 'Global nutrition transition and the pandemic of obesity in developing countries', vol. 70, no. 1, pp. 3–21. doi:10.1111/j.1753-4887.2011.00456.x.

Popkin, B.M., Adair, L.S. and Ng, S.W. (2012) 'Global nutrition transition and the pandemic of obesity in developing countries', *Nutrition Review*, vol. 70, no. 1, pp. 3–21.

Reardon, T., Chen, K., Minten, B. and Adriano, L. (2012) *The Quiet Revolution In Staple Food Value Chains*. Asian Development Bank (ADB) and IFPRI, Manila and Washington DC.

Ruel, M.T., Alderman, H. and the Maternal and Child Nutrition Study Group (2013) 'Nutrition-sensitive interventions and programmes: How can they help to accelerate progress in improving maternal and child nutrition?' *The Lancet*, vol. 382, no. 9891, 536–551.

Saksena, R. and Kariotis, T. (2018) 'World Economic Forum global agenda: Adolescent health has been overlooked for too long' https://www.weforum.org/agenda/2018/10/adolescent-health-overlooked-too-long/.

Shekar, M., Jakub, K., Dayton, J., and Walters, D. (2017) *An Investment Framework for Nutrition: Reaching the Global Targets for Stunting, Anemia, Breastfeeding, and Wasting*. International Bank for Reconstruction and Development and World Bank, Washington DC.

Smith, L.C. and Haddad, L. (2015) 'Reducing child undernutrition: Past drivers and priorities for the post-MDG era', *World Development*, vol. 68, pp. 180–204.

Springmann, M., Mason-D'Croz, D. Robinson, S. Garnett, T., Godfray, H.C., Gollin, D., Rayner, M. Ballon, P. and Scarborough, P. (2016) 'Global and regional health effects of future food production under climate change: a modelling study', *Lancet*, vol. 387, no. 10031, 1937–1946.

Suryanarayana, M.H. (2013) 'The pursuit of food security in India: Policies sans concept and commitment?', http://www.ipc-undp.org/pub/IPCOnePager207.pdf

UN (United Nations) (2011) *Political Declaration of the High-level Meeting of the General Assembly on the Prevention and Control of Non-Communicable Diseases*. UN, New York.

UN (2015) *Transforming our World: The 2030 Agenda for Sustainable Development*. UN, New York.

UN (2016) *UNDecade of Action on Nutrition (2016–2025) (A/RES/70/259)*. UN, New York.

WHO (2018) *Global Nutrition Policy Review 2016–2017: Country progress in creating enabling policy environments for promoting healthy diets and nutrition.* WHO, Geneva.

WHO (2019). Nutrition: Global targets 2025. https://www.who.int/nutrition/topics/nutrition_globaltargets2025/en/.

World Bank. (2018) 'Agriculture, value added (% of GDP)', https://data.worldbank.org/indicator/NV.AGR.TOTL.ZS?locations=XM&view=chart.

7

MITIGATING NEGATIVE NUTRITION TRANSITIONS

Cultivating diversity in food systems

Angela M. McIntyre

7.1 Introduction

Malnutrition arising from nutrition transitions brings food policy success, failures, contradictions and unintended outcomes into sharp focus. The phenomenon of nutrition transition is explained as change in the nutritional profile of populations resulting from food consumption and lifestyle shifts, driven by economic, demographic, environmental, and cultural changes (Popkin, 2015).

A major health risk associated with nutrition transitions is higher body overweight and obesity. But for low and middle-income countries, energy over-consumption can co-exist with micro-nutrient (vitamins and minerals essential for metabolism and development) under-consumption to produce what has been named 'hidden hunger'. Obesity and childhood stunting are related to over- and under-consumption and yet these can be found within the same populations, the same households and can even affect the same individuals over the life course. At the heart of this contradiction is the quality and variety of foods required to meet nutritional needs. Although humans have found infinitely innovative ways to exploit environments for survival, creating a great diversity of food systems, this diversity is diminishing rapidly. (Lachat et al., 2018).

Food systems have become difficult to govern in ways that promote good nutrition. Fewer and fewer people are active participants in food systems beyond their roles as consumers. This notion is central to the 'broken food system' hypothesis, which suggests that a loss of broad-based agency and control and over-concentration of power and financial interests in profit-making are perpetuating the ongoing global food crisis (Holt-Giménez and Peabody, 2008). One symptom of this malfunction is the co-existence of hunger and obesity, which is confounding food policymakers.

7.2 The food system: broken or highly vulnerable?

The 'broken food system' narrative suggests that a global order undermines local economies and decimates food cultures, allowing industrial food production to have unchecked, detrimental effects on ecosystems and human health (Holt-Giménez and Peabody, 2008). This is the result of too much control by corporate monopolies, underwritten by global trade agreements, who are engaged in profit-driven, industrial-scale production not of food, but of raw materials for food processing and animal feed (Holt-Giménez and Peabody, 2008). This concentration is facilitated by trade liberal-isation, commodity speculation, land dispossession and exclusion of smaller scale food producers (Araghi, 2009). These trends have profound livelihood and nutrition impacts on everyone, not only smallholders in low-income countries.

This configuration makes for a vulnerable global food system. The number of coun-tries dependent on food imports due to changes in local production, national and regional trade and energy policies is growing, creating a global food system that is precariously susceptible to shocks and stresses of market volatility, climate change and other global dynamics (Suweis et al., 2015). Where food supplies and availability are closely coupled to global markets, consumers can experience price shocks that impact food accessibility (Suweis et al., 2015).

The food system also determines quality, including diversity, of diets. Within indus-trialising food systems, the conglomeration of land, farming enterprises, supply chains and marketing are concentrating the provenance of food. Food travels ever greater dis-tances before reaching consumers, while local food cultures are becoming diluted, along the way shedding the knowledge related to production, consumption and nutrition that contributes to dietary diversity. Although affluent consumers have a bewildering array of food choices from across the globe, including fresh produce, access to dietary variety and quality is highly inequitable and the poor often have far fewer choices.

Countries' food systems are increasingly interconnected, responding to global pres-sures such as economic fluctuations and climate change. Policies governing such a massive and complex system that crosses borders and hemispheres are bound to be uncoordinated and even discordant, creating unintended patterns of scarcity and abundance that negatively influence nutrition outcomes and population health. As scales of production and industry concentration increase and globalisation takes food production farther away from consumers, the food system and all its interlinkages has fallen out of the reach of those sectors traditionally governing nutrition, such as health and agriculture. Food environments are being shaped by forces far beyond the control of consumers and healthy choices are often not there for people on limited incomes.

There are no top-down or one-size-fits-all solutions for any form of malnutri-tion, much less the conundrum of concurrent obesity and hunger. No single policy, food crop or miracle supplement is likely to fix a global food system failing to sustainably meet human needs. The solutions to problematic nutrition transi-tions, it is suggested in this chapter, might lie in restoring diversity in ways that builds greater resilience into all three dimensions of food systems: production, consumption and nutrition.

7.3 Production: the rise of the monoculture

In the past century, "assumptions about the causes of famine" and the need to re-tool wartime post-war industrial economies came together to mobilise "what came to be known as the green revolution". Malnutrition was perceived as a problem of undernourishment, or inadequate intakes of protein and energy, to be addressed by boosting food production. Part of the solution was to produce more energy-rich staple crops, which was done on a massive scale with unprecedented volumes of chemical fertilisers and pesticides, water, newly engineered grain varieties and the conversion of land to intensive farming. From the perspective of production, dramatic increases in grain tonnage indicated resounding success. But the longer term gains from the green revolution in reducing global hunger and malnutrition, along with its various economic, technological and nutritional offspring remain topics of controversy.

The agriculture-driven 'calorie project', was arguably a triumph from a purely production point of view. In addition to boosting staple crop yields, the green revolution opened up vast possibilities for the production of raw materials and animal feed. New food-processing technologies made edible plant oils and refined sweeteners cheaper, more available in greater quantities and found more ingenious places to put them. Grain-derived sugars and oils are now ubiquitous in processed and long-shelf-life foods and unprecedented numbers of animals are grown in factory farms. The availability of durable processed food is widened by regulatory environments that influence the free flow of goods and enable the expansion of modern supermarkets and agricultural intensification, operating on economies of scale that make manufactured food more affordable (Popkin et al., 2012).

Deficits in national food supplies, even for the world's poorest countries, have become rarer, yet undernourishment persists, accompanied by rising rates of overweight and obesity. Low-income consumers are susceptible to shocks and stresses generated by a precariously interconnected food system, threatened also by climate change. These are systemic problems on the grandest possible scale, but their solutions might require us to actually think smaller, not bigger, and to consider the role of diversity in diets, food systems, and in ecosystems in general.

7.4 Policy silos and nutrition paradoxes

The combination of micronutrient deficiencies, overweight and protein-energy malnutrition is described as the 'triple burden' of malnutrition. There is currently no country in the world that does not suffer at least one of the three forms of malnutrition (Gómez et al., 2013). No country has yet succeeded in reversing the growth of overweight and obesity (Roberto et al., 2015). In many low- and some middle-income countries, health systems still grapple with hunger, infectious disease and delivering basic primary care are now confronting increasing burdens of chronic disease, including cancer, cardiovascular disease and type II or adult-onset diabetes. Nutrition transition is linked also to epidemiological transitions, which see a move away from infectious diseases towards chronic diseases at the population level. High prevalence of infectious diseases is associated with malnutrition, so it is for chronic diseases, albeit a different form.

In some low- and middle-income countries, stunted children and overweight mothers can be found living together, and stunted children can become obese. It is difficult to discern the causes of this paradox – is it associated with income poverty or affluence, urbanisation or rural marginalisation? The solutions have so far evaded food security policy and conventional health and agricultural interventions, because these have failed to keep pace with nutrition transitions and rapidly changing food systems.

But this is not a new problem. Policymakers have struggled with finding nutrition a 'home' ever since it became a global development issue in the 1970s. Different forms of malnutrition have been addressed by different sectoral efforts aimed at improving access not to food, but to specific nutrients. The agricultural contribution to alleviating malnutrition has aimed primarily at increasing yields to meet food energy needs. Meanwhile, vitamin and mineral deficiencies were treated as medical problems to be addressed with supplementation programs. Health sector-driven supplementation programs are short-term, unsustainable interventions that are have no long-term effects on diets. Supplementation has no effect on structurally rooted problems of food accessibility, for example land dispossession and income poverty. The productivist approach exemplified by the green revolution exacerbated the triple burden by boosting food energy availability simultaneously reducing diversity in agriculture, ecosystems and diets.

National-level nutrition planning continues to pose great challenges to governments, with their discreet policy sectors, professional disciplines and power bases (Berg and Austin, 1984). Where national policies succeed in coordinated action, the tendency is for these to be economically-focused. Food policy has not focused on nutrition or consumption, but on self-sufficiency, national supplies, prices and purchasing power. Issues around income disparities and the social determinants that interact with malnutrition, fall varyingly into other sectors or are simply overlooked (Berg and Austin, 1984). Fragmented, partial or mono-disciplinary policy thinking is unlikely to capture all facets of even one form of malnutrition, let alone the triple burden of malnutrition.

In the example of micronutrient deficiency in otherwise energy-sufficient diets, referred to as hidden hunger, malnutrition hides within bodies that are not visibly emaciated and behind apparently adequate food supplies. In effect, hunger is hidden because of the way it has been conceptualised and how information is gathered. Understanding the apparent paradox of obesity and poverty is constrained by opposing ideas that also limit policy responses. It is often simplified into a problem of either poor lifestyle choices or uncontrollable environmental factors. This is a simplistic and misleading dichotomy, when in fact people's interactions with food environments have elements of both (Roberto et al., 2015)

Economic prosperity itself has de-coupled from healthy eating. The rising global consumption rates of certain products, for example, sugar-sweetened beverages, are indication of their growing accessibility and affordability. Between 1990 and 2016, consumption increased in LMICS as relative income costs (as percentage of GDP) fell, a change that occurred more quickly in low than in high-income countries (Blecher et al., 2017). 'Empty calories', have never been more accessible to consumers in low and middle-income countries. At the same time, local, fresh food markets in low and middle-income countries are on the decline (Popkin, 2015). These 'obesogenic' (promoting obesity) environments are shaped by economic policies rather than dietary preferences, health priorities or local culture, and reinforced by policies that are often outdated.

Policies in low- and middle-income countries are especially falling behind nutrition transitions. A 2014 scan of 139 low and middle-income countries revealed that less than half included both under- and over-nutrition (overweight and obesity) in policies (Sunguya et al., 2014). Where policies do occasionally target obesity, they still reflect the understanding of obesity as consequence of lifestyle choices associated with urbanisation and modernisation. Obesity is growing among the poorest in low-income countries, and particularly in rural, agrarian settings. This shows most dramatically among children and reproductive-aged women in low income countries. Volatile food prices, changing climates and intensification (requiring land and water appropriation) and declining smallholder production cause diets to be pared down to only cheap, energy-rich staples (Garrett and Ruel, 2005).

7.5 Food consumption: the missing policy link?

Consumption is as important a facet of food systems as nutrition and production. It is the critical interface between people and food systems. Yet in policy terms, food consumption is something of a poor cousin of nutrition and production. Malnutrition responses often address nutrients, rather than food in all its possibilities. In low-income countries, health can be predicted by national production diversity, more so than in middle- and high-income countries, where incomes and trade have a greater influence (Remans et al., 2014).

The populations at greatest risk of obesity and chronic disease are 'those' experiencing changes in dietary patterns over which they have little control, namely the world's agrarian poor, dispossessed from land and traditional food systems and the urban poor living in 'food deserts', relyin on cheap, ultra-processed food or fast food. Where supermarket expansion occurs, processed, long-shelf-life foods may replace the products of diverse, local food systems. Dietary diversity comes under further pressure in poor rural areas with diminished access to Indigenous or wild harvested plants and animals. As small-scale farming and local industries give way to wage-labour incomes, reliance on purchased food increases. Both urban and rural poor people are coming to rely on cheap food from uniform ingredients supplied by highly concentrated industries. Local food growers, processors and marketers cannot compete with these economies of scale of industrialised supply chains.

From a policy perspective, consumption is challenging to regulate. Policies most often address consumption from the perspective of behaviour and lifestyle choices, relying mostly on nutrition guidelines and education. For the poor who cannot afford healthy diets, these policies are inadequate. If energy-dense, micronutrient-poor diets are all that is accessible, choices are very few. Aside from this, policies governing what people eat by regulating the quality and diversity of food supplies, are patchy. Some countries have introduced taxes on sugary drinks and restricted advertising to children and regulated food labelling, but reducing harm is a long way from promoting good food.

7.6 Is greater diversity the answer?

Thinking about malnutrition in the context of modern food systems needs to progress in the same way as thinking about famines did decades ago – through better understanding of structural factors that reinforce inequitable patterns of scarcity and (over)abundance. By now it is accepted that food shortages and famines are man-made, structurally-embedded phenomena and simply increasing food supplies is unlikely to affect root causes. The negative effects of nutrition transitions are just as unlikely to be mitigated by approaches that treat symptoms rather than structural causes.

Like famines, negative nutrition transitions are a political problem, and one related to food quality as much as quantity. Obesity and hidden hunger are also the outcomes of precarious and poorly-governed food systems. As a whole, the global food system has shown itself to lack resilience in being vulnerable to shocks and stresses that push people into food crisis or keep them states of chronic malnutrition. Of course many factors – social determinants of health, climate change, energy and water – are implicated in malnutrition. Different configurations of these at local levels make it highly unlikely that problems can even be accurately defined, let alone solved, at national levels.

Some activist food movements argue that the problems of malnutrition, including obesity resulting from 'industrial' diets, are caused by too much concentration of power. Proponents of food sovereignty, for example, argue for less control by the global, industrial food system. Only by putting food systems back in the hands of those whose vested interests are in food rather than profit, can malnutrition, poverty and environmental degradation begin to be addressed. The technical counterpart of this political agenda is different approaches to production; smaller scale, local ownership of land and resources, cultural revitalisation and protection of local seed varieties. In short, greater diversity in food systems, stakeholders and localised accountability are ingredients for the interconnected outcomes of health, resilience and socioeconomic and political empowerment. Whether these approaches lead to improved dietary diversity and nutrition outcomes is an important topic for research.

In the meantime, it is widely accepted that policies, strategies and programs can also benefit from 'diversity' thinking, with multi-sectoral coordination, multi-disciplinary, and transdisciplinary approaches. One way to begin understanding the structural causes of food insecurity, including negative effects of nutrition transition, is to re-examine roles, responsibilities and potential of different stakeholders. These include industrial food producers, small producers and custodians of traditional food systems, small-scale marketers and processors, consumers, non-human species and ecosystems. Representing many, rather than only few, food system interests, cultivates diversity in thinking and ownership, and therefore sustainability, of solutions.

In its current configuration, the global food system is failing on the nutrition front by reinforcing the patterns of production, consumption and nutrition that put populations at risk of chronic disease and hidden hunger. These patterns have in many ways been resistant to policy interventions because they are reproduced by systems that are not governable by conventional sectoral approaches. Responses need to address nutrition, consumption and production in order to create structural shifts towards resilience, sustainability and diversity. More than ever there is a need for innovation, which is always the product of a multitude of ideas and diversity in thinking.

References

Araghi, F. (2009) 'Accumulation by displacement: Global enclosures, food crisis, and the ecological contradictions of capitalism', *Review (Fernand Braudel Center)*, vol. 32, no. 1, pp. 113–146.

Berg, A., and Austin, J. (1984). 'Nutrition policies and programmes. A decade of redirection', *Food Policy*, vol. 9, no. 4, 304–312. https://doi.org/10.1016/0306-9192(84)90066-6.

Blecher, E., Liber, A.C., Drope, J.M., Nguyen, B. and Stoklosa, M. (2017) 'Global trends in the affordability of sugar-sweetened beverages, 1990–2016', *Preventing Chronic Disease*, vol. 14, no. E37, pp. 1–13.

Garrett, J. and Ruel, M.T. (2005) 'The coexistence of child undernutrition and maternal overweight: Prevalence, hypotheses, and programme and policy implications', *Maternal & Child Nutrition*, vol. 1, no. 3, pp. 185–196.

Gómez, M.I., Barrett, C.B., Raney, T., Pinstrup-Andersen, P., Meerman, J., Croppenstedt, A., Carisma, B. and Thompson, B. (2013) 'Post-green revolution food systems and the triple burden of malnutrition', *Food Policy*, vol. 42, pp. 129–138.

Holt-Giménez, E. and Peabody, L. (2008) 'From food rebellions to food sovereignty: Urgent call to fix a broken food system', *Food First Backgrounder*, vol. 14, no. 1, pp. 1–6.

Lachat, C., Raneri, J.E., Smith, K.W., Kolsteren, P., Van Damme, P., Verzelen, K., Penafiel, D., Vanhove, W., Kennedy, G. and Hunter, D. (2018) 'Dietary species richness as a measure of food biodiversity and nutritional quality of diets', *Proceedings of the National Academy of Sciences*, vol. 115, no. 1, pp. 127–132.

Popkin, B.M. (1993) 'Nutritional patterns and transitions', *Population and Development Review*, vol. 19, no. 1, pp. 138–157.

Popkin, B.M. (2015) 'Nutrition transition and the global diabetes epidemic', *Current Diabetes Reports*, vol. 15, no. 9, pp. 64.

Popkin, B.M., Adair, L.S. and Ng, S.W. (2012) 'Global nutrition transition and the pandemic of obesity in developing countries', *Nutrition Reviews*, vol. 70, no. 1, pp. 3–21.

Remans, R., Wood, S.A., Saha, N., Anderman, T.L. and Defries, R.S. (2014). 'Measuring nutritional diversity of national food supplies', *Global Food Security*, vol. 3, no. 3–4, pp. 174–182.

Roberto, C.A., Swinburn, B., Hawkes, C., Huang, T.T., Costa, S.A., Ashe, M., Zwicker, L., Cawley, J.H. and Brownell, K.D. (2015) 'Patchy progress on obesity prevention:

emerging examples, entrenched barriers, and new thinking', *The Lancet*, vol. 385, no. 9985, pp. 2400–2409.

Sunguya, B.F., Ong, K.I., Dhakal, S., Mlunde, L.B., Shibanuma, A., Yasuoka, J. and Jimba, M. (2014) 'Strong nutrition governance is a key to addressing nutrition transition in low and middle-income countries: Review of countries' nutrition policies', *Nutrition Journal*, vol. 13, no. 1, pp. 65.

Suweis, S., Carr, J.A., Maritan, A., Rinaldo, A. and D'Odorico, P. (2015) 'Resilience and reactivity of global food security', *Proceedings of the National Academy of Sciences*, vol. 112, no. 22, pp. 6902–6907.

8

CONTEMPORARY POLICY ISSUES IN FOOD ASSISTANCE

Steven Were Omamo, Lorenzo Motta and Chelsea Graham

8.1 Introduction

Food crises of the twenty-first century are symptomatic of a complex and challenging global food security context. Climate change, migration, conflict and political instability contribute to rising levels of chronic hunger and spreading food crises, creating greater demands on food assistance and a need for new approaches. Risk factors in food crises often work together in vicious cycles. Climate change has become an important influence on food insecurity as well as a driver of migration, particularly where vulnerable ecosystems are degraded. Households resort to seasonal migration to cope with poor harvests but extreme climate events such as droughts and destructive storms can drive long-term or permanent displacement. It is estimated that by 2050, 200 million people could become permanently displaced 'environmental migrants' (Raskin, 2005). Migration creates social tensions and localised conflict over control of natural resources, accounting for many intra-state conflicts (UNCCD, 2014). Conflict, migration and erratic weather leave food systems weak and unable to function effectively, even as peace and stability are restored and livelihoods and productivity begin to recover. Unsustainable livelihoods, eroded resilience and poorly functioning food systems create long-term development challenges for food security and heighten the risk of further food crises.

Food assistance has evolved beyond 'aid' and a purely emergency response. It is a tool for post-conflict recovery, for building resilience among vulnerable populations and a catalyst for economic development, intersecting in multiple ways with the Sustainable Development Goals. Innovations in the analysis of food assistance show how weak food systems interact with other drivers of food insecurity to create food crises, revealing why hunger sometimes persists in spite of abundant harvests and relative stability. With adequate investments in humanitarian assistance, social protection and longer-term interventions that help to build resilient food systems, food assistance can drive progress towards development goals.

8.2 What is food assistance?

Food assistance includes a number of measures aiming to improve access to food, of a given quantity, quality or value, to insecure and vulnerable populations (Omamo et al., 2010). Although food accessibility is short-term goal in itself, in-kind food, vouchers or cash transfers can also work towards achieving longer-term development objectives, for example, better nutrition outcomes, education or disaster risk reduction. While needs assessments, good information management and efficient logistics make these successful initially, strategies for handover that include engagement with national safety nets can make programs sustainable and adaptable to changing food security contexts (Omamo et al., 2010).

8.3 What constitutes a food crisis?

The severity and magnitude of acute food insecurity can be classified, compared over time and across countries, according to an internationally harmonised protocol known as the Integrated Food Security Phase Classification (IPC), shown in Figure 8.1. The

Phase	Description	Priority Response Objectives
Phase 1: Minimal	At least four in five households are able to meet their food and non-food needs without engaging in atypical coping strategies or relying on humanitarian assistance.	Action required to build resilience and reduce disaster risk.
Phase 2: Stressed	Even with humanitarian assistance, at least one in five households in the area have the following or worse: reduced and minimally adequate food consumption but unable to afford some essential non-food expenditures without engaging in irreversible coping strategies.	Action required to reduce disaster risk and protect livelihoods.
Phase 3: Crisis	Even with humanitarian assistance, at least on in five households in the area have the following or worse: large food shortages and acute malnutrition at high or higher-than-normal rates; OR are marginally able to meet minimum food needs by depleting livelihood assets, which will lead to food consumption gaps.	Protect livelihoods, prevent malnutrition, and prevent deaths.
Phase 4: Emergency	Even with humanitarian assistance, at least one in five households in the area have the following or worse extreme food consumption gaps resulting in very high acute malnutrition or excess mortality; OR extreme loss of livelihood assets that will lead to food consumption gaps in the short term.	Save lies and livelihoods.
Phase 5: Famine	Even with humanitarian assistance, at least on in five households in the area have total lack food an/or other basic needs and are clearly exposed to starvation, death and deprivation. (Note: Evidence for all three criteria of food consumption, wasting and CBR are required to classify Famine).	Prevent large-scale deaths and avoid total collapse of livelihoods.

FIGURE 8.1 Integrated Food Security Phases Classification
Source: WFP, 2018a

IPC is a set of analytical tools that support decision-making by describing the objectives of different responses for different phases, or states of food insecurity.

Acute Malnutrition Classification (ACM) can complement IPC with a situation analysis of malnutrition, usually indicated by prevalence of wasting (acute malnutrition) and stunting (chronic malnutrition), including information on immediate and underlying causes. Other sources of nutrition data employed in acute food insecurity diagnosis include various subnational surveys, demographic and health surveys (DHS), multiple-indicator cluster surveys (MICs) and National Vulnerability Assessments and Analyses. Stunting and wasting together are used as proxies for the prevalence of malnutrition in communities (Table 8.1).

8.4 Causes of food crises

Underlying causes of food insecurity, such as poverty, unemployment, low educational attainment and gender inequality can combine with short-term or catastrophic events such as conflicts and natural disasters to drive food crises. Disasters, moreover, have long-term impacts on agriculture including loss of harvest and livestock, disease outbreaks and destruction of infrastructure and irrigation systems (Conforti et al., 2018). Preventing them requires short-term actions as well as long-term investments, although how to prioritise these in different contexts is not always clear. Expenditures on food assistance have been especially high in conditions of political instability, poor education and weak infrastructure, especially when natural disasters and weak food systems are also factors. A food crisis is more likely when a greater proportion of the population is affected by a natural disasters and food availability is already limited by poor infrastructure, market access and services. Conversely, higher education levels and political stability are associated with smaller scale outbreaks. The relative importance of food crisis risk factors is illustrated in Figure 8.2, where the outer contour represents countries experiencing crisis, compared to the inner contour, representing those without (WFP, 2018a).

In 2017, some of the countries facing the most acute food insecurities experienced concurrent conflict and extreme climate events, provoking mass internal and external displacements (WFP, 2017). Conflict was the major driver in terms of scale, creating the need for food assistance for 74 million people in 18 countries, with the greatest

TABLE 8.1 WHO severity indices for wasting and stunting

Wasting			*Stunting*		
Global acute malnutrition	<5%	Acceptable	Chronic malnutrition	<20%	Acceptable
	5–9%	Poor		20–29%	Poor
	10–14%	Serious		30–39%	Serious
	≥15%	Critical		≥40	Critical

Source: WHO (2019)

FIGURE 8.2 Food crisis risk factors
Source: WFP, 2018b

numbers found in northern Nigeria, the Democratic Republic of Congo, Somalia and South Sudan. In terms of severity, Yemen, Syria, Iraq and Palestine, all affected by conflict, experienced crisis conditions (IPC phase 3 or above). Drought affected 23 countries, creating food crises that affected 39 million people. African countries counted for two-thirds of these, where 32 million people needed urgent food assistance. Other extreme climate events such as destructive tropical storms and flooding affected Latin America, the Caribbean and South Asia. Conflict and extreme climate events affect food availability and accessibility, creating crop production shortfalls and food price spikes. Conflict disrupts agricultural activity and the functioning of markets, contributing to economic decline and currency devaluation (WFP, 2017).

It is important to note though, that migration in itself, and even environmentally induced migration is not always a cause of food insecurity. The IOM defines this as:

> … persons or groups of persons who, predominantly for reasons of sudden or progressive change in the environment that adversely affects their lives or living conditions, are obliged to leave their habitual homes, or choose to do so, either temporarily or permanently, and who move either within their country or abroad.
>
> *(IOM, 2007)*

Migration towards better economic opportunities is also an adaptive response that can actually have a positive outcome for food security (Rechkemmer et al., 2016). The urgency of the situation, for example in the case of forced migration induced by conflict or natural disasters can make a great difference in whether migration is

Policy issues in food assistance   65

adaptive or renders people more vulnerable to food insecurity and result in food crisis (Renaud, et al., 2011). Among the largest-scale and most severe food crises unfolding between 2016 and 2018, conflict was the most important factor, with displacement following close behind (WFP, 2018a). Box 8.1 illustrates a multi-country food crisis driven mainly by conflict, which caused massive displacement, disruption of livelihoods and markets, resulting in widespread malnutrition and an extreme situation characterised as famine.

8.5 From food aid to food assistance: preventing food crises

Susceptibility to food crises and the need for food assistance are linked to multiple development issues. This is reflected in the SDGs approach to eliminating hunger and creating food security. Zero Hunger targets link some of the issues that directly contribute to food crises, but several other goals and targets address major risk factors for food crises, including those related to climate change, education, migration and protecting biodiversity. SDG targets also address many of the risk factors modelled in food assistance planning, with targets that link directly and indirectly to food security, shape food systems and affect their functioning (UN, 2017). These linkages were recognised prior to the new global development agenda, when food assistance was already beginning a shift away from the old style of food 'aid', which was unable to address, and may have even exacerbated some of the underlying drivers of food crises (WFP, 2010). Food assistance is now expected to not only protect lives and livelihoods through transfers of food and cash, food procurement but also to help in addressing the root causes of hunger (WFP, 2017).

Food assistance has become more sophisticated in working with what is arguably one the most important causes of hunger and components of food security, the food system. Food crises are driven in part by particular features of food systems and how they perform in relation to food demand and supply. Figure 8.3 illustrates a food system as characterised by three subcomponents, production, transformation and consumption. An effectively functioning food system should contribute to food security and nutrition at the household level (HLPE, 2012). Food assistance can work systemically by addressing problems that are widespread, affecting availability and accessibility of food for large groups of people, at the same time, improving the functioning of food systems (Zhou and Hendriks, 2017).

Some of the key innovations in food assistance in the twenty-first century involve targeting instruments of food assistance such as cash transfers, vouchers and insurance mechanisms in ways that improve food production, transformation and consumption. But targeting alone is not sufficient; food assistance also has a thematic dimension, where interventions can centre on supporting livelihoods, education, promoting gender equality, improving food technology and mitigating the impacts of HIV epidemics. The activities and platforms involved in implementing food assistance programs, such as assessments, disaster preparedness, logistics, strategic planning, safety nets, and the handover of food assistance programs and activities from humanitarian agencies to national entities can all support more effective functioning of food systems.

66 Steven Were Omamo et al.

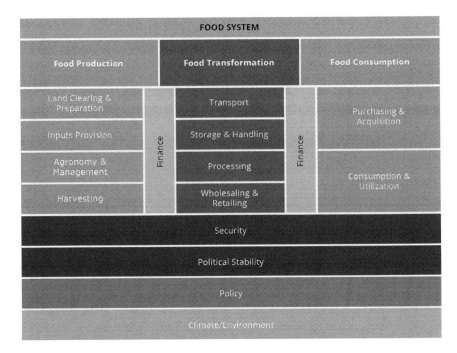

FIGURE 8.3 A functional and contextual view of food systems
Source: WFP 2017

8.6 Systemic problems, food insecurity and food assistance

Food systems are an important structural factor contributing to food crises and require long-term strategic and policy interventions to function effectively. But they can also be positively influenced with well-targeted shorter-term responses to food crises that help break the cycles that undermine resilience and create vulnerability. Closer examination of the workings of food assistance has revealed some of these systemic problems (WFP, 2017).

The volume and quality of food assistance are mitigated by the particular financial, logistical and security challenges of humanitarian action, especially where access is difficult, for example due to conflict or geographical remoteness. But the volume and quality of food assistance are also shaped by the structure and functioning of food systems which are usually implicated in food insecurity and food crises to begin with. These particular challenges have been described as "the good year", "the bad year" and "the last mile" problems, illustrated in Figure 8.4 (WFP, 2017).

8.6.1 The good year scenario

With good weather conditions and access to inputs, farmers produce food surpluses, driving prices down and leaving producers unable to recoup production costs. High transport and transactions costs prevent food from being moved.

Policy issues in food assistance 67

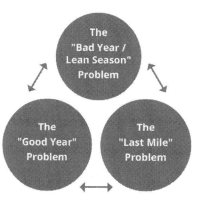

FIGURE 8.4 The good year, the bad year, and the last mile
Source: WFP 2017

Poor telecommunications and a lack of market information inhibit trade, so markets do not absorb abundant harvests. Large quantities of food stored on-farm or in inadequate facilities goes to waste. The result is that food surpluses and food insecurity exist in close proximity to one another, while government agencies may not have the resources to purchase surpluses. In response to these food system flaws, governments often respond as if to food shortages and exacerbate the problem with further disincentives such as export bans and trading practices that favour urban consumers and disadvantage small producers. Ironically, the outcome of a good harvest can be eroded livelihoods and mass food spoilage (WFP, 2017).

8.6.2 The bad year scenario

In the 'bad year' scenario, the destructive impacts of natural disasters, armed conflict, civil strife, economic shocks on lives and livelihoods can overwhelm people's capacity to cope. Increasing frequency and intensity of bad years leaves little recovery time in between, eroding resilience over time (UNISDR, 2015). Food systems can be implicated in these dynamics, amplifying the effects of both good and bad years. Poor and marginalised households in rural and urban areas lack sufficient food to meet nutritional needs because of access constraints, such as low incomes and purchasing power or too few resources or assets to produce food. These households are especially vulnerable to shocks, stress and even seasonal fluctuations, enduring periods of food shortage, hunger and wasting in lean seasons, or bad years. Women with extensive care duties and heavy workloads are especially vulnerable.

In rural areas, where food security is reliant on crop and livestock yields, fragile environments and unfavourable weather contribute to lean seasons. Lean seasons bring extra hardship when they endure through several production cycles. For city dwellers, lean seasons are created by unemployment as well as unanticipated or uneven expenses for school fees, health care or funerals, that consume small incomes (Mohiddin et al., 2012).

8.6.3 The last mile scenario

Poverty and hunger are often associated with physical, social, political and economic isolation (Gatzweiler et al., 2011). Widely dispersed rural smallholders often have insecure land tenure, poor storage facilities, tenuous links to markets and little bargaining power. They trade in bulky, low-value products, at a disadvantage in relation to buyers with access to better information. The gap between farmers' access to services, inputs and technologies and service providers and investors is the "last mile" to sustainably improving production, which persists because of these different forms of isolation. The low returns and high risks of subsistence farming are affirmed by hunger and poverty. Environmental and natural resource degradation, political conflict, poor physical infrastructure and a range of economic shocks linked to macroeconomic policy, trade and globalisation exacerbate the "last mile" problem (WFP, 2017). This problem affects both producers and consumers (Figure 8.5).

8.7 Solutions and innovations in food assistance

Confronting the problems created by bad years, good years (where production cannot be absorbed) and the last mile (isolation from support and services) involves careful targeting of food assistance instruments with the right thematic focus, appropriate platforms, and strategic changes in policy. Food assistance interventions that can help re-shape food systems include:

- Nutrition-specific and nutrition-sensitive interventions;
- Food safety nets within shock-responsive social protection systems;
- Purchase-based support platforms for smallholder farmers and small-scale and medium-scale agrifood enterprises;
- Physical, technical and organisational upgrading of food retailers;
- Digital innovations in value-chain integration and tracking;
- Physical, technical and organisational upgrading of public food reserves;
- Physical, technical and organisational upgrading of food supply chain infrastructure and services;
- Food safety and quality standards and regulations; and
- Market and trade policy reform (WFP, 2017).

Applying instruments thematically lends food assistance a special focus on reducing particular risk factors and mitigating drivers of food insecurity. Appropriate support to smallholder farmers can reduce risks, enhance production and protect rural livelihoods. In drought-prone communities, this might include enhancing critical infrastructure such as roads, or conservation technologies for water and soil.

Policy issues in food assistance 69

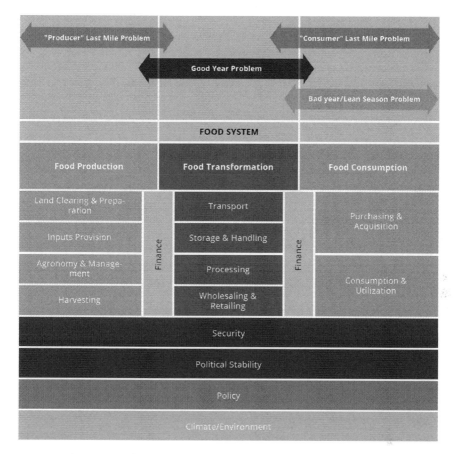

FIGURE 8.5 Systemic problems in food systems
Source: WFP, 2017

Smallholder farmers can be linked to markets to access better quality inputs, but also to trade opportunities in public and private sector food procurement, for example school meal programs or World Food Program procurement through digital technology. Financial services such as microfinance and insurance that are affordable to smallholders can protect and promote food production, improving livelihoods and resilience.

A focus on nutrition can include developing skills in communities for producing and preparing more diverse and nutritious foods, complemented by messaging that raises awareness of health and social protection services. Developing capacity for local processing and fortification of food, adds value for local producers and processors while improving the nutritional quality of food. Addressing food quality and safety gaps in policies ensures that meal programs have good nutritional content while reducing risks of contamination and food-borne illness.

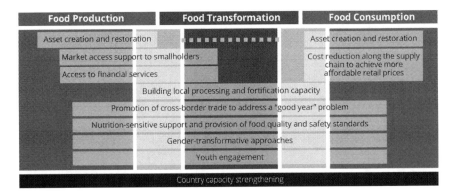

FIGURE 8.6 WFP interventions across the food system in Kenya
Figure source: WFP, 2017

Promoting trade and enhancing the efficiency of supply chains go hand-in-hand to moderate the fluctuations of good and bad years, ensuring that surpluses can be absorbed and demands met. Regional integration and cross-border corridors can facilitate movement, while better storage, aggregated transport and collective buying reduce transaction costs, while leveraging the demand created by cash transfers.

Gender inequality contributes to the 'last mile' problem. Women are often excluded from owning land, accessing agricultural inputs and extension services and participation in farmers' organisations and there are fewer women traders in agricultural commodities (WFP, 2009). Empowering women with cash transfers and asset-building gives them greater roles in the retail sector, as well as control over food and dietary diversity at the household level. Pregnant and lactating women have additional nutritional needs that can also be met with access to fortified foods. Supporting mothers is an investment in preventing childhood malnutrition. Giving women a voice in food assistance decision-making can ensure that their views and needs are reflected. This is particularly important in conflict and natural disaster situations, which exacerbate gender inequality when social structures break down and women become victims of violence (Michels, 2006).

Cross-cutting interventions can also strengthen country capacity, where government-led food assistance programs are self-sufficient and relief assistance is needed only when crises exceed their capacities. Table 8.2 illustrates food-system focused solutions to bad year, good year and last mile problems, by cross-cutting platform and policy-based solutions that address all three.

8.8 Policies for preventing and mitigating food crises

Food system-based policy interventions focussed on the problems of good years, lean seasons and the last mile can prevent and buffer shocks. These include policies and

Policy issues in food assistance 71

TABLE 8.2 Summary of food assistance-based responses and solutions to systemic problems in food systems

FOOD ASSISTANCE-BASED SOLUTIONS TO SYSTEMIC PROBLEMS IN FOOD SYSTEMS

Bad year/lean season solutions	*Last mile solutions*	*Good year solutions*
• Nutrition-specific and nutrition-sensitive productive – skill and asset building – food-based and cash-based transfers to vulnerable consumers	• Nutrition-specific and nutrition-sensitive productive – skill and asset building – food-based and cash-based transfers to vulnerable consumers	• Purchase of quality food from trader-processors, including locally fortified nutritious foods
• Transfer-based capacity development for enhanced household and community resilience and risk management	• Purchase of quality food from producer-traders	• Demand-led investments to fill food transformation gaps for trader-processors
• Transfer-based nutrition education and self and family care for women	• Purchase-based coordination and facilitation of supply-side, aggregation, and financing support for smallholders and rural small-to-medium enterprises	• Demand-led upgrading of market and supply chain physical infrastructure
• Demand-led, ICT-based, benchmark-driven investments to upgrade retailer supply chain management	• Demand-led, ICT-based, benchmark-driven investments to upgrade retailer supply chain management	• Digital innovations in value chain integration and tracking
		• Demand-led, ICT-based, benchmark-driven investments to upgrade retailer supply chain management

Cross-cutting solutions

- Food fortification and development, and enforcement of food safety and quality standards
- Digital platforms to enhance quantity, quality and flow of market data and information
- Reform and strengthening of food platforms in shock-responsive social protection systems
- Reform of structure and functioning of public food reserves
- Reform of market and trade policy standards and implementation
- Improvement of food market infrastructure
- Preparedness and early warning systems

Figure source: WFP, 2017

standards for food fortification, food safety and quality; platforms for the flow of higher quantities of adequate market data; shock-responsive social protection systems; effective and well-structured public food reserves; appropriate trade policies; adequate market infrastructure and early warning systems and preparedness for emergencies. In general, food systems must also become more productive and more efficient to meet food security demands necessary to eliminate chronic hunger (Figure 8.7).

Food insecurity is implicated as both a driver and an outcome of conflict, therefore promoting peace and ending conflict is imperative to restoring livelihoods and building resilience. Markets cannot function effectively in conditions

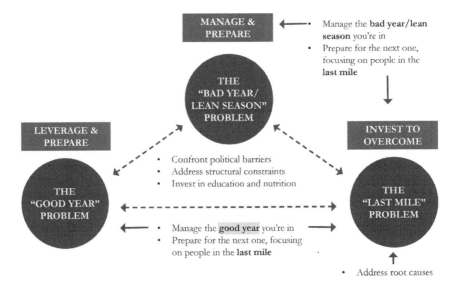

FIGURE 8.7 Managing good years, bad years and the last mile
Source: WFP, 2018b

of insecurity and unstable environments do not attract investments. Food assistance programming can be conflict-sensitive by understanding contexts, avoiding doing harm, ensuring inclusivity and equity, following humanitarian principles and supporting peace building at local and national levels (WFP, 2013).

Sudden surges in levels of hunger and food insecurity usually occur against a backdrop of chronic hunger. With numbers of chronically hungry people growing worldwide, it is a matter of urgency to promote livelihoods that enable people to meet their food and nutrition needs and to build resilience. This includes investing in developments that reduce underlying risk factors, such as better educational attainment, gender equity, decent work and incomes, health and social infrastructure and inclusive rural development.

References

Conforti, P., Ahmed, S. and Markova, G. (2018) *Impact of Disasters and Crises on Agriculture and Food Security 2017*. Food and Agriculture Organisation (FAO), Rome.
HLPE. (2012) 'Social protection for food security', A report by the HLPE, Rome.
IOM (International Organisation for Migration) (2007) 'Migration and the environment', A discussion note-MC/INF/288, IOM, Geneva.
Michels, A. (2006). *Gender and Protection in the Context of World Food Programme (WFP) Uganda Operations*. WFP, Rome.
Mohiddin, L., Phelps, L. and Walters, T. (2012) *Urban Malnutrition: A Review of Food Security and Nutrition among the Urban Poor*. Nutrition Works, International Public Nutrition Resource Group at London, London.

Omamo, S.W., Gentilini, U. and Sandström, S. (2010) *Revolution: From Food Aid to Food Assistance: Innovations in Overcoming Hunger*. WFP, Rome.

Raskin, P.D. (2005) 'Global scenarios: Background review for the millennium ecosystem assessment', *Ecosystems*, vol. 8, no. 2, pp. 133–142.

Rechkemmer, A., O'Connor, A., Rai, A., Decker Sparks, J.L., Mudliar, P. and Shultz, J.M. (2016) 'A complex social–ecological disaster: Environmentally induced forced migration', *Disaster Health*, vol. 3, no. 4, pp. 112–120.

Renaud, F., Bogardi, J.J., Dun, O. and Warner, K. (2007) *Control, Adapt or Flee: How to Face Environmental Migration?*, United Nations University, Institute for Environment and Human Security, Germany, Richmond.

UN (United Nations) (2017) *The Sustainable Development Goals Report 2017*. UN, New York.

UNCCD (United Nations Convention to Combat Desertification) (2014) *Desertification: The Invisible Frontline*. UNCCD, Bonn.

UNISDR (United Nations Office for Disaster Risk Reduction) (2015) 2015*Disasters in Numbers*. UNISDR, Geneva.

WFP (2009) *WFP Gender Policy: Promoting Gender Equality and the Empowerment of Women in Addressing Food and Nutritional Challenges*. WFP, Rome.

WFP (2010) *Revolution from Food Aid to Food Assistance: Innovations in Overcoming Hunger*. World Food Programme, Rome.

WFP (2013) 'WFP's role in peace building in transition settings: Policy issues', Rome 4–7 November 2013, WFP, Rome.

WFP (2017) *World Food Assistance 2017: Taking Stock and Looking Ahead*. WFP, Rome.

WFP (2018a) *Global Report on Food Crisis 2018*. Food Security Information Network, Rome.

WFP (2018b) *World Food Assistance: Preventing Food Crises*. WFP, Rome.

WHO (2019) 'Global database on child growth and malnutrition', https://www.who.int/nutgrowthdb/about/introduction/en/index5.html

Zhou, A.C. and Hendriks, S.L. (2017) 'Does food assistance improve recipients' dietary diversity and food quality in Mozambique?', *Agrekon*, vol. 56, no. 3, pp. 248–262.

PART II

Practical guidance on in the components of evidence-based food security policy analysis

9

ASSESSING THE COHERENCE OF BROADER DEVELOPMENT POLICIES FOR FOOD SECURITY

Nic J.J. Olivier and Nico J.J. Olivier

9.1 Introduction: the global call for policy coherence

The United Nations Decade for Nutrition was announced in 2016 with an important theme: policy convergence and coherence to ensure that government sectors and food system actors are working together towards achieving food security and improved nutrition worldwide (HLPE, 2017; FAO and WHO, 2017). The challenge for food security might seem overwhelming for policy-makers and researchers. How can we possibly solve the complex, multi-sectoral problems of food security and malnutrition, with their diverse, localised, national, sub-regional, regional (continental) and global (international) drivers and determinants? Countries typically have conflicting priorities and multi-level obligations and commitments.

Comprehensive food security policymaking is still a relatively new endeavour for many governments. Even in countries with food security policies, these may have become outdated as climate unpredictability, nutrition transitions and global economic volatility impact livelihoods, health and resilience in different ways. Historically, governments have not been structured or equipped for the kind of collaboration needed to confront food insecurity. Due to the complexity and cross-cutting nature of food insecurity and malnutrition challenges, the issues need to be addressed as multi-level (sometimes referred to multi-tier) obligations that involve governance at the local (such as community) level, the aggregated level (such as provincial or federal government), as well as multi-sphere (across sectoral lines) obligations that cut across traditional sectoral governance structures.

Among the wealth of new approaches to policy in the age of the SDGs are new ways of assessing, monitoring and evaluating food security policy. The importance of policy coherence is underscored by SDG 17, which states that "inclusive partnerships built upon principles and values, a shared vision, and shared goals that place people and the planet at the centre, are needed at the global, regional, national and local level" (UNGA, 2016). The targets for Goal 17 include addressing systemic issues underlying sustainable development, which include policy coherence and coordination, forging multi-stakeholder partnerships and respecting each country's policy space and leadership (UNDG, 2017). The multisectoral nature of food security makes policy coherence a central concern.

In the majority of (if not all) democracies a specific process is followed in the formulation of policies, the enactment of legislation and the implementation of programmes and projects. This process is often referred to as a "policy loop".

This chapter offers a more in-depth look at the importance of policy coherence for food security. It begins with a look at how policies articulate within countries, sub-regions, regions (continents) and global (international) frameworks and why this presents so many challenges. It provides a brief overview of the organisation of government, with reference to the three arms of government (the Legislature, the Executive and the Judiciary) and the three levels (or spheres) of government (national, provincial and local (municipal)), the content of a public policy and the need for the alignment of policies to achieve food security.

9.2 How government is organised

A typical characteristic of democracies is the distinction between the three arms or branches of government (sometimes referred to the *trias politica* doctrine):

- The Legislature, composed of elected representatives (mostly) from political parties, which is responsible for the carrying out of the following four key roles:
  - Adoption and enactment of legislation as well as approval of medium-term strategies, short term implementation plans and related budgets
  - Oversight in respect of the executive as regards policy implementation and the effective use of approved resources
  - Domestication (incorporation in the national legal system concerned) of global (international), regional (continental) and sub-regional legally binding obligations and commitments
  - Awareness raising as representatives of the electorate concerned (in a proportional, constituency or mixed system basis)
- The Executive, consisting of the Head of State and ministers appointed by the Head of State. Each minister is responsible for one or more government departments, which employ public servants. Each government department has specific powers, functions and duties that are determined by the Constitution and other legislation of the country concerned.
- The Judiciary, which is responsible for all judicial matters. This arm of government is autonomous and does not account to the Legislature and/or

the Executive. Furthermore, the Executive is obliged to ensure the full implementation of all final decisions of the courts. A distinction is made between criminal matters (where a person or persons are prosecuted, and if found guilty, convicted for crimes allegedly committed) and civil matters (where the disputes between individuals, legal entities and between the State and individuals and/or legal entities are considered and resolved).

Another typical characteristic of most democracies is the existence of different tiers (sometimes referred to as spheres) of government:

- The national sphere of government, consisting of the National Executive (referred to as Cabinet, comprising the President as chairperson and Ministers) and supported by a number of national government departments. In addition, the National Legislature (usually referred to as Parliament) is responsible for the legislative function and the three other roles discussed above.
- The provincial or regional sphere of government, consisting of the Provincial Executive (comprising, in South Africa, the provincial Premier as chairperson and Members of the Executive Council) and supported by a number of provincial government departments. The Provincial Legislature (consisting of elected representatives) is responsible for the provincial legislative function and the three other roles discussed above.
- The local sphere of government, consisting of municipalities. In some jurisdictions municipalities are implementers of national and regional (provincial) programmes. In other countries (such as South Africa) each municipality has an elected municipal council (consisting of elected councillors), which has both executive and legislative powers, functions and duties. Municipal mayors form the head of the municipal executive, whilst the municipal speaker is in charge of meetings of the municipal council. As regards the carrying out of its executive powers and duties, and the performance of its executive functions, the municipal council is supported by the municipal administration (that is headed by the municipal manager – referred to, in the case of larger cities, as the city manager).

9.3 Articulating policy: local, national, sub-regional, regional (continental) and international (global) links

Broadly defined, policy includes a wide range of instruments, including legislative and implementation frameworks and plans. Although policies as such are not enforceable, they are supported by legislation (that establishes the rules of the game and sets out incentives and punitive measures for enforcement) and implemented through medium-term strategies and shorter-term work (performance) plans of varying scope and duration (for example, five-year strategies and annual work plans).

At the national level, developing new and reviewing existing policies are subject to the Constitution and legal framework of the country concerned. In addition, national policy development must take into account all relevant sub-regional, regional (continental) and international (global) (a) instruments (with their concomitant legal obligations) and (b) agreements and declarations (with their concomitant commitments). Ratification of these above instruments, agreements and declarations by a national legislature (in accordance with the constitution of the country concerned) generally means that countries have incorporated them into national policy and legal frameworks.

From the *national perspective*, every country-specific policy must also be aligned, and coherent with, the current long-term, transversal National Development Plan (NDP; sometimes referred to as the National Vision) and the medium-term National Growth and Development Strategy (NGDS; sometimes referred to as a Medium-Term Strategic Framework – MTSF). Both these long- and medium-term transversal (across sectors) plans and strategies have implications for what policies are adopted, the necessary legislation enacted and other transversal and sectoral strategies and plans formulated (and implemented) during the five-year government period (the period between each national election in a particular country).

In similar vein, at regional (continental) and sub-regional (e.g. Regional Economic Communities – RECs) levels both (a) binding, legally enforceable, instruments and (b) declarations and agreements creating commitments, exist.

Figure 9.1 provides a graphic representation of the close interrelationship between global (international), regional (continental) and national elements of the framework determining policy development.

At national level, governance models usually mandate long-, medium- and short-term instruments, such as (Figure 9.2):

- Long-term visions or development plans (usually ten years +) for the country as a whole
- Medium-term growth and development strategies or medium-term strategic frameworks (usually five-years) for the country as a whole (based on the political platform of the ruling party)
- Sectoral policies (usually of a five-year duration and which in themselves are not legally binding but provide direction for all the instruments listed below). A policy sets out the political goals of the ruling party (usually found in the election manifesto of the ruling party). In principle, policies are aimed at providing frameworks on how to address an issue identified at the political level.
- Sectoral legislation (which is binding and enforceable, and forms the basis for all subsequent instruments as well as for the allocation of public funding) provides the framework for delivering and enforcing the policy goals and initiatives through both incentives and punitive measures.
- Sectoral (implementation) strategies – sometimes also referred to as plans or action plans (usually of a five-year duration, and which contain the

FIGURE 9.1 An illustration of the interrelationship between global, regional and national elements of the framework determining policy development
Source: Authors

implementation modalities as regards programmes, beneficiary groups, targets, funding, implementation agents as well as human and other resources). It is important to differentiate a policy from a strategy.
- Sectoral implementation plans – sometimes also referred to as annual performance plans, annual plans, annual action plans or annual work plans (usually of a one-year duration and which contain the detailed implementation modalities for projects within approved and funded programmes)
- Monitoring and evaluation, resulting in reports and, in some cases, possible interventions and the taking of remedial steps
- The above evaluation report often results in the review and amendment of existing, or the drafting of new, policy, regulatory, strategic and implementation frameworks (Hendriks et al., 2019).

In most democracies, the policy formulation process begins with a political decision to address a current failure, gap, or shortcoming in some current policy or regulatory framework, or to meet the obligations of a new international, continental or regional

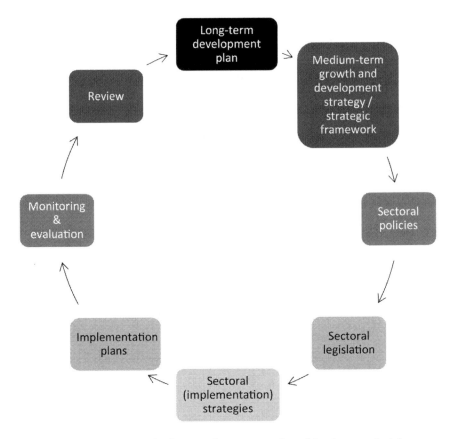

FIGURE 9.2 The governance (policy, regulatory, strategic and implementation) loop
Source: Hendriks et al. (2019, p. 64)

agreement. This might begin with a status quo report providing an overview of issues – gaps, failures, shortcomings or new requirements – with which to inform the new policy. A policy framework provides the higher-order values, principles, objectives, expected outcomes and an overview of proposed regulatory, institutional and implementation frameworks. Ideally this is accompanied by the review of existing legislation and formulation of appropriate new legislation, followed by the drafting, approval and implementation of a strategy. Monitoring and evaluation, and hopefully, feedback into policy renewal, completes the governance cycle.

In the majority of (if not all) democracies, a specific process is followed in the formulation of policies, the enactment of legislation, the formulation of short-term implementation plans as well as the implementation of approved programmes and projects (Figure 9.3):

i The decision to formulate a new policy or revise an existing policy (agenda setting) is based on a political decision of the government of the day. Such decisions are often

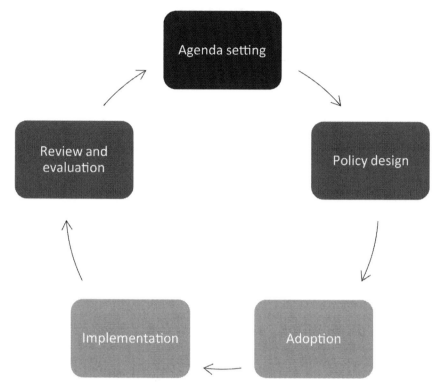

FIGURE 9.3 The policy development loop/cycle
Source: Hendriks et al., 2019, p. 64

part of the political platform of the majority party, sometimes a result of failures/ gaps/shortcomings of the current policy and regulatory framework and its implementation, and sometimes on account of (new) international (global), regional (continental) and subregional binding obligations and commitments.

ii Developing a status quo report and collecting the evidence to support the design of the policy (design stage). The status quo report provides an overview of the current policy, regulatory and implementation framework with its failures, gaps and shortcomings to inform the review and design of the policy.

iii The actual drafting of the new policy framework (in the adoption stage). The policy framework is the new proposed (higher order) framework with its respective values, principles, objectives, expected outcomes, as well as providing an overview of proposed regulatory, institutional and implementation frameworks, etc. In principle, the approval of a policy should be followed by the review of existing and formulation of appropriate legislation and subsequently by the drafting, approval and implementation of a strategy.

iv The next step is the adoption (approval) of the policy framework by the executive arm of government. This is followed by the drafting of a new (or amended) regulatory framework (as part of adoption). The statement of a policy usually requires review and revision of all relevant regulatory measures. The new and/or amended regulatory (statutory/legal) framework then gives effect to the new policy framework.

v Also part of the adoption stage is the drafting of the medium-term strategic framework and short-term (usually annual) implementation plan which, as a detailed roadmap, sets out the detailed timelines, transitional measures, change management processes, structures, systems, programmes (with detailed projects), resource allocation, execution, and monitoring and evaluation of the implementation of the new policy and regulatory framework.

vi During the implementation stage, all key activities specified in the short-term implementation plan are executed (including, amongst others, the continuous monitoring of implementation and the production of regular performance reports).

vii During the review and evaluation stage, evaluation take place, resulting in evaluation reports, and importantly, also of review reports that may have a direct impact on perceptions and approaches regarding the need for either resetting the current policy framework or developing a new policy framework.

A policy document usually includes explanations of:

- The nature of the document
- The role of government (executive and legislative arms) and other stakeholders and partners
- The process for policy review and (re)formulation
- The process for regulatory environment review and reformulation
- How the development of programmes will take place and who is responsible for their design, implementation and monitoring and review
- Structures and institutions
- Resource allocation
- Mutual accountability and coordination
- Risk and mitigation (finance, institutional, environmental, etc.)
- A monitoring and evaluation framework
- Responsibilities about reporting for action (Hendriks et al., 2019).

Medium-term strategies (often of a five-year duration) lay out the details of policy implementation, including the structures, programmes (and sometimes also concomitant projects), funding, human resources, infrastructural resources, beneficiaries, activities and a robust programme-level monitoring and evaluation framework. A typical strategic plan includes an overview, vision and mission statements, legislative and other mandates, a situational analysis, strategic outcome-oriented goals and programs and links to other departmental and institutional plans.

An annual (action) plan (also referred to as an annual performance plan or annual work plan) sets out what a department/institution intends to do in an upcoming financial year and during the medium term to implement its strategic plan. It provides performance indicators and targets for programmes and sub-programmes, and often includes a quarterly breakdown of performance targets for an upcoming financial year. A departmental or institutional budget is submitted to the relevant national/regional legislature together with the annual plan through a process that is known in some jurisdictions as a departmental (institutional) vote.

Table 9.1 provides a summary of the above-mentioned categories of national instruments linked to the institutions responsible for the approval and/or implementation of these instruments.

9.4 What makes policy coherence challenging?

The term 'policy coherence' often occurs in conjunction with the terms 'policy alignment', 'policy integration' and 'policy convergence'. These concepts are interrelated and are sometimes used interchangeably. For clarity, policy coherence in this context is used to describe consistency, harmony and compatibility of outcomes of policies across sectors (Dubé et al., 2014). For food security, this means agreement on common objectives for sectoral policies, ensuring that outcomes of different policies do not undermine one another and are mutually reinforcing or beneficial (Hawkes, 2017).

Synergies, contradictions and trade-offs between policy goals come into sharp focus around food security and nutrition. Vulnerabilities in the global food system

TABLE 9.1 Summary of national instruments linked to the institutions responsible for the approval and/or implementation of these instruments

INSTRUMENT CATEGORY	APPROVAL ENTITY	IMPLEMENTATION ENTITY
National vision (national development plan)	National Executive (political level: Cabinet) + National Legislature	National Executive (public service) Provincial (regional) executive Local Government
National policies	National Executive (political level: Cabinet)	National Executive (public service) Provincial (regional) (public service) executive Local Government
Medium-term national strategies	National Executive (political level: Cabinet) + National Legislature	National Executive (public service) Provincial (regional) (public service) executive Local Government
Annual national (work/ performance) plans and related budget allocation	National Executive (political level: Cabinet) + National Legislature	National Executive (public service) Provincial (regional) (public service) executive Local Government
Monitoring and evaluation framework	National Executive (political level: Cabinet)	National Executive (public service) Provincial (regional) (public service) executive Local Government

can be seen as evidence of the shortfalls of sectoral policies: food price volatility, biodiversity loss, persistent malnutrition and social unrest (Sonnino et al., 2016). These globalised problems are all, in some ways, the outcomes of policy gaps, contradictions and unintended consequences. Achieving food security, on the other hand, is assumed to be the result of the convergence of policy interests (Sonnino et al., 2016).

> [...] It is then crucial to ensure that food security strategies facilitate an integration of technical, environmental, social and political interests around collective goals. The social and spatial processes of generation of public and social legitimacy and consent that this entails raise critical questions, especially around food security governance.
>
> *(Sonnino et al., 2016, p. 478)*

Policy incoherence, or contradictions and conflicts that negate the actions of different policies, arise for many reasons. Sectoral agendas within countries differ. Development partners, such as multilateral and bilateral cooperation agencies exert influences, as do private sector actors. Forums that bring all actors together, including civil society groups, are still relatively few and top-down policymaking tends to be the norm. Evidence-informed policymaking requires knowledge translation, which is time-consuming. Public engagement mechanisms around food security is still rare, in part because it is painstaking and time-consuming. Political change often creates discontinuity in agendas and institutional turnover, which can further dampen political commitment (Dufour and Dodé, 2016).

Food security information systems have tended to be fragmented and piecemeal, with over-emphasis on policy outcomes, and little understanding of processes, potential synergies or contradictions and impacts outside the scope of data collection. Poor information systems are a reflection of the lack of coordination and the 'silo' phenomenon that has afflicted food security. Health, agriculture and social development, the sectors most immediately linked to food security, have difficulties aligning policies to one another. The more distal policy areas, energy, water and trade, for example, further complicate coordination.

Nevertheless, monitoring and evaluation frameworks are emerging as important focal points for accountability, coordination and alignment of policy objectives and are therefore of key concern to policymakers. Without them, it is difficult to monitor progress towards milestone and targets, to assess outcomes and to understand what creates positive (or negative) impacts. Integrated development, including integrated food security policies, requires indicators drawn from across sectors. Governments can streamline monitoring and evaluation processes and enhance transparency by aligning indicators with sectoral, national, regional and international objectives. This makes information management and reporting more efficient and economical (Hendriks et al., 2018).

9.5 Conclusion

Supporting policy coherence for food security and nutrition requires wider awareness and agreement on key concepts, not least of all food security itself. This is a fundamental step towards focusing sector policies on food security and nutrition and harmonising policy objectives. Although perfect harmony or synergy between policy objectives is unlikely across sectors, the aim of policy coherence can be to reduce contradictions and conflicts while identifying and maximising the opportunities arising from synergy.

Stakeholders may need incentives to work in more integrated ways, not only across sectors, with researchers and development partners, but also more 'vertically' to ensure policy beneficiaries are included. This ensures that the problems being addressed by policy are grounded in real social problems and reflect diversity within countries. Wider stakeholder diversity, including public engagement as well as expert panels and private and public interests, brings richness to dialogue, resulting in deeper understandings of impacts, implications of trade-offs and possibilities for synergy. A solid understanding of context requires extensive mapping of existing policies and stakeholder interests and the dynamics shaping the policy environment.

References

Dubé, L., Addy, N.A., Blouin, C. and Drager, N. (2014) 'From policy coherence to 21st century convergence: A whole-of-society paradigm of human and economic development', *Annals of the New York Academy of Sciences*, vol. 1331, issue 1, pp. 201–215.

Dufour, C. and Dodé, M.C. (2016) 'Mapping and analysis policies to inform food security and nutrition planning: Towards more coherent and cross-sectoral policies', Powerpoint presentation, Agriculture, Nutrition and Health Academy Week.

FAO and WHO (2017) *United Nations Decade of Action on Nutrition (2016–2025)*. United Nations, New York.

Hawkes, C. (2017) 'Policy coherence across the food system for nutrition: From challenge to opportunity?' *GREAT Insights Magazine*, vol. 6, no. 4, pp. 23–24.

Hendriks, S.L., Olivier, N.J.J., Mkandawire, E., Mabuza, N., Olivier, N.J.J., and Makhura, M.N. (2019) 'Creating the necessary policy context for progress on the Malabo Declaration: A review of food security and nutrition policy changes in 11 African countries', Food Security Policy Innovation Lab working paper No. 122, Michigan State University and the University of Pretoria, East Lansing and Pretoria.

Hendriks, S. L., Mabuza, N., Hendriks, K.R., Olivier, N.J.J., Makhura, M.N., Mkandawire, E., Mkhwanazi, Z., Mkusa, L. and Vilakazi, N. (2018) 'An evaluation of the level of integration and Aaignment of the Malabo commitments, Africas Agenda 2063 and the SDGs in 10 National Agricultural Food Security Investment Plans', Feed the Future Innovation Lab for Food Security Policy Research Paper No.107, Michigan State University, IFPRI and University of Pretoria at East Lansing, Washington DC and Pretoria.

HLPE (2017) 'Nutrition and food systems', Report no. 12, HLPE, Rome.

UNDG (United Nations Development Group) (2017) *Mainstreaming the 2030 Agenda for Sustainable Development: Reference Guide to UN Country Teams*. United Nations Development Group, New York.

UNGA (United Nations General Assembly) (2016) *The Sustainable Development Goals*. UNGA, New York. https://www.un.org/sustainabledevelopment/globalpartnerships/.

10

THE POLICYMAKING PROCESS

Introducing the Kaleidoscope Model for food security policy analysis

Steven Haggblade, Suresh C. Babu, Danielle Resnick and Sheryl L. Hendriks

10.1 Increased interest in evidence-based policymaking

Since policy decisions shape the incentives and actions of key farmer, consumer and industry groups, policies become central determinants of overall economic performance as well as progress towards key agricultural, nutrition and food security goals. Governments across the globe increasingly recognise that favourable policy environments facilitate economic growth, while unfavourable policy regimes can easily stymie development outcomes. The policy systems in which stakeholders interact to formulate and implement policies, therefore, become critical to effective development outcomes. For this reason, donors show interest in policy systems, particularly in the wake of the recently adopted SDGs, the Paris Declaration for Aid Effectiveness and the ensuing demands to achieve and measure policy impact (see OECD/DAC, 2014 and White 2014). The predictability, stability, and transparency of policy processes likewise serve to promote the Paris Declaration goals of mutual accountability among donors, partner governments and their citizens. (USAID, 2013). As a result, national governments and donors are interested in understanding policymaking processes and outcomes.

In response to growing interest in developing country policy systems, the Kaleidoscope Model (KM) was developed to provide a systematic framework for evaluating key drivers of policy change and identifying opportunities for stakeholder interventions to improve the functioning and outcomes of developing country policy systems (Resnick et al., 2015; 2017; 2018). The KM provides a simple, applied framework for analysing key drivers of policy change in food security, agriculture and nutrition. The model offers flexibility sufficient to accommodate application across a broad range of policy domains and political systems.

This chapter introduces the Model, describing its origins, structure and key hypotheses. Using four sets of tools, the discussion below describes how interested stakeholders – including policymakers, farmer representatives, business organisations,

The policymaking process **89**

civil society groups, donors or researchers – can use the model to help better understand and intervene in specific policy systems.

10.2 Kaleidoscope model of food security policy change

Two large bodies of experience have informed the structure and content of the KM. First, the model draws on literature on theoretical constructs as well as empirically documented episodes of policy change, primarily in the fields of public administration and political science. Second, the model derives insights from international development policy experience on episodes of policy change in developing countries. This evidence encompasses a range of policy domains related to food security, including agriculture, education, healthcare, nutrition and social protection (Resnick et al., 2015).

Pulling together evidence and experience from both the academic and donor communities, the KM inductively derives a set of core variables that prove consistently important in motivating policy reform and influencing policy design, implementation and reform. The framework spans all five stages of the policy cycle:

- Agenda setting
- Design
- Adoption
- Implementation and
- Evaluation and reform.

As the model's architects explain, they have named this framework "the 'Kaleidoscope Model' because just as shifting a kaleidoscope refracts light on a new pattern, so does focusing on a particular stage of the policy process reveal a different constellation of key variables" (Resnick et al., 2015, p. 26). Like the pieces of coloured glass inside a kaleidoscope, many underlying variables remain relevant as policy dynamics unfurl, yet some factors play a disproportionately larger role in providing illumination and driving policy change at a particular point in time.

Testable propositions about key drivers of policy change centre on the 16 hypotheses listed in light grey inner circle in Figure 10.1. In addition to these primary causal variables, an array of contextual conditions envelops the policy environment and shapes its contours. For example, macro-economic conditions often shape prices, private sector motivations and government budgets. Similarly, material conditions (such as asset distribution, poverty rates, available technologies, soil structure and climate), shape the intensity of specific policy problems as well as feasible design options. To highlight the importance of these situation-specific contextual conditions, the outer circle of the KM wheel includes an illustrative list of contextual conditions.

The module was tested in different operational and policy settings and refined (see Resnick et al., 2018). Researchers and practitioners have applied the model, each aimed broadly at understanding policy processes and improving the effectiveness of policy systems, research, advocacy and implementation. For specific applications and examples,

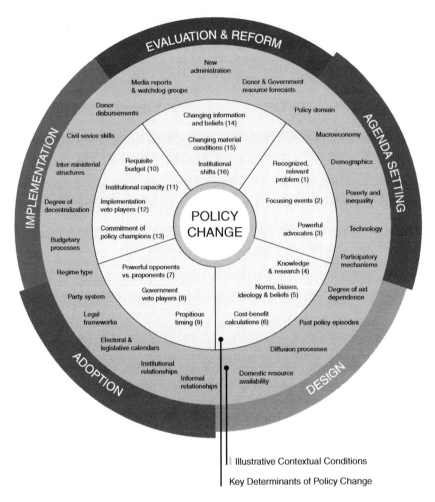

FIGURE 10.1 The Kaleidoscope Model
Source: Resnick et al. (2018).

see Babu et al. (2016), Haggblade et al. (2016), Hendriks et al. (2016), Mather and Ndyetabula, (2016), Resnick and Mason, (2016) and Resnick and Mather, (2016).

For each purpose, a variety of tools exist. 'The User's Guide to the Kaleidoscope Model' provides a good starting point (Haggblade and Babu, 2017). The guide and other web-based learning materials are available to interested stakeholders (see www.http://foodsecuritypolicy.msu.edu/resources).

10.3 Diagnostic tools

The Kaleidoscope Model (KM) provides a structured framework for identifying the key factors that drive policy change. The model includes four basic diagnostic tools:

- Policy chronology
- Stakeholder mapping
- Circle of influence
- Hypothesis testing.

Interested stakeholders can apply the KM diagnostic tools to look forward or backwards. Looking backwards, the tools help to trace policy changes and understand the reasons for past policy outcomes. Looking forward, the diagnostic tools can help to identify promising opportunities for future policy reform.

The policy chronology provides a starting point in both applications. The chronology identifies major policy decisions as well as key individuals, interest groups, information and events shaping these policy changes. The policy chronology provides several benefits to stakeholders. It serves to identify the key players in a given policy system. In addition, the reconstruction of policy events, debates and outcomes helps to distinguish the highly influential players from the less influential and marginal actors. Moreover, the timing of key decisions and key influencing factors often helps to understand how to contribute most effectively to future policy discussions.

Policy processes involve multiple actors. In agricultural policy systems, government decision makers typically interact with stakeholder groups such as farmer organisations, major agribusiness firms and scientists involved in agricultural research systems. Nutrition policy often involves a broader set of interest groups, including civil society advocacy groups, the food industry, nutritionists and public health specialists. In both policy arenas, donor agencies frequently play an outsized role in developing countries through their financial support for technical assistance, research and even host country budgets.

The KM deploys several related tools for identification and mapping of the key stakeholders, namely a stakeholder inventory, a policy system schematic (Figure 10.2) and a circle of influence (Figure 10.3). The stakeholder inventory explores the key involved parties, their roles, resources and policy stances. Decision makers include government entities responsible for authorising and codifying key policy decisions. Implementation may involve government agencies or the private sector. For example, some fertiliser subsidy programs rely on direct government delivery of low-priced inputs. In other situations, policy designs incentivise private traders to deliver low-cost farm inputs via the transfer of purchasing power to target groups; often through vouchers that farmers then take to their preferred agrodealer, who in turn assumes responsibility for physical distribution and delivery of the commodities to the final consumer.

Advocates for nutrition policy reform include public health groups, church groups, civil society groups as well as medical and academic researchers. International researchers and agencies have proven especially effective as advocates of nutrition policy reform in developing countries over the past several decades (Hendriks et al., 2017). In the agricultural policy arena, advocates often include farmer groups, specific agribusiness interests, environmental advocacy groups and agricultural researchers.

In turn, the policy system schematic describes how these players interact: setting policy agendas, designing policy options, decision-making, implementation and monitoring. The schematic in Figure 10.2 highlights key differences in implementation responsibility

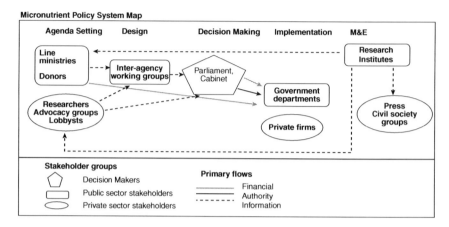

FIGURE 10.2 Policy system schematic
Source: Haggblade and Babu (2017)

across different nutrition policies. While government agencies (clinics and schools) may implement micronutrient supplementation programs, biofortification involves government breeders and farmers, while food fortification requires implementation by private sector food processors. Where implementation depends on private sector compliance, trade organisations and even powerful individual firms become de facto veto players.

The circle of influence graphic, adapted from Grindle (2014), illustrates the key players and their policy positions (Figure 10.3). Supporters and opponents appear in their respective segments in the diagram. Those with the greatest power to sway decision makers appear closest to the 'bull's eye'. This graphic provides a quick, visual summary of key actors and their relative levels of influence on policy outcomes.

Recent empirical applications of the KM suggest that positions may change over time. For example, pro-subsidy groups may become advocates for reform in instances where widespread pilferage and rent-seeking emerge (Resnick et al., 2018).

Together these elements enable existing stakeholders or prospective advocates to intervene more effectively in policy debates of specific interest. Identification of the advocates who have proven most effective historically or who share your perspective will help to narrow the range of potential allies and collaborators. A review of the key advocates and circumstances driving past change can help to identify strategies for future advocacy. Similarly, a review of the types of evidence that have proven persuasive in the past or gaps constraining our understanding of key outcomes can help focus future research and make evidence-based advocacy more effective.

Even with well-conceived policies, implementation frequently falls short of expectations. As a result, monitoring and periodic feedback by stakeholders and their advocates can become critical to effective policy outcomes. A comparison of micro-nutrient and input subsidy policies in Zambia by Resnick et al. (2018) provides examples of implementation bottlenecks that enable advocacy groups to successfully lobby for subsequent rounds of policy reform.

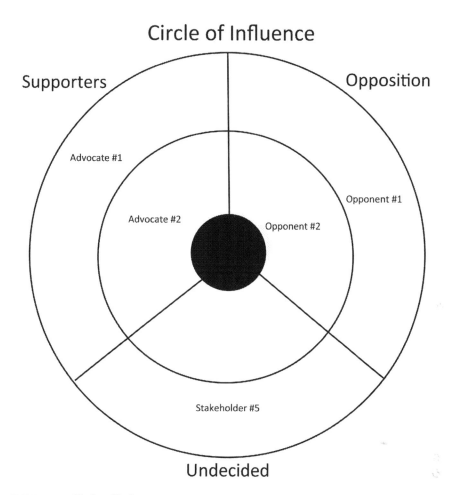

FIGURE 10.3 Circle of influence
Source: Haggblade and Babu (2017)

10.4 Testable hypotheses

For many operational purposes, the simple diagnostic tools presented above will suffice. However, systematic efforts to promote knowledge accumulation and improve understanding of policy processes requires more rigorous academic research and formal hypothesis testing. For this reason, a growing body of analytical work has used the KM to formally test hypotheses about what factors prove critical in enabling past policy changes (Haggblade et al., 2017).

As knowledge accumulates and as patterns emerge from the formal hypothesis testing, it may become possible to develop simple rating tools for ranking policy reform opportunities in terms of likelihood of successful reform. Two reviews summarise and generalise from findings available to date (Resnick et al., 2018) and

(Haggblade et al., 2017). The following discussion presents the KM hypotheses, data requirements and standards of evidence required to accept or reject hypotheses about the key factors driving policy reform.

The Kaleidoscope Model revolves around 16 testable hypotheses about the proximate causes of policy reform. The inner circle in Figure 10.1 enumerates these 16 hypotheses, while Table 10.1 formally describes them. The model lists each variable at the policy stage where it typically influences outcomes most directly. Nonetheless, as many scholars of the policy process have observed, policy change often involves iterative and nonlinear trajectories, with substantial feedback loops as past decisions influence future policies (see Sabatier, 2007). Likewise, individual variables may influence outcomes at multiple stages. For example, knowledge and research (Kaleidoscope Model Variable number 4, KMV4) clearly affects design options but also frequently motivates agenda setting as well as monitoring and evaluation. Rather than listing each variable multiple times, at every point where it may potentially prove relevant, the KM lists each variable only once, at the stage in the policy process where it typically takes precedence.

Data for testing the KM hypotheses comes from two principal sources. The first includes a range of secondary resources, including academic articles, parliamentary records, media reporting, donor reviews, working papers, and other grey literature. In addition, full understanding of policy processes and outcomes requires qualitative, semi-structured interviews with knowledgeable stakeholders and observers. Although interview numbers vary according to the complexity of the system under review, past work with the KM has involved interviews with roughly 20 to 30 policy system stakeholders. It is important to include representatives from all major stakeholder groups, including decision makers, advocates, opponents, implementers and beneficiary groups.

Unlike quantitative statistical analysis, qualitative research such as this requires that researchers establish explicit criteria for hypothesis testing and clear standards of evidence for assessing the significance (or insignificance) of each key variable. This requires triangulation among respondents and across sources to identify points of disagreement and consensus. Although a detailed discussion of hypothesis testing protocols and standards of evidence is beyond the scope of this chapter, Haggblade and Babu (2017) provide a detailed discussion of evidence requirements and the measurement protocols developed for formal testing of key KM hypotheses.

The initial case studies (see Babu et al. 2016; Haggblade et al., 2016; Hendriks et al., 2016; Mather and Ndyetabula, 2016; Resnick and Mason, 2016; Resnick and Mather, 2016) conducted with the model involved multiple instances of policy reform, redesign and implementation adjustments. As a result, these pilot studies compiled evidence on 50 policy reform episodes, including 38 micro-nutrient policies and 12 agricultural input policy reforms. Three papers (Haggblade et al., 2017; Hendriks et al., 2017; Resnick et al., 2017) review the key findings of this work. Table 10.2 and the discussion below provides a short synopsis of these early results.

TABLE 10.1 Kaleidoscope Model hypotheses about key drivers of policy change

Policy stages	Key variables driving policy change	Hypothesis
Agenda setting	1. Recognised, relevant problem	A concerned constituency identifies a relevant problem based on credible evidence or popular perception.
	2. Focusing event	A well-defined event focuses public attention on a problem or creates a window of opportunity for policy change.
	3. Powerful advocates	Strong individuals, organisations, or companies support a new or changed policy to key decision makers.
Design	4. Knowledge and research	Evidence-based knowledge shapes feasible design options.
	5. Norms, biases, ideology and beliefs	Beliefs and biases shape the range of acceptable designs.
	6. Cost-benefit calculations	Expected benefits and costs (political, economic and social) influence the preferred design.
Adoption	7. Powerful opponents vs. proponents	For a policy to be adopted, supporters must be relatively more powerful than opponents.
	8. Government veto players	For a policy to be adopted, government agents with ultimate decision-making power must be supportive or neutral. For a policy to be vetoed, government agents with ultimate decision-making power must be an opponent.
	9. Propitious timing	Supporters wait for opportune moments (political, economic, social) to push policy change.
Implementation	10. Requisite budget	Government or donors provide fund sufficient to carry out the new policy or program as intended.
	11. Institutional capacity	Government or other intended implementing organisations managed the new policy or program as it was intended.
	12. Implementing stage veto players	Designated implementers – from the private sector, NGO or local agencies – have both incentives and willingness to implement the policy program.
	13. Commitment of policy champions	Strong individuals, organisations, or companies continued to publicly support the program.
Evaluation and Reform	14. Changing information and beliefs	New learning emerges that influences how decision makers believe the policy/program should be structured.
	15. Changing material conditions	Available resources, technology, or policy needs have changed since the policy was originally implemented.
	16. Institutional shifts	New actors enter the policy arena as the result of elections, cabinet reshuffle, or new staffing.

Agenda setting

Policy reform requires a burst of energy to overcome the inertia of existing vested interests. At the agenda-setting stage, evidence from these 50 episodes of policy reform indicates that three main factors routinely provoke rethinking of current policy positions (Table 10.2). High-profile focusing events (KMV1) enable powerful advocates (KMV2) to place recognised, relevant problems (KMV3) squarely in the view of decisions makers and the general public.

In the case of micro-nutrient policies, international advocates led by UNICEF convened the 1990 World Summit for Children at the UN General Assembly, while a coalition of nutrition advocates followed up with a series of international summits (on universal salt iodisation, for example) followed by several *Lancet* special issues documenting the pervasiveness of micro-nutrient deficiencies as well as potential solutions. With agricultural input policies, high-profile advocates (often country presidents) responded to the world food and petroleum price hikes of 2008 by initiating or scaling up politically popular input subsidies.

Design

At the design stage, forces driving the formulation of new policies differ across policy domains. The design of agricultural input subsidy modalities depends to a large extent on norms, core beliefs and ideology (KMV5), in particular deeply held beliefs about the fairness (or unfairness) and efficiency (or inefficiency) of private markets. In contrast, micro-nutrient supplementation policies have proven less controversial and more frequently founded on international best-practice medical and nutritional scientific research and knowledge (KMV4) as well as empirical evidence concerning the costs and benefits (KMV6) of alternative solutions.

Adoption

Decisions to adopt a new policy depend on two primary factors: the relative power of proponents and opponents (KMV7) and agreement of government veto players (KMV8). Both of these variables proved important in the majority of both micro-nutrient and input subsidy policy changes reviewed.

Implementation

Implementation depends fundamentally on the availability of requisite budget resources (KMV10), institutional delivery capacity (KMV11) and the on-going commitment of policy champions (KMV13). With input subsidy programs, budget and implementation capacity constraints have proven especially acute. Indeed, changing budgetary resources (including donor support) frequently trigger reforms. In micro-nutrient supplementation policy reforms, budget and implementation capacity constraints have proven less dominant, piggy backing on health system delivery systems.

TABLE 10.2 KM Hypothesis tests (percentage of cases in which variables proved significant)

		Policy Domain	
Policy stage	Kaleidoscope hypotheses	Micro-nutrients	Fertilizer subsidy
Agenda setting	1 Focusing event	82%	58%
	2 Powerful advocates	84%	100%
	3 Recognized, relevant problem	84%	100%
Design	4 Knowledge, research and ideas	89%	58%
	5 Norms, biases, ideology, beliefs	16%	100%
	6 Cost-benefit, risk calculations	55%	75%
Adoption	7 Powerful opponents vs. proponents	68%	92%
	8 Government veto players		
	+ affirmative decision	88%	100%
	- exercise veto	12%	0%
	9 Propitious timing	3%	27%
Implementation	10 Requisite budget	61%	82%
	11 Institutional capacity	53%	100%
	12 Implementing stage veto players		
	+ facilitate implementation	87%	45%
	- stymie implementation	13%	55%
	13 Commitment of policy champions	50%	91%
Evaluation, reform	14 Changing info and beliefs	50%	82%
	15 Changing material conditions	42%	82%
	16 Institutional changes	32%	18%
Number of cases		38	12

Source: Haggblade et al. (2017)

In the case of fortification policies, the bulk of these reforms involved food fortification mandates, which rely on private – rather than public sector – delivery and consumer – rather than government – financing. In these cases, private sector implementing agents become potential veto players (KMV12). Across the policy domains studied, budget and implementation capacity constraints pose major constraints on the monitoring and evaluation of these programs as well as on compliance. Despite their importance, these elements do not always receive careful consideration in the design and implementation of these programs.

Evaluation and reform

Reform of existing policies results from three major causes. Changing material conditions (KMV15) have proven important in micro-nutrient policies, as when early iodisation efforts in all three Southern Africa countries resulted in not only the expected rapid reduction of iodine deficiency disorders but also in an unexpected emergence of excessive urinary iodine. This changing reality, in turn, triggered a reduction in mandated fortification levels in Malawi and Zambia. Changing information and beliefs (KMV14) have proven critical to agricultural input subsidy reforms, particularly evidence on leakage, poor targeting and late deliveries. Institutional changes (KMV16) contributed to roughly one-third of policy reform efforts.

New presidents, new governments and new agriculture ministers routinely open up opportunities for input subsidy reform. In micro-nutrient policy, a series of cross-ministerial institutional reforms have proven decisive, most notably with the creation of Malawi's Department of Nutrition and HIV and AIDS (DNHA) at the Office of the President, which afforded nutrition advocates unprecedented visibility and political access (Babu et al., 2016).

10.5 Conclusion

The Kaleidoscope Model provides a practical tool for stakeholders interested in improving policy outcomes. Governments, farmers, civil society advocacy groups, donors and academics can all make use of these Kaleidoscope Model findings to orient and align their policy advocacy efforts. Some stakeholders express interest in improving the overall performance of a given policy system. Others seek to influence outcomes by engaging more effectively in specific policy debates.

References

Africa Lead (2015) 'African Lead II update', http://dai.com/our-work/projects/africa%E2% 80%94africa-lead-ii.

Babu, S.C., Haggblade, S., Mkandawire, E., Nankhuni, F. and Hendriks, S.L. (2016) 'Micronutrient policy process in Malawi', Discussion paper no. 01568, IFPRI, Washington DC.

Grindle, M. (2014) *Tools for the Political Analysis of Reform Initiatives*. Kennedy School of Government, Harvard University, Cambridge.

Haggblade, S. and Babu, S. (2017) 'A user's guide to the Kaleidoscope Model: Practical tools for understanding policy change', Research paper no. 46, Feed the Future Innovation Lab for Food Security, Michigan State University, East Lansing.

Haggblade, S., Babu, S., Harris, J., Mkandawire, E., Nthani, D. and Hendriks, S. (2016) 'Drivers of micronutrient policy change in Zambia: An application of the Kaleidoscope Model', Working paper C3–3, Innovation Lab for Food Security Policy, Michigan State University, East Lansing.

Haggblade, S., Babu, S., Hendriks, S., Mather, D. and Resnick, D. (2017) 'What drives policy change? Evidence from six empirical applications of the Kaleidoscope Model', Policy research brief no. 31, Feed the Future Innovation Lab for Food Security, Michigan State University, East Lansing.

Hendriks, S. L., Babu, S. C. & Haggblade, S. (2017) 'What drives nutrition policy reform in Africa? Applying the Kaleidoscope Model of food security policy change', Policy research brief no. 30, Feed the Future Innovation Lab for Food Security, Michigan State University, East Lansing.

Hendriks, S.L., Mkwandawire, E., Hall, N., Olivier, N.J., Schönfeldt, H.C., Randall, P., Morgan, S., Olivier, N.J., Haggblade, S. and Babu, S.C. (2016) 'Micronutrient policy change in South Africa: Implications for the Kaleidoscope model for food security policy change', Research paper no. 18, Feed the Future Innovation Lab for Food Security, Michigan State University, East Lansing.

Mather, D. and Ndyetabula, D. (2016) 'Assessing the drivers of Tanzania's fertilizer subsidy programs from 2003–2016: An application of the Kaleidoscope Model of policy change', Research paper no. 34, Feed the Future Innovation Lab for Food Security Policy, Michigan State University, East Lansing.

Nelson, J.M. (1984) 'The political economy of stabilization: Commitment, capacity, and public response', *World Development*, vol. 12, no. 10, pp. 983–1006.

Organisation for Economic Co-operation and Development (OECD)/ Development Assistance Committee (DAC) (2014) 'Measuring and managing results in development co-operation: A review of challenges and practices among DAC members and observers', Review, OECD, Paris.

Resnick, D., Babu, S., Haggblade, S., Hendriks, S. and Mather, D. (2015) 'Conceptualizing drivers of policy change in agriculture, nutrition, and food security: The Kaleidoscope Model', Discussion paper no. 01414, IFPRI, Washington.

Resnick, D., Haggblade, S., Babu, S., Hendriks, S.L. and Mather, D. (2018) 'The Kaleidoscope Model of policy change: Applications to food security policy in Zambia', *World Development*, vol. 109, pp. 101–120.

Resnick, D. and Mason, N. (2016) 'What drives input subsidy policy reform?: The case of Zambia, 2002–2016', Research paper no. 28, Feed the Future Innovation Lab for Food Secuiryt Policy, Michigan State University, East Lansing.

Resnick, D. and Mather, D. (2016) 'Agricultural inputs policy under macroeconomic uncertainty: Applying the kaleidoscope model to Ghana's fertilizer subsidy programme (2008–2015)', Research paper 19, Feed the Future Innovation Lab for Food Security, Michigan State University, East Lansing.

Resnick, D., Mather, D., Mason, N. and Ndyetabula, D. (2017) 'What drives agricultural input subsidy reform in Africa? Applying the Kaleidoscope Model of food security policy change', Policy research brief no. 27, Feed the Future Innovation Lab for Food Security Policy, Michigan State University, East Lansing.

Sabatier, P. (2007). 'The need for better theories', in P. Sabatier (Ed.), *Theories of the policy process*. Westview Press, Boulder, CO.

USAID (2013) *Feed the Future Guide to Supporting Sound Policy Enabling Environments.* USAID, Washington DC.

White, H. (2014) 'Current challenges in impact evaluation', *The European Journal of Development Research*, vol. 26, no. 1, pp. 18–30.

11

DEVELOPING AND APPLYING A THEORY OF CHANGE ASSESSMENT

Angela M. McIntyre

11.1 Target setting in the SDG era

The Sustainable Development Goals, more so than any previous international consensus, reflect the complexity and interconnectedness of human development issues. For this reason, setting SDG targets involved a great many stakeholders and a long consultative process in order to determine universally meaningful indicators. The expansiveness of the SDGs is also a result of the process by which they were designed:

> Throughout 2012 and 2013, the United Nations facilitated what seemed like the first exercise in global participatory democracy, organising fifty-plus country consultations, multiple global thematic consultations, and a worldwide online citizen survey—all of which were accompanied by numerous parallel NGO, expert, and state initiatives
>
> *(Langford, 2016, p. 170)*

The SDGs include 17 interconnected goals, each with multiple targets and indicators. Alone, SDG 2, which aims to end hunger, achieve food security, improve nutrition and promote sustainable agriculture, has eight targets, each with multiple indicators. Together, they intend to address drivers of hunger and food insecurity by reaching various targets for reducing malnutrition, improving agricultural productivity in more diverse and inclusive ways, making production systems more sustainable and resilient and removing market distortions and disincentives.

Although the outcome of the SDGs is of universal benefit and the indicators universally meaningful, the processes, stakeholders and pathways required for effecting change are likely to be very different for each country. The economic, social, environmental and political constraints faced by decision-makers differ widely. Meaningful changes in global indicators require that countries

Applying a theory of change assessment **101**

adopting the SDGs embark on their own particular trajectories of policymaking, planning, programming and monitoring and evaluation.

Many of the difficulties of designing sustainable responses to complex social problems like food insecurity revolve around complexity and uncertainty. Using theories of change (ToC) is a way of recognising that development work has complexity, uncertainty and ambiguity (Valters, 2014). It is a method for making these explicit, clarifying possibilities and limitations, establishing transparency and accountability and ensuring that action is supported by evidence and research. Building a ToC begins with the desired state of things, working backwards to establish pathways of change that take complexity, uncertainty and ambiguity into account.

Related to complexity, uncertainty and ambiguity is the challenge of inclusion: which sectors, which stakeholders, what assumptions, what rationale, which pre-conditions must be met and what targets must be reached along the way to achieve the desired impact? This challenge is the same in virtually every development context, from the community to the global levels. ToC can also be a way of addressing the challenges of inclusivity and stakeholder diversity that are so important to planning sustainable interventions for addressing socio-economic problems like food insecurity and malnutrition. Building a ToC can bring unheard or under-represented voices into development planning. It can bring stakeholders together in multi-sectoral initiatives, overcoming some of the problems of policy 'silos' in food security, where collaboration between agricultural, health and water and sanitation, for example, is essential. Research teams can employ theories of change to bring disciplines, development paradigms and society together in transdisciplinary approaches (Maru et al., 2018).

Modelling change can happen before, during and after interventions, in planning, monitoring and evaluation stages. ToC can be used to build consensus, to mainstream issues into planning by including a range of different stakeholder perspectives. They can be used to develop monitoring systems for adaptive management and learning during implementation. ToC are increasingly used in evaluation process. A ToC developed at the end of a project cycle can provide a mode for scaling up interventions (Mayne, 2015).

11.2 A theory of change as a means to shift from outputs and outcomes to impact in development planning, monitoring and evaluation

Policies, programs and projects all aim to create change. Along the way, they may generate various outputs and outcomes, which all add up to a desirable effect – a change in the overall state or condition of things. The achievement of national food security, for example, can rest on a complex and interconnected array of outcomes, for example, institutions that perform better, resilient food systems, sustainable production models and gender equity. The outcomes might generate many different outputs, including goods, services, new skills and abilities of individuals and institutional capacities (Bester, 2012). These can be accounted for in ToC, as well as the ways in which they are linked, as cause and effect or through feedback loops, to create the changes that add up to positive impact.

Development planning, monitoring and evaluation tools are all challenged with managing complexity. Highly linear models that rely heavily on quantifiable outputs can have serious limitations in unpredictable political, economic and social contexts. The failure to account for contingencies can quickly derail the best-intentioned initiatives. Change pathways are not always clear, stable or linear, for example, where improving nutrition requires behaviour change or farmers are asked to adopt new technologies to increase yields (Mayne and Johnson, 2015; Douthwaite and Hoffecker, 2017). Acknowledging uncertainty and complexity and making assumptions explicit from the outset can make programs more flexible, more responsive to change and more accountable.

Success can mean very different things to a government, development partner and community member. Policies and development programs have long faced the criticisms of being 'donor-driven' or 'top-down'. This is also the case in food security, where highly integrated and globalised markets, climate change and political instability exercise influences along pathways that are often poorly understood. Ecological, social and cultural characteristics of local contexts are key to the understanding of food security challenges. Local communities have critical insights into the success and failure of past initiatives and have current experience of the impacts of climate change, global economic shocks and political upheaval (McIntyre and Hendriks, 2018). All of these factors shape assumptions about causality.

New kinds of stakeholder engagement, measurement tools and types of data must be brought into planning and evaluation to generate the outcomes and impacts envisioned in the SDGs. Theories of change are gaining popularity and acceptance as ways of dealing with complexity and uncertainty in development.

11.3 The elements of a theory of change approach

A ToC is a map that begins with identifying long-term goals, mapping out steps or causal links and making explicit the assumptions, preconditions and requirements necessary for change. It explains strategically how and why the theory will work through a logical progression of steps and supporting assumptions, using diagrams and narratives to summarise logic (Taplin and Clark, 2012).

Complexity presents many practical and theoretical challenges. Solving problems by working 'backwards' to map out the preconditions and pathways of change allows for different kinds of evidence to be brought into the theory. Capturing all the significant assumptions, linkages and dimensions of change can require both qualitative and quantitative data. For this reason, a ToC is often supported by both, in addition to information generated by consultative processes involving different actors within the system.

The generic ToC diagram in Figure 11.1 depicts a causal pathway leading to changes in wellbeing arising from actions. The actions (1), or activities are undertaken by the different actors involved in the intervention might produce goods or services (2), sometimes referred to as outputs, which are interim effects of the intervention. Reach and reaction (3) is a concept developed by Mayne (2015) to describe the target group of an intervention, for example, gender, geographical spread or socioeconomic characteristics, and their anticipated initial reaction, all of which carry different assumptions. Immediate changes in capacity or knowledge (4) give rise to behaviour changes or changes in practices (5). These can have direct benefits (6) that support the overall shift in wellbeing (7).

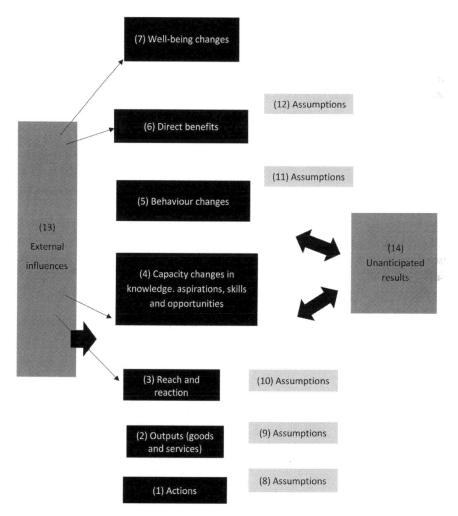

FIGURE 11.1 Generic theory of change model
Source: Adapted from (Mayne, 2015)

This causal chain is mediated by assumptions (8–12), which are understandings about the conditions necessary for the causal pathway to work as anticipated. These could include evidence and theories from natural or social sciences, but may also derive from stakeholder knowledge and experience (Mayne and Johnson, 2015). What is taken for granted by one stakeholder might be a make-or-break assumption for another. For example, a project supporting small-scale or household food production to improve nutrition rests on many different assumptions, a possible one being that all households equally access agricultural extension services. But barriers such as gender discrimination might exclude some families entirely if female household heads are excluded in some way from accessing programs, land or inputs, for example. Thinking critically, employing evidence and inviting the views of different stakeholders brings assumptions into view. Assumptions may also be derived from evidence generated by prior research, but often this is not enough. Using a ToC to replicate or scale interventions across different contexts should generate new sets of assumptions.

Unanticipated results (14) are inevitable where there is uncertainty and complexity. Income generating activities aimed at improving purchasing power, for example, demand time that might be spent on childcare, a trade-off that could negatively impact children's wellbeing (Mayne and Johnson, 2015). Including relevant assumptions about gender and childcare in the design of the project could mediate this effect. Sometimes unanticipated results are positive, especially where new skills and capacity inspire initiative and innovation outside the scope of a project (Douthwaite and Hoffecker, 2017).

11.4 Challenges and limitations of theories of change

While ToCs are useful tools in multi-sectoral, multidisciplinary and multi-stakeholder situations, doing them well can make relatively greater demands on time and resources than more linear or top-down management tools. Ideally, a ToC is an iterative process that takes place in an environment conducive to learning, where organisational cultures encourage reflection (Maru et al., 2018). There is no standard approach to the ToC and it is subject to different interpretations and applications and is easily confused with other tools such as logical frameworks. Skills and practice are required, including the 'soft' skills need for community engagement, negotiation and conflict management (Maru et al., 2018). Facilitators working with diverse stakeholders need to maintain objectivity and impartiality in brokering power relations (Maini et al., 2018). Getting buy-in and ownership is a challenge where stakeholders have different priorities. Adequate time needs to be invested in ensuring that everyone understands and trusts the process and that it is genuinely a creative one, rather than a 'rubber-stamp' exercise to fast-track plans designed in advance (Maini et al., 2018). Studies of ToCs in agricultural innovations for food security and nutrition in developing countries suggest that factors such as quality, sustained research partnerships, relationships between stakeholders and researchers and research strategies are important determinants of impact (Joly et al., 2015; Schut et al., 2016).

Applying a theory of change assessment **105**

Ultimately, ToCs are subject to forces within wider systems and therefore always have limitations; no ToC can ever capture all assumptions or calculate all the potential risks in development or research initiatives.

11.5 Applications of theories of change in food security research and development: biofortified food crops to increase micronutrient intake

Theories of change have many uses in development, from planning to guiding implementation processes to evaluation and are used in organisational learning, communication and program accountability. They are gaining popularity in research-for-development initiatives linking government sectors, including health, social development, food and agriculture and environment, and at many levels, from community development initiatives to national policies. ToCs have gained traction in research with strong multidisciplinary and participatory components, for example in agricultural interventions for improving nutrition. ToCs are proving especially useful to agricultural research for development, for demonstrating pathways between agricultural research and social impact.

Micronutrient deficiency is a serious global public health nutrition concern, resulting in stunted growth and development among children, weakened immune systems and poor metabolic functioning. It is linked to poor diet quality and efforts to address it raise important questions about the role of food systems in food insecurity and malnutrition. Agriculture and food security are important determinants in health and nutrition, but in order for agriculture to positively impact nutrition, the research and development emphasis must shift from supply-side productivity goals to food consumption and diet quality issues (McDermott et al., 2015). A promising field of agricultural research to promote micronutrient consumption is the biofortification of crops with the nutrients necessary for growth and development, for example iron and vitamin A. Causal chains between developing fortified crop varieties and healthy growth is, however, complex, resting on multiple assumptions and relying on the inclusion of diverse stakeholders.

The following example (Figure 11.2) of iron-fortified beans in Rwanda is drawn from a CGIAR initiative to address high rates of iron deficiency and anaemia among children 6–59 months old and women. In this case, a ToC is employed to illustrate the causal chain between the introduction of seeds and reduced prevalence of inadequate iron intake (Johnson et al., 2015). In this model, risks are included alongside assumptions as mediators of causality.

Each link along the pathway carries assumptions, and alongside these, risks. If assumptions are incorrect or weak, the risks might weaken the impact of the initiative. Farmers will only adopt the seeds if they are convinced of the benefits (4) and produce will not be readily available in local markets if traders do not see any demand from consumers (11–12). The consumption of biofortified produce (7) rests on its accessibility, either by way of own production, purchase or some other entitlement enabling exchange. This assumption can be informed by information

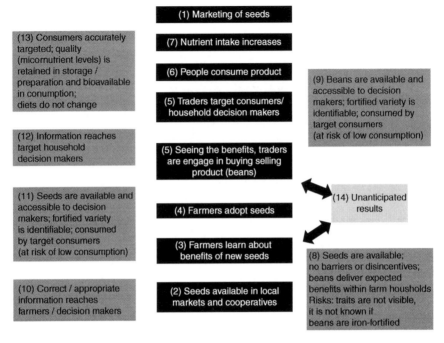

FIGURE 11.2 Theory of change for increasing micronutrient consumption through biofortified crops
Source: Adapted from (Mayne and Johnson, 2015) and (Johnson et al., 2015).

about livelihoods, income and dietary preferences. That consumption of the crop is actually adding to micronutrient intake rests on assumptions about nutrient retention in storage, preparation and bioavailability in consumption (13).

There could be many more risks, assumptions and other external factors working for or against success, but it is simply not feasible to include all of the political, economic and environmental factors in a theory of change at this level. But research evidence, social science theory and stakeholder experience are informed assumptions and understandings of risk (Johnson et al., 2015). A diversity of stakeholders, which in this case could include farmers, market sellers, non-farming household decision makers, enriches the ToC by grounding it in local reality and experience. In this example a health issue (micronutrient deficiency) is addressed by situating the problem in local context where knowledge, capacity, entitlements and preferences are made explicit. It demonstrates clear links between the agriculture, health and economic sectors, along a pathway that is not confined by sectoral, donor or commercial interests or theoretically confined by a particular discipline.

As an *ex-post* evaluation tool, this theory of change can inform the design of future interventions, the need for further research, or local, participatory action towards nutrition-sensitive agriculture (Johnson et al., 2015). It is a segment of a longer pathway between research on biofortification and improved micronutrient status. It could be one of several ToCs making up a multi-faceted approach to improving overall nutrition outcomes, for example, aimed at improving accessibility to diverse diets through social protection, or building capacity and skills with nutrition education, which are mutually reinforcing.

11.6 Conclusion

Working towards high-level international development targets like the SDGs can seem impossibly complex. There is little hope of approaching hunger, food insecurity and malnutrition sectoral issues or by posing mono-disciplinary research questions; the problems simply cannot be approached from the top down. Widespread, localised, environmentally, culturally and politically appropriate efforts to creating local impact will add up to the collective effort needed to reach global development targets and goals. Grounding complex social problems like hunger, malnutrition and food insecurity calls for new kinds of tools, novel collaborations and wider stakeholder inclusivity. Using ToC can help articulate the demand-led, participatory and multisectoral initiatives involving diverse stakeholders that are necessary for working towards international development targets (Thornton et al., 2017). ToC can be an effective tool for managing complexity because it begins by framing problems within particular spheres of actors and stakeholders at appropriate scales, creating common ground for research and development planning.

References

Bester, A. (2012) 'Results-based management in the United Nations Development System: progress and challenges', A report prepared for the United Nations Department of Economic and Social Affairs (UNDESA), for the Quadrennial Comprehensive Policy Review, UNDESA, New York.

Douthwaite, B. and Hoffecker, E. (2017) 'Towards a complexity-aware theory of change for participatory research programs working within agricultural innovation systems', *Agricultural Systems*, vol. 155, pp. 88–102.

Johnson, N.L., Guedenet, H. and Saltzman, A. (2015) 'What will it take for biofortification to have impact on the ground? Theories of change for three crop-country combinations', Discussion paper no. 01427, IFPRI, Washington DC.

Joly, P.B., Gaunand, A., Colinet, L., Larédo, P., Lemarié, S. and Matt, M. (2015) 'ASIRPA: A comprehensive theory-based approach to assessing the societal impacts of a research organisation', *Research Evaluation*, vol. 24, no. 4, pp. 440–453.

Langford, M. (2016) 'Lost in transformation? The politics of the sustainable development goals', *Ethics and International Affairs*, vol. 30, no. 2, pp. 167–176.

Maini, R., Mounier-Jack, S. and Borghi, J. (2018) 'How to and how not to develop a theory of change to evaluate a complex intervention: Reflections on an experience in the Democratic Republic of Congo', *BMJ Global Health*, vol. 3, no. 1, pp. 1–6.

Maru, Y.T., Sparrow, A., Butler, J.R., Banerjee, O., Ison, R., Hall, A. and Carberry, P. (2018) 'Towards appropriate mainstreaming of "Theory of Change" approaches into agricultural research for development: Challenges and opportunities', *Agricultural Systems*, vol. 165, pp. 344–353.

Mayne, J. (2015) 'Useful theory of change models', *Canadian Journal of Program Evaluation*, vol. 30, no. 2, pp. 119–142.

Mayne, J. and Johnson, N. (2015) 'Using theories of change in the CGIAR Research Program on Agriculture for Nutrition and Health', *Evaluation*, vol. 21, no. 44, pp. 407–428.

McDermott, J., Johnson, N., Kadiyala, S., Kennedy, G. and Wyatt, A.J. (2015) 'Agricultural research for nutrition outcomes – rethinking the agenda', *Food Security*, vol. 7, no. 3, pp. 593–607.

McIntyre, A. and Hendriks, S.L.(2018) 'Interpreting food security research findings with rural South African communities', *Global Journal of Health Science*, vol. 10, no. 5, pp. 183–196.

Schut, M., Klerkx, L., Sartas, M., Lamers, D., Mc Campbell, M., Ogbonna, I., Kaushik, P., Atta-Krah, K. and Leeuwis, C. (2016) 'Innovation platforms: experiences with their institutional embedding in agricultural research for development', *Experimental Agriculture*, vol. 52, no. 4, pp. 537–561.

Taplin, D.H. and Clark, H. (2012) 'Theory of change basics: A primer on theory of change', Technical Paper, ActKnowledge, New York.

Thornton, P.K., Schuetz, T., Förch, W., Cramer, L., Abreu, D., Vermeulen, S. and Campbell, B.M. (2017) 'Responding to global change: A theory of change approach to making agricultural research for development outcome-based', *Agricultural Systems*, vol. 152, pp. 145–153.

Valters, C. (2014) 'Theories of change in international development: communication, learning, or accountability'. Justice and Security Research Programme paper 17, The Asian Foundation, San Francisco.

12

THE ESSENTIAL ELEMENTS OF ASSESSMENT, MONITORING AND EVALUATION TO DETERMINE THE IMPACT OF POLICIES AND PROGRAMMES

Sheryl L. Hendriks and Hunadi Mapula Nkwana

12.1 Introduction

In order to adequately assess public policy and programme effectiveness, it is imperative for policymakers to engage in monitoring and evaluation of food security policies, strategies and programmes. Evidence is essential to improve policies and programmes, identify successful models for scaling up and application in other contests and for redirecting funds from failed and less successful policies and programmes to those that are more likely to be effective (Evidence-based Policymaking Collaborative, 2016). Assessment and evaluation are important tools to promote innovation and test new approaches (Evidence-based Policymaking Collaborative, 2016). They are also essential for streamlining policies, strategies and programmes as well as actors in these processes. They play an important role in facilitating more efficient use of resources (Goldman et al., 2012). In complex crosscutting matters like food security, these systems can act as crucial drivers of coordination between sectors and between the public sector and other stakeholders.

The assessment, monitoring and evaluation of food security policies and programmes, is complicated by the fact that there is no 'perfect single measure that captures all aspects of food insecurity' (see Chapter 2). Food insecurity is not a homogeneous condition easily measured in economic, energy-availability or anthropometric terms (Webb et al. 2006, p. 1405S). After decades of intensive discussion and indicator development, we still do not have a universally accepted food security measurement system that we can apply across emergency and non-emergency contexts (Hendriks, 2015). This chapter defines what assessment, monitoring and evaluation is and what it involves. It sets out the importance of continuously applying these concepts within the food security context to learn from experiences and inform future policy decisions. The chapter concludes by providing the essential elements of a food security monitoring and evaluation system.

12.2 What is assessment, monitoring and evaluation?

Sound policies should include targets. Setting targets demands input data that establish the baseline or starting point at the publishing of a policy or the implementation of a programme. Baseline data provides a useful benchmark for setting targets for measuring progress (Rabie and Cloete 2018, p. 283). Targets are expressed as measurable changes that determine the success of a public policy and its implementation. These targets should align and support the achievement of national, regional or international targets.

In the case of the SDGs, the setting of targets involved a complicated process and months of deliberation to identify the most universal indicators that could provide a comparable measurement across countries worldwide. Just as with food security, each SDG can be measured in multiple ways. Not only is this necessary due to the complexity of the issue, that cannot simply be distilled into one indicator, but the multiple dimensions are important to achieve the four key elements of food security (refer to Chapter 2 for a discussion of these four elements). Given the different elements of food security, the ability to develop appropriate and effective policies is largely dependent on clearly defined indicators.

If we are to target our interventions effectively, we need to define the experiences, causes and consequences of food insecurity clearly and understand how the multiple dimensions reinforce each other and compound the problem. **Assessment** helps us understand the contextual situation specific to the community or area. It also identifies the most affected and vulnerable people to be able to target the programme towards these people. Assessments determine the depth and severity of food insecurity (see Chapter 3). They may be conducted for research purposes to obtain a snap shot of the situation at one particular time (context) or pre- (cause) and post intervention assessments to determine the impact (see Figure 12.1).

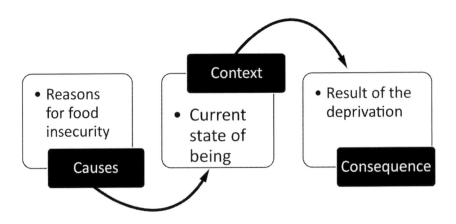

FIGURE 12.1 Differentiating between causes, context and consequences
Source: Authors

Food security assessments are typically carried out when:

- A problem is identified and we need to know more about the problem, its causes and consequences to identify potential solutions to the problem
- A new programme is implemented in order to establish a baseline against which to set targets and measure progress
- Mid-term evaluations are conducted
- End-term evaluations are conducted.

Assessments support policy and programme design as well as review stages. Assessments need to take consideration of the causes of food insecurity, the context (situation and experience) and the consequence of food insecurity (the impact) (see Figure 12.2). They should, therefore, include input, output and impact measures.

One of the challenges of food security assessment, monitoring and evaluation is that most observable measures capture the recent past, while policymakers are most interested in the likely future effects of prospective interventions (Barrett, 2010). An ideal food security indicator would reflect the forward-looking time series of probabilities (Barrett, 2010). An important question to ask in policy evaluation is whether policies are implemented based on sufficient and accurate information about the problem; its causes and consequences as well as the efficacy of existing policies (Nkwana and Malan, 2018).

Monitoring is defined as a process of monitoring, analysis and interpretation of indicators and causal factors, in order to make appropriate decisions that will lead to effective interventions to improve the food security and the nutrition status of the population. Monitoring is not a once-off action; rather it is a process that is aimed at continuously checking and tracking activities in progress (Ile, 2014). Monitoring is carried out over the duration of a policy and programme cycle to conduct

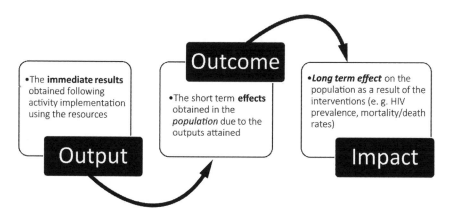

FIGURE 12.2 Differentiating between inputs, outcomes and impacts
Source: Authors

periodic checks of how effective and efficient the policy or programme is. Monitoring comprises two actions that are complementary to one another: monitoring that takes place during the implementation process as well as monitoring the extent to which the results have been attained (de Coning, Wissink and Rabie, 2018). Monitoring helps identify problems and constraints to achieving the goals and targets of policies and programmes. Continuous monitoring is important to identify necessary adjustments to improve the effectiveness and impact of the programme.

Monitoring helps support accountability by making sure the programmes are being implemented as planned. It allows timely measures to be taken to address bottlenecks and challenges. It facilitates the modification of programme actions to improve the likelihood of achieving programme goals and targets.

Monitoring systems in food security programmes also include the establishment and management of early warning systems. Babu (2005, p. 3) explains that:

> The main objective of an early warning system is to monitor food security and nutritional status so to inform decision makers of impending food shortages at national and local levels. The response that an early warning system triggers is an important indicator of its success. The appropriateness of this response, in turn, depends on the links between the information generated by the system and the policy making process.

These systems continually monitor a set of indicators – often using sentential sites – to monitor trends and patterns in weather, climate, food supply and prices. The early detection of changes helps decision makers anticipate crises and prepare for disasters. Long-term data supports this function, providing a sound base for predictions and forecasts to support disaster and development planning. The evolution of big data offers many opportunities to strengthen early warning systems in domains such as food security where complexity demands the monitoring of a range of indicators.

Evaluation of public policies or programmes takes place in different phases from the design, the process of implementation as well as at the end of the policy process in order to ascertain the results of the intervention (Rabie Cloete, 2018). There is a difference between formative and summative evaluation. Formative evaluation takes place during the implementation process (i.e. while the process is still ongoing) whereas summative evaluation takes place at the end of the implementation process to enable lessons to be learnt from the policy cycle (Ile, 2014).

Summative evaluation determines the impact of a policy or programme, seeks to determine the change that has occurred because of a particular policy or programme. Summative evaluation occurs at the end of the policy cycle or end of a project and informs the review and revision of the next policy cycle. The focus on impacts helps drive attention beyond the modalities and processes of implementing policies and programmes to emphasising impacts or how to produce better results (Evidence-based Policymaking Collaborative, 2016). Policy evaluation has a dual role in that it provides an assessment of past actions in order to inform future decisions.

Goldman et al. (2012) sets out six types of evaluations that are relevant for food security:

i Diagnostic evaluations that identifying the root cause of problems and potential options to address them
ii Design evaluations to evaluate the design of policies, programmes and systems is robust
iii Implementation assessments to measure if an intervention's progress and determining how it can be strengthened
iv Impact evaluations identifying the impact of interventions
v Economic evaluations the cost-effectiveness or cost benefit of interventions and
vi Evaluation synthesis – drawing lessons across a number of evaluations.

Babu (2005) explains the imperative to constantly assess food security monitoring systems in terms of the quality and accuracy of data, the appropriateness of data processing procedures, the effectiveness of the information disseminated and its use for planning and policymaking purposes to facilitate keeping abreast of changing needs for these systems and, indeed, the changing nature of food security systems.

Monitoring and evaluation systems should be closely linked to planning and budgeting as well as to performance systems (Goldman et al., 2012). In systems where mutual accountability is promoted, monitoring and evaluation frameworks should not be limited to the performance of programme implementers or government only, but should engage all parties as actors responsible for achieving the required impact. Scorecards and the publication of these for public access promotes mutual accountability at all levels of society.

Mutual accountability is a tool for holding all stakeholders accountable. Mutual accountability allows governments, the private sector and citizens to hold each other accountable to following through on commitments. The concept recognises that the accountability of all stakeholders is crucial to driving development outcomes (Oehmke, et al., 2018). It is achieved through the implementation of institutional and policy changes led by countries in an inclusive manner involving all stakeholders, including beneficiaries and civil society.

Institutions also play a vital role in enforcement and the quality management of monitoring evaluation systems. Legislation could enforce the collection, capture, analysis and publishing of information essential to food security monitoring and evaluation, such as having statutory reporting on certain indicators. Some examples of relevant statutory indicators include infant birth weights and lengths, child anthropometry, micronutrient deficiency prevalence etc.

The best data is not useful if it does not feed back into the learning and planning cycle. Institutions should ensure that the outcomes of assessments – both monitoring and evaluation components – feedback vital information into the policy cycle and programme planning system. Institutions also act as coordinating bodies to avoid unnecessary duplication and the sharing of data and information. Without this function, there may be excessive duplication of systems, with multiple sectors supporting duplicate systems and collecting the same data.

12.3 Learning from successes and failures

Learning from past successes and failures is one purpose of monitoring and evaluation. In addition, assessment, monitoring and evaluation can also:

- Provide rigorous evidence about what works. This could be produced by randomised control trials or quasi-experiments to determine impact.
- Build and compile evidence of what works or success stories using a range of methodologies that can be use in policy and programme design and help build a menu of options for policymakers to consider when looking for potential solutions to problems.
- Determining the costs and benefits of policies and programmes per unit outcome achieved. This allows for comparisons of options and their relative benefits (Evidence-based Policymaking Collaborative, 2016).

These activities could also include assessment of the costs of not acting. This evidence can be very persuasive in supporting decision-making and moving discussions into policy actions and processes. Some of recent reports that set out the compelling case on why nutrition is important for development include the:

- Cost of Hunger in Africa Study (AU et al. 2014)
- Global Nutrition Report 2017 (DI, 2017)
- Global Panel on Agriculture and Food Systems for Nutrition (GloPan) report *The Cost of Malnutrition: Why policy is urgent* (GloPan, 2016)
- Hoddinott's (2016) report on *The Economics of Reducing Malnutrition in Sub-Saharan Africa* for GloPan
- Horton and Ross' (2003) *Economics of Iron Deficiency*
- Scaling Up Nutrition's *What Will It Cost?* report (Horton et al., 2009)
- World Bank Group's (2016) *Investment Framework to Reach the Global Nutrition Targets: Investing in Nutrition the Foundation for Development.*

Multiple statistical tools and approaches could be used for these analyses, the choice depends on the nature of the data and the purpose of the analysis. Multiple texts exist to support the identification of appropriate analytical methods. Some sources of these include:

- Timmer et al.'s (1983) *Food Policy Analysis*
- Delgado et al.'s (1998) *Agricultural Growth Linkages in Sub-Saharan Africa*
- WFP's (2009) *Emergency Food Security Assessment Handbook (EFSA)* (second edition)

Determining the impact of policies and programmes **115**

- Babu and Sanyal's (2009). *Food Security, Poverty and Nutrition Policy Analysis: Statistical Methods and Applications* (first edition)
- Babu et al.'s. (2014) *Food Security, Poverty and Nutrition Policy Analysis: Statistical Methods and Applications* (second edition)
- Moltedo et al.'s (2014) *Analyzing Food Security Using Household Survey Data: Streamlined Analysis with ADePT Software*
- Babu et al.'s (2016) *Nutrition Economics: Principles and Policy Applications.*

Table 12.1 illustrates the diversity of indicators that can be included in food security assessments, monitoring and evaluation frameworks. Detail on how these are calculated and the purpose for their application is presented in Chapter 17.

12.4 The essential elements of a comprehensive food security monitoring and evaluation framework

Achieving the goals related to food security requires a robust comprehensive national agriculture, food security plan as well as policy reform to ensure that a resilient food system is capable of delivering nutritious food for all people at all stages of the life cycle. The key questions an evaluation of food security policies, strategies and programmes answers some of the following questions:

a   Are the planned actions likely to lead to **improved risk management**?

- Is there a framework or policy that proactively identifies and acts on risk, mitigation and management?
- Is there an operational Early Warning System (EWS) that allows a country to measure, monitor and track groups who are vulnerable to food insecurity and shocks (e.g. droughts, floods, market and other shocks), their characteristics and where they live?
- Is this system sufficiently resourced and functioning programme (including time-bound targets and indicators of progress) to reduce vulnerability to droughts, floods, market and other shocks and are you making progress towards the targets?
- Is there a crisis response system in place including mechanisms, triggers, teams/actors and emergency resources at national and community levels?
- Do the Government and Development Partners have a framework and commitment that are supportive of the risk management items outlined above?

b   Will the planned actions **increase the supply of, and access to, nutritious food year-round through a sustainable food system**?

- What are the primary sources of food for the acute and chronically food insecure or those vulnerable to chronic food insecurity? For example, is it known if they are net purchases of food?

TABLE 12.1 List of potential indicators

Component	Example	Individual	Household	Aggregate
Cause	Poverty (economic and purchasing power) Social (care, exclusion) Inequality (access, entitlements) Environmental (access to services, production potential) Markets (price, distribution etc.)			
Context (status or outcome)	Availability Access Nutrition Resilience	Nutrition (Anthropometry, clinical micronutrients) Experience of hunger/child hu nger Food consumption and food frequency, nutrient intakes Dietary Diversity/FCS	Source of food Food consumption/frequency Income/Expenditure Share of expenditure spent on food Experience of hunger/the Food Insecurity Experience Scale (FIES) Household Dietary Diversity/Food Consumption Score/ Coping Strategies Index (including debt patterns) Assets	Average supply Average stocks/deficit CPI and Food price index Level of service delivery (not just infrastructure) Level of malnutrition (Body Mass Index for adults and stunting, wasting, underweight, over-weight and obesity for children)
Impact	Changes in status			Improved health, productivity, economic growth, reduced mortality and morbidity, reduced malnutrition, employment rate

- What are their current production and consumption (amount and types of foods) practices and are these adequate and sustainable?
- What are appropriate and sustainable options for increasing food production?
- What are the options to improve market access and operations in the areas where the vulnerable are located to improve food availability?
- What are the policy constraints to increasing production and improving markets for the target groups?
- Are the actions 'pathways' to nutrition-sensitive food systems?

c   Will the planned actions lead to **increased economic opportunities for the vulnerable** (including women and youth)?

- Are the current sources and levels of incomes and assets of these targeted groups increasing sufficiently to sustainably achieve/improve their food security status?
- Do other opportunities exist to improve their food security status, resilience and contribution to growth beyond what is possible under their current activities?
- Do environmental, institutional and policy constraints prevent them from effectively protecting, using and expanding their assets, incomes and livelihood opportunities to sustainably improve their food security status?

d   Will the planned activities lead to an improvement in the **nutritional status of vulnerable groups (women, children, the elderly and adolescent girls) year-round**?

- What are the levels of micro-nutrient deficiencies among the vulnerable groups (e.g. iron, vitamin A, iodine)?
- What are the viable options and actions to increase the access by vulnerable groups to diversified food production and supply to improve micro-nutrient intake?
- To what extent are bio-fortification, fortification, food processing and safety technologies being applied at all levels of the food chain to improve dietary quality of the target groups?
- What are the environmental, institutional and policy constraints to food fortification?

In consultation with various stakeholders, the potential policy and programme options identified need to be prioritised in terms of what is the best way to increase assets and incomes and improve food security and nutrition against the following criteria. One can ask, does the option:

- Build resilience to food insecurity of the target groups?
- Reduce food insecurity AND build assets for the target group?
- Help achieve the rate and level of growth required to meet the SDGs and regional targets as well as national targets?

- Have a direct impact on inclusive agricultural growth and improve livelihoods?
- Have potential to operate at a scale that leads to a significant and widespread impacts on the targeted groups?
- Build and/or strengthen the capacity for sustainability of development actions?
- Provide evidence-based cost-effective investments to achieve the objective?

To answer these questions, a stocktaking assessment is necessary. This requires assessment of the following elements:

- The current status of food security and malnutrition (in all its forms – amongst others, under nutrition, micronutrient deficiencies as well as overweight and obesity).
- A theory of change assessment of the potential for the priority programmes to achieve the outcomes desired.
- Assessment of the adequacy of the set of indicators for monitoring and evaluating progress towards established goals and targets.
- Identification of risks (covariate and idiosyncratic) and vulnerable populations that these risks affect.
- Assessment of the adequacy of current policies and programmes to address food insecurity, malnutrition (including biofortification) and associated risks.
- Assessment of the broader development, agriculture, food safety, trade and health policies to determine if these support the transformation of current agriculture and food systems in inclusive ways to deliver safe and nutritious food year-round to all people.
- Institutional assessment to determine the adequacy of the coordination, implementation management and accountability system.

Stocktaking involves gathering information on the current state and severity of food insecurity and malnutrition in the country to establish the magnitude of change required to attain the established targets. Despite the increasing availability of open access datasets, up-to-date food security and nutrition data are not always available. Recent Demographic and Health surveys have helped improve the availability of food security and nutrition-related data. However, the collection of detailed nutrition data is expensive and irregular.

Both qualitative and quantitative components should be included, as quantitative components provide crucial information about the experience and state of the situation with respect to hunger, food security and nutrition-related indicators. In addition, both policy and programme monitoring and evaluation should both include process indicators to determine how efficiently the process has been.

Levinson and Herfoth (2014) suggest that monitoring and evaluation for food security and nutrition should include geographically representative sentinel sites, where baseline data are followed by the collection of quantitative and qualitative data at six-month intervals. Data collected in these areas, plus comparable control sites should include:

Determining the impact of policies and programmes **119**

- Information indicating programme participation and the extent to which households and individuals within households have been reached/affected by the policy or programme (Levinson and Herforth, 2013)
- Data on household food insecurity levels, nutritional deficiencies and dietary quality (see Chapter 17)
- Where appropriate, data on young child nutritional status (collected annually if the budget allows)
- Agricultural production diversity and food availability
- Information on women's empowerment (qualitative and quantitative)
- Information that might indicate harm to food security or nutrition (e.g. increased time constraints or inadequate protection of natural resources) (Levinson and Herforth, 2013).

References

Barrett, C.B. (2010) 'Measuring food insecurity', *Science*, vol. 327, no. 327, pp. 825–828.

Babu, S.C., Gajanan, S.N., Hallam, J.A. (2016), *Nutrition Economics: Principles and Policy Applications*. Elsevier, London

Babu, S.C., Gajanan, S.N. and Sanyal, P. (2014) *Food Security, Poverty and Nutrition Policy Analysis: Statistical Methods and Applications*. Academic Press, Cambridge, Massachusetts.

Babu, S.C. and SanyalP. (2009). *Food Security, Poverty and Nutrition Policy Analysis: Statistical Methods and Applications*. First edition. Academic Press, Cambridge, Massachusetts.

Cloete, F. (2018). Policy evaluation. In Cloete, F., de Coning, C., Wissink, H. and Rabie, B. (eds). *Improving Public Policy for Good Governance*. Fourth edition. Van Schaik, Pretoria.

De Coning, C., Wissink, H., and Rabie, B. (2018). Institutionalisation of public policy management. In Cloete, F., de Coning, C., Wissink, H. and Rabie, B. (eds). *Improving Public Policy for Good Governance*. Fourth edition. Van Schaik, Pretoria.

Delgado, C.L., Hopkins, J. and Kelly, V.A. (1998). *Agricultural Growth Linkages in Sub-Saharan Africa*. IFPRI, Washington DC.

Development Initiatives (DI). (2017). *Global Nutrition Report 2017: Nourishing the SDGs*. Development Initiatives, Bristol.

Evidence Based Policymaking Collaborative (EBPC) (2016) *Principles of Evidence-based Policymaking*. Brookings Institute, Washington DC.

Global Panel on Agriculture and Food Systems for Nutrition (GLOPAN) (2016) *The Cots of Malnutrition: Why policy is urgent?*. GLOPAN, London.

Goldman, I., Engela, R., Akhalwaya, I., Gasa, N., Leon, B., Mohamed, H. and Phillips, S. (2012) 'Establishing a national M&E system in South Africa'. PREM Notes 21, World Bank, Washington DC, USA.

Hendriks, S.L. (2015) 'The food security continuum: A novel tool for understanding food insecurity as a range of experiences', *Food Security*, vol. 7, no. 3, pp. 609–619.

Hoddinott, J. (2016) 'The economics of reducing malnutrition in Sub-Saharan Africa', Working Paper, GLOPAN, London.

Horton, S. and Ross, J. (2003) 'The economics of iron deficiency', *Food Policy*, vol. 28, no. 1, pp. 51–75.

Horton, S., Shekar, M. and Ajay, M. (2009) *Scaling up Nutrition: What Will It Cost?*. World Bank, Washington DC.

Ile, I. (2014). Monitoring and evaluating the quality of policy implementation. In Thornhill, C., Van Dijk, G. and Ile, I. (eds). *Public Administration and Management in South Africa: A Developmental Perspective*. Southern Africa Oxford University Press, Cape Town.

Levinson, F.J. and Herforth, A. (2013) *Monitoring and Evaluation of Food Security and Nutrition Effects of Agricultural Projects*. FAO and WHO, Rome and Geneva.

Oehmke, J.F., Young, S.L., Bahiigwa, G., Keizire, B.B. and Post, L.A. (2018) 'The behavioral economics basis of mutual accountability to achieve food security', *Politics and Policy*, vol. 46, no. 1, pp. 32–57.

Moltedo, A., Troubat, N., Loshin, M., Zurab, S. (2014). *Analyzing Food Security Using Household Survey Data: Streamlined analysis with ADePT Software*. World Bank, Washington DC.

Nkwana, H.M. and Malan, L.P. (2018). Analysing the monitoring and evaluation of the Household Food and Nutrition Security Strategy in South Africa. In De Vries, M., Van Dijk, H.G., and Chitiga-Mabugu, M. (eds). *Public Administration: Reflection, readiness and relevance*. NISPACEE, Bratislavia.

Rabie, B. and Cloete, F. (2018). Policy evaluation. In Cloete, F., de Coning, C., Wissink, H. and Rabie, B. (eds). *Improving Public Policy for Good Governance*. Fourth edition. Van Schaik, Pretoria.

Timmer, C.P., Falcon, W.P. and Pearson, S.R. (1983). *Food Policy Analysis*. Johns Hopkins University Press for the World Bank, Baltimore, MD.

Webb, P., Coates, J., Frongillo, E.A., Rogers, B.L., Swindale, A.Bilinsky, P. (2006) 'Measuring household food insecurity: Why it is so important and yet so difficult to do', *The Journal of Nutrition*, vol. 136, no. 5, pp. 1404–1408.

WFP (2009) *Emergency Food Security Assessment Handbook* (EFSA). Second edition, WFP, Rome.

13

IDENTIFICATION OF RISKS AND VULNERABLE POPULATIONS

Filippo Fossi

13.1 Introduction

Food security is the outcome of the ability of livelihoods and systems of production, storage, processing, marketing and trade to consistently provide people with food. Risk, the potential of occurrence of negative events, is inherent in livelihoods and is an important part of food security analysis. Every food security intervention attempts to manage risks. Their impacts can lead to a direct loss to the means by which people obtain food and income, or may arise from the mere presence of risks. Risks are described as 'covariate', affecting everybody in a community or 'idiosyncratic', affecting particular individuals or households. A hazard is a latent danger or risk factor that is external and to livelihoods and not manageable.

The study of risks is fundamentally about vulnerability. All concepts of risk have a common element – the distinction between reality and possibility. Risks imply the possibility of undesirable states of reality, implicitly referring to the connections between actions or events and their effects or consequences (Cardona, 2004). The identification of events that affect food security starts from the question of what risks a person or group of the population is vulnerable to? People are not vulnerable to food insecurity, but rather to specific events that drive it. A household may be 'vulnerable' to a particular hazard, but not necessarily at 'risk' of food insecurity depending on how their basic needs are met. The magnitude of the hazard is also important to consider. If the magnitude of the hazard is low, people may still be able to respond, or cope, drawing on existing resources. But for those with few resources, eve a small shock or stress can put them deeper into food insecurity.

In food security analysis, it is important not to only look at past and current food security outcomes, but also to identify groups or individuals who are at risk in the future. Risk management and vulnerability analysis are part of food security analysis. The objective of risk management is to identify, quantify and address risks and

122 Filippo Fossi

their effects. Vulnerability analysis aims at identifying who is more susceptible, for how long, to certain events.

13.2 Risk management

Risks can be expressed as the probability of occurrence of certain events, of certain intensity, at a specific site, and during a certain period of exposure. Risk management aims to answer the following questions:

- What hazards are more likely to affect the ability of the population to produce and obtain food?
- At what frequency and intensity will the hazard affect the availability, access and nutrition of people?
- How exposed is the population to these risks?
- What mechanisms are in place to mitigate the risk and/or facilitate the recovery?
- What interventions, and by whom, need to be implemented for mitigation and response?

Risk management has been studied in finance since the 1950s (Crockford, 1982) and is now widely practised in food security analysis. It generally involves five steps (McNeil et al., 2005):

i   Identification of risks likely to affect livelihoods, including events in the wider political and economic system;
ii Risk analysis – where likelihood and consequences are determined;
iii Evaluation of risks, by determining their magnitude or the combination of likelihood and intensity, identifying which events should be monitored and treated;
iv Risk treatment, activities minimising the probability of occurrence and response plans;
v   Monitoring and reviewing key events.

Table 13.1 shows a conventional typology of risks and their treatment, based on intensity and frequency.

Table 13.1 also shows the potential management options. These include a variety of mechanisms aiming at prevention, transfer and coping (OECD, 2009; Cervantes-Godoy et al., 2013). Risk mitigation strategies are *ex ante* measures designed to stabilise livelihoods, income, or prices, pest management and economic diversification. Risk transfers are *ex ante* actions to transfer potential financial consequences from one party to another, for example insurance and future market contracts in agriculture. Coping strategies are *ex post* measures that bear welfare costs for example arising from consumption volatility.

The options available also differ by the level of decision-making power. It is important to consider all possible interventions; whether they be mutually reinforcing public policies or contingency planning efforts and their funding and predictability.

TABLE 13.1 Typology of risks and response options Adapted from (Hatch et al., 2012)

		Frequency		
		Low	Medium	High
Intensity	Low	Normal risks → risks bearing and prevention/mitigation	Normal and transferable → risk bearing and prevention/mitigation	Normal → risks bearing and prevention/mitigation
	Medium	Transferable risks → risk bearing, prevention/mitigation and risk transfer	Transferable and normal → risk bearing, prevention/mitigation and risk transfer	Catastrophic → risk coping and prevention/mitigation
	High	Catastrophic → risk prevention/mitigation, transfer and coping	Catastrophic → risks bearing and prevention/mitigation	Catastrophic → LH failure/stop activity

Direct policy approaches deal with the likelihood of risks and responses (like safety nets or contingency plans), but it is important to consider in the analysis the whole range of institutions affecting risks. In policymaking, econometric approaches such as simulations (such as the Value-at-Risk approach) to rank different options (Scaramozzino, 2006; Crouhy et al., 2006; Dowd, 1998). Vulnerability provides a basis for tracing causality and physical processes (Ribot, 2010).

13.3 Vulnerability frameworks

With risk management, vulnerability is part of food security analysis. If vulnerability is assumed homogeneous and constant, food security analysis would be limited to the estimation of physical damages from hazards. On the other hand, without the notion of risk, emphasis on vulnerability would only result in social and economic profiling of a population.

Vulnerability is an imprecise term with no single definition. Over time, researchers and practitioners have emphasised its multi-dimensionality, but also widened and broadened the concept (Figure 13.1). In general, vulnerability refers to the potential for loss (Cutter, 1996) and susceptibility to not having enough coping capacity when facing stress and shocks.

Vulnerability and poverty must be distinguished (Cardona, 2004; Scaramozzino, 2006). Poverty can be a contributing factor to vulnerability and vice-versa (Turner et al., 2003; Adger, 2000). Poverty exacerbates inequalities and condemns households to high price volatility and lower growth, thwarting the payoffs of risk management and coping mechanisms. Although most global food insecurity is associated with chronic poverty (Barrett, 2010), severe food insecurity is typically associated with disasters. However, vulnerability is a forward-looking concept. It cannot be considered a household characteristic without the notion of risk.

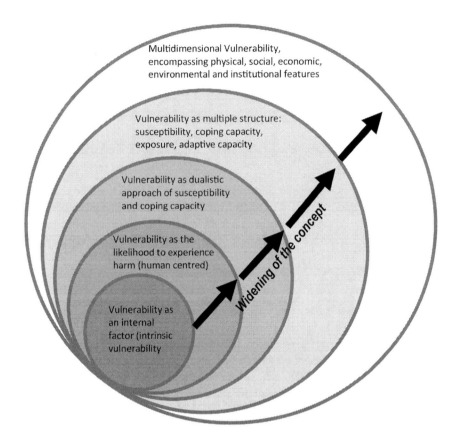

FIGURE. 13.1 The spheres of vulnerability
Source: Birkmann, 2005

Vulnerability can be understood in terms of entitlements, or the resources available based on own production, assets or reciprocal arrangements, where livelihoods are vulnerable to shocks when there is a breakdown in endowments (Sen 1984). Risks (the probability of occurrence of a certain hazard) are seen as function of hazard (the threat to humans) and exposure and susceptibility to losses (vulnerability). How people suffer from calamities depends on how livelihoods are exposed to hazards or shocks and their capacity to withstand them (Dilley and Boudreau, 2001).

Seeing vulnerability through the lens of food systems highlights the interconnectedness and iterative nature of human-environment systems (Adger, 2000; Turner et al., 2003). Risks can originate from dependency on globalised markets, production and market failures, distorting price formation and the choices individuals and households make. Risks can arise due to the inter-relationships between people, assets, income and livelihood opportunities. They are also rooted in the precarious natural resource base of agriculture, all of which can lead to fluctuations in production, prices and rural employment (Cannon, 1991).

The World Economic Forum's (WEF, 2016) Global Risks Interconnectedness Map illustrates the complex interactions of environmental, societal, geopolitical and economic risks in relationships across sectors and countries. Trade is influenced by local and global economic and political environments and infrastructure. Exchange rates, income stability, food prices, inflation and food safety concerns impact consumers. Events affecting one group's livelihoods creates feedback effects on other groups. A focus on food systems (rather than just food production) has the advantage of identifying links among components and various feedbacks. Cascade effects and consequences on different segments of the population should be taken into consideration when assessing risks and vulnerability. For example, in drought, farmers feel immediate environmental effects, but these also impact other livelihoods (e.g. traders, livestock keepers, consumers, etc.) through higher prices and transaction costs. The framework in Figure 13.2 illustrates how changes in the environment affect the elements of the food system in different ways.

The framework in Figure 13.2 (based on Bohle et al. (1994), Combs et al. (1996) and Carter et al. (2001)), illustrates how changes on the environment (both negative and positive) affect the elements of the food system disproportionally. However, it is very likely that their effects are also reflected in the other elements. In addition, people usually react to negative changes, and different individuals, communities, or groups of households will react in different ways, according to their exposure to such events, their capacity to respond and the opportunities presented to them.

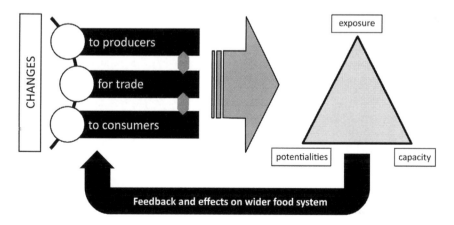

FIGURE 13.2 How changes in the environment affect the elements of the food system in different ways
Source: Adapted from Bohle et al., 1994; Combs et al., 1996; Carter et al., 2001

126 Filippo Fossi

The analysis of vulnerability in the context of food insecurity is complex. Traditional planning methods have a limited ability to engage with uncertainty in complex systems (Van der Sluijs, 2005; Wilkinson and Eidinow, 2008). More sophisticated techniques such as scenario development can explore uncertainty and complexity more effectively than a single forecast can (Kok et al., 2006; Van der Sluijs, 2005). Simulation models are characterised by their own assumptions about systems: while exploratory scenarios, developed as narratives and other formats, can incorporate a wide range of factors and interactions, the scope of simulation models is pre-defined (Reilly and Willenbockel, 2010).

Scenarios can be developed at various levels, for different timeframes and with different levels of sensitivity. They have the advantage of outlining scenarios in ways that can be used for the analysis of the impact of policies, investments and strategies. However, some aspects of future developments can be difficult to explore (Vervoort et al., 2014). Scenarios can be qualitative and developed in stakeholder consultations or quantitative; where assumptions allow the use of simulation models. Qualitative and quantitative approaches are not mutually exclusive, but complementary. Caution is necessary in the consideration of scenarios generated by groups of stakeholders that could be biased towards the groups' perspectives (Schoemaker, 1993).

These techniques are used in food security analysis and early warning (Vervoort et al., 2014), for example by Famine Early Warning Systems Network (FEWSNET, 2010). The current food security conditions and outcomes are summarised, estimating people's ability to meet basic food needs in a chosen geographic area and time period to assess the capacity and duration of households' ability to sustain changes in livelihoods. Analysts often make assumptions in order to assess the consequences to particular populations or areas. Vulnerability frameworks can establish assumptions about shocks and effects (including timing, duration and severity), using historical data. The direct and indirect effects on households are estimated and their external response options are considered, guiding assumptions about probable impact, including on coping strategies, the level, timing, and duration of external response. Household responses and prior household-level outcomes are considered within the context of local livelihoods to estimate food security outcomes.

13.4 Identification of vulnerable populations

A vulnerability assessment should answer five questions (Hoddinott and Quisumbing, 2010, p. 8):

- What is the extent of vulnerability?
- Who is vulnerable?
- What are the sources of vulnerability?
- How do households respond to shocks?
- What gaps exist between risks and risk management mechanisms?

Table 13.2 lists a number of available approaches and methodologies for assessing risk and vulnerability.

TABLE 13.2 Summary of main vulnerability estimates

Approaches	Characteristics and applications
Population-level approaches	
Social Vulnerability Index (SVI) (Shirley et al., 2012)	Examines spatial patterns of social vulnerability to natural hazards (used mainly in the United States); draws on socio-economic and demographic data to identifies specific demographic groups and geographic locations with higher vulnerability to environmental and public health hazards; used for emergency preparedness and public-health planning
World Risk Index (Welle et al., 2013)	A function of exposure to hazards and vulnerability, measured as susceptibility (the likelihood of suffering from the hazard), coping and adaptive capacity; used in cross-country analysis, for prevention and preparedness
The Methods for the Improvement of Vulnerability Assessment in Europe (MOVE) framework (Birkmann et al., 2013)	A generic framework for integrated vulnerability assessment, includes indicators specific to each type of assessment; used in evaluations of preparedness actions and is particularly useful for communicating the complexity of linkages among vulnerability, disaster risk, risk management and adaptation; not used for cross-country assessment.
The Prevalent Vulnerability Index (PVI) (Cardona, 2006)	Uses three weighted complex sub-indexes of exposure and susceptibility, socio-economic fragility and lack of resilience; used in Latin America, by highlighting the three sub-indexes it can draw attention and compare different dimensions
The Hunger and Climate Vulnerability Index (Krishnamurthy et al., 2014)	Focusing on climate events and combining information about exposure to present-day hazards and food security measures of sensitivity and adaptive capacity; can be used for comparative analysis as well as graphically emphasising the relative importance of different indicators included in the index at the national level
Specific to food security	
The Household Economy Approach (HEA) (Holzmann et al., 2008)	A livelihood-based analytical framework for determining how people access food and income (Boudreau et al., 2008). Works between population- and household-level approaches, Using secondary data, quantitative primary data, and participatory and qualitative approaches; used to predict the impact of shocks and disasters in a livelihood zone across different wealth groups; although developed for large-scale segmentation, it can be modified in the Individual Household Model (IHM), to provide detailed vulnerability analysis at household level

Approaches	Characteristics and applications
Household-level approaches	
Consolidated Approach to Report Indicators of Food Security (CARI) (WFP, 2015)	Involves development of a console reporting indicators in different domains, i.e. 'economic vulnerability', capturing households' capacity to access food in the future (through poverty measure or food expenditure shares), and 'assets depletion', using a categorisation of coping mechanisms according to the level and sustainability of decapitalisation; not commonly used in vulnerability analysis, but it can contribute in quickly estimating food security outcomes after a shock, by using assessing economic vulnerability and the livelihood stress
The Household Vulnerability Index (HVI) (FANRPAN, 2011)	Developed by the Food, Agriculture and Natural Resources Policy Analysis Network (FANRPAN) in response to impacts of HIV/AIDS pandemic on household agriculture; discerns levels of external (exposure to shocks or hazards) and internal vulnerability (the capacity to cope with or withstand those shocks) (Kureya, 2013); limited to agriculture, but can be used as a census-type instrument for individual and household level monitoring and targeting (Moret, 2014)
The Southern African Vulnerability Initiative (SAVI), (O'Brien et al., 2009; Casale et al., 2010).	A framework that emphasises interconnections of multiple stressors; examines dynamism of vulnerability, including how coping mechanisms and responses change vulnerability, rather than seeing vulnerability as an 'end point'; provides a set of research questions for assessment; useful for strategic planning, project design, and policy
Participatory methods, e.g. Participatory Wealth Ranking (Moret, 2014; Simanowitz and Nkuna, 1998)	With the facilitator ensuring that both risk and coping mechanisms are considered by participants in their criteria for vulnerability, it can define different profiles; due to representivity bias, not recommended for household targeting; used for wealth ranking, but expandable to vulnerability

There is no established consensus on the best approach to measure vulnerability. Population-level measures are used mostly to segment a population into different categories of vulnerability for policy-planning and intervention design. This approach makes use of vulnerability indexes, intended as a synthetic overview of components and factors of vulnerability. For targeting, household-level methods are usually preferred, but the approaches in Table 13.2 can complement each other. In general, both vulnerability indexes and household-level methods can be used for covariate risks, while idiosyncratic risks are usually assessed with survey data. However, food security analysis should not use 'off-the-shelf' tools, but must tailored these to specific contexts, eventually combining approaches (while aware of their limitations), especially when risks cannot be anticipated and are difficult to quantify (Fiksel, 2015).

13.5 Conclusion

This chapter provides an overview of different tools for capturing different types of risks and vulnerability measures. Any food security intervention aims at managing risks, whatever its scope of action. Interventions should be based on a clear picture of needs. It is difficult to generalise methods across the wide range of hazards affecting increasingly complex food systems and socio-economically diverse populations. People are not vulnerable to food insecurity, but rather to specific events that create it. Food security analysis tools, including those for assessing vulnerability, must be tailored to specific contexts, combining approaches where necessary and remaining aware of limitations.

References

Adger, W.N. (2000) 'Social and ecological resilience: Are they related?', *Progress in Human Geography*, vol. 24, no. 3, pp. 347–364.

Barrett, C.B. (2010) 'Measuring food insecurity', *Science*, vol. 327, no. 5967, pp. 825–828.

Birkmann, J. (2005) *Danger Need Not Spell Disaster: But How Vulnerable Are We?* United Nations University Press, Bonn.

Birkmann, J., Cardona, O.D., Carreño, M.L., Barbat, A.H., Pelling, M., Schneiderbauer, S., Kienberger, S., Keiler, M., Alexander, D. and Zeil, P. (2013) 'Framing vulnerability, risk and societal responses: The MOVE framework', *Natural Hazards*, vol. 67, no. 2, pp. 193–211.

Bohle, H.G., Downing, T.E. and Watts, M.J. (1994) 'Climate change and social vulnerability: Toward a sociology and geography of food insecurity', *Global Environmental Change*, vol. 4, no. 1, pp. 37–48.

Boudreau, T., Lawrence, M., Holzmann, P., O'Donnell, M., Adams, L., Holt, J., Hammond, L. and Duffield, A. (2008) *The Practitioners' Guide to the Household Economy Approach*. The Food Economy Group, Potten End, Herts, UK.

Cannon, T. (1990) 'Hunger and famine: Using a food systems model to analyse vulnerability'. In: Bohle, H., Cannon, T., Hugo, G., and Ibrahim, N.N. (Eds), *Famine and Food security in Africa and Asia: indigenous Response and External Interventions to Avoid Hanger*. University of Bayreuth, Naturwissenschaftliche Gesellschaft Bayreuth.

Cardona, O.D. (2006) 'A system of indicators for disaster risk management in the Americas', in J. Birkmann (ed) *Measuring Vulnerability to Natural Hazards: Towards disaster resilient societies*. United Nations University Press, New Delhi.

Cardona, O.D. (2004) 'The need for rethinking the concepts of vulnerability and risk from a holistic perspective: A necessary review and criticism for effective risk management', in G. Bankoff, G. Frerks and D. Hilhorst (eds) *Mapping Vulnerability: Disasters, development and people*. Earthscan, Routledge, Oxon, USA.

Carter, T.R., La Rovere, E.L., Jones, R., Leemans, R., Mearns, L., Nakicenovic, N., Pittock, A., Semenov, S. and Skea, J. (2001) 'Developing and applying scenarios', in J.J. McCarthy, K.S. White, O. Canziani and D.J. Dokken (eds) *Climate Change 2001: Impats, adaptation and vulnerability*. Cambridge University Press, Cambridge.

Casale, M., Drimie, S., Quinlan, T. and Ziervogel, G. (2010) 'Understanding vulnerability in southern Africa: Comparative findings using a multiple-stressor approach in South Africa and Malawi', *Regional Environmental Change*, vol. 10, no. 2, pp. 157–168.

Cervantes-Godoy, D., Kimura, S. and Antón, J. (2013) 'Smallholder risk management in developing countries', OECD Food Agriculture and Fisheries Papers no. 61, OECD Publishing, Paris, France.

OECD (2009) *Managing Risk in Agriculture: A Holistic Approach.* OECD Publishing, Paris.

Combs, D.L., Parrish, R.G., Mcnabb, S.J. and Davis, J.H. (1996) 'Deaths related to hurricane Andrew in Florida and Louisiana, 1992', *International Journal of Epidemiology*, vol. 25, no. 3, pp. 537–544.

Crockford, G.N. (1982) 'The bibliography and history of risk management: Some preliminary observations', *Geneva Papers on Risk and Insurance*, vol. 7, no. 23, pp. 169–179.

Crouhy, M., Galai, D. and Mark, R. (2006) *The Essentials of Risk Management.* McGraw-Hill, New York.

Cutter, S.L. (1996) 'Vulnerability to environmental hazard', *Progress in Hhuman Geography*, vol. 20, no. 4, pp. 529–539.

Dilley, M. and Boudreau, T.E. (2001) 'Coming to terms with vulnerability: A critique of the food security definition', *Food Policy*, vol. 26, no. 3, pp. 229–247.

Dowd, K. (1998) *Beyond Value at Risk: The New Science of Risk Management, Frontiers in Finance Series.* John Wiley and Sons, London.

FANRPAN. (2011) 'The household vulnerability index', http://www.fanrpan.org/projects/seccap/vulnerability_assessment/HVI_Pilot_Summary_20110829.pdf

FEWSNET. (2010) *Scenario Development for Food Security Early Warning: Guidance for Famine Early Warning Systems Network (FEWSNET) Staff and Partners.* USAID, Washington DC.

Fiksel, J. (2015) *Resilient by Design: Creating Businesses that Adapt and Flourish in a Changing World.* Island Press, Washington DC.

Hatch, D., Nunez, M., Vila, F. and Stephenson, K. (2012) *Agricultural Insurance in the Americas: A Risk Management Tool.* Inter-American Institute for Cooperation on Agriculture at San Jose, Costa Rica.

Hoddinott, J. and Quisumbing, A. (2010) 'Methods for microeconometric risk and vulnerability assessment', in R. Fuentes-Nieva and P.A. Seck (eds) *Risk, Shocks, and Human Development: On the Brink.* Springer, New York.

Holzmann, P., Boudreau, T., Holt, J., Lawrence, M. and O'Donnell, M. (2008) *The Household Economy Approach: A Guide for Programme Planners and Policy-Makers* . Save the Children, London.

Kok, K., Rothman, D.S. and Patel, M. (2006) 'Multi-scale narratives from an IA perspective: Part I. European and Mediterranean scenario development', *Futures*, vol. 38, no. 3, pp. 261–284.

Krishnamurthy, P., Lewis, K. and Choularton, R. (2014) 'A methodological framework for rapidly assessing the impacts of climate risk on national-level food security through a vulnerability index', *Global Environmental Change*, vol. 25, pp. 121–132.

Kureya, T. (2013) 'Household vulnerability index background document'. Unpublished document: FANRPAN.

McNeil, A. J., Frey, R. and Embrechts, P. (2005) *Quantitative Risk Management: Concepts, techniques and tools.* Princeton University Press, Princeton.

Moret, W. (2014) *Vulnerability Assessment Methods: A Review of Literature.* ASPIRES, Washington DC.

O'Brien, K., Quinlan, T. and Ziervogel, G. (2009) 'Vulnerability interventions in the context of multiple stressors: Lessons from the Southern Africa Vulnerability Initiative (SAVI)', *Environmental Science and Policy*, vol. 12, no. 1, pp. 23–32.

Reilly, M. and Willenbockel, D. (2010) 'Managing uncertainty: A review of food system scenario analysis and modelling', *Philosophical Transactions of the Royal Society of London B: Biological Sciences*, vol. 365, no. 1554, pp. 3049–3063.

Ribot, J. (2010) 'Vulnerability does not fall from the sky: Toward multiscale, pro-poor climate policy', in R. Mearns and A. Norton (eds) *Social Dimensions of Climate Change: Equity and Vulnerability in a Warming World*. World Bank, Washington DC.

Scaramozzino, P. (2006) 'Measuring vulnerability to food insecurity', ESA Working Paper, FAO, Rome.

Schoemaker, P.J. (1993) 'Multiple scenario development: Its conceptual and behavioral foundation', *Strategic Management Journal*, vol. 14, no. 3, pp. 193–213.

Sen, A. (1982) *Poverty and Famines: An Essay on Entitlement and Deprivation*. Oxford University Press, New York.

Sen Amartya, K. (1984) *Resources, Values and Development*. Harvard University Press, Cambridge.

Shirley, W.L., Boruff, B.J. and Cutter, S.L. (2012) *Hazards Vulnerability and Environmental Justice*. Routledge, London.

Simanowitz, A. and Nkuna, B. (1998) *Participatory Wealth Ranking Operational Manual*. Small Enterprise Foundation, Tzaneen.

Turner, B.L., Kasperson, R.E., Matson, P.A., Mccarthy, J.J., Corell, R.W., Christensen, L., Eckley, N., Kasperson, J.X., Luers, A. and Martello, M.L. (2003) 'A framework for vulnerability analysis in sustainability science', *Proceedings of the National Academy of Sciences*, vol. 100, no. 14, pp. 8074–8079.

UNDRO (United Nations Disaster Relief Organ) (1980) 'Natural disasters and vulnerability analysis', Report of Expert Group Meeting (9–12 July, 1979), United Nations Disaster Relief Organ, Geneva, Switzerland.

Van Der Sluijs, J. (2005) 'Uncertainty as a monster in the science–policy interface: Four coping strategies', *Water Science and Technology*, vol. 52, no. 2, pp. 87–92.

Vervoort, J.M., Thornton, PK., Kristjanson, P., Förch, W., Ericksen, P.J., Kok, K., Ingram, J.S., Herrero, M., Palazzo, A. and Helfgott, A.E. (2014) 'Challenges to scenario-guided adaptive action on food security under climate change', *Global Environmental Change*, vol. 28, pp. 383–394.

WEF (World Economic Forum) (2016) *The Global Risks Report 2016, 11th edition*. WEF, Geneva.

Welle, T., Birkmann, J., Rhyner, J., Witting, M. and Wolfertz, J. (2013) 'World Risk Index 2013', in Alliance Development Works, *World Risk Report, 2013*. UNU-EHS.

WFP (2015) *Consolidated Approach to Reporting Indicators of Food Security (CARI): Technical guidelines*. World Food Programme, Rome.

Wilkinson, A. and Eidinow, E. (2008) 'Evolving practices in environmental scenarios: A new scenario typology', *Environmental Research Letters*, vol. 3, no. 4, pp. 1–11.

14

INSTITUTIONAL ARRANGEMENTS FOR GOVERNANCE, COORDINATION AND MUTUAL ACCOUNTABILITY

Moraka N. Makhura and Nosipho Mabuza

14.1 Comprehensive development approaches raise the need for collaboration, coordination and cooperation

The SDGs bring about a strong focus on the integration of development objectives across sectors (United Nations General Assembly (UNGA), 2015). They prioritise five areas of importance (the so-called five Ps):

- **People**: Ending poverty and hunger and ensuring dignity and equality in a healthy environment.
- **Planet**: Protecting the planet through ensuring sustainability to support the needs of the future.
- **Prosperity**: Ensuring prosperous lives and economic, social and technological progress in harmony with nature.
- **Peace**: Fostering peaceful, just and inclusive societies.
- **Partnership**: Mobilising means to implement the Agenda through a global partnership.

The principles of the SDGs extend the 2011 Busan Partnership for Effective Development Co-operation that recognised two types of partnerships that are a requirement for effective sustainable development (Makhura et al., 2019):

- Partnership between the country and donor institutions – moving from donor led to country led development, and
- Internal partnerships within the country to bring about sustainable development in the country. This recognises four foundational principles, namely ownership of development priorities by developing countries, focus on results, inclusive development partnerships and transparency and accountability to each other.

In order to reach the common goal of effective development co-operation, the Busan Partnership identified the need to:

- Include new actors in development on the basis of shared principles and differential commitments
- Improve the quality and effectiveness of development co-operation through ownership, results and accountability; transparent and responsible co-operation; promote sustainable development in situations of conflict and fragility; and partnering to strengthen resilience and reduce vulnerability in the face of adversity (OECD 2011).

Multi-stakeholder partnerships emerged during the 1990s through the adoption of Agenda 21 at the Earth Summit in Rio de Janeiro (Pattberg & Widerberg, 2014), which called for a "Global Partnership for Sustainable Development" and constantly highlighted partnerships between "public, private and community sectors" to implement sustainable development (UNCED, 1992). Agenda 21 recognised the complexity of food security challenges, which requires the involvement of all relevant stakeholders so that 'no one is left behind' as per the SDG mandate. Active participation of stakeholders helps guarante effective use of resources, benefitting from all stakeholders' comparative advantage and resources – whether technical, human or financial.

Caron (2018) explains that the 2030 Agenda for the SDGs and the Addis Ababa Action Agenda (AAAA) promote multi-stakeholder partnerships (MSPs) as a way to complement the efforts of national governments and international organisations and to "mobilise and share knowledge, expertise, technology and financial resources, to support the achievement of the SDGs in all countries and in particular developing countries". MSPs are now recognised (UN, 2015; AAAA, 2015) as one of the means of implementation of the 2030 Agenda (HLPE, 2018).

Partnership requires the active participation of a range of stakeholders. Brem-Wilson (2015) qualifies participation as "effective" if stakeholders: (i) are able to intelligibly and persuasively communicate their views, (ii) can participate physically and timely at key meetings, (iii) are sufficiently informed, (iv) are psychologically comfortable with the multi-stakeholder partnerships, and (v) have the right to speak and be heard.

This is supported by evidence from the Malabo Montpellier Panel's assessment of seven countries in Africa that have made the most progress on reducing malnutrition in period between 2000 and 2015. The Panel found that these countries were able to carry out successful interventions at the political, institutional and programmatic level. This included adopting a comprehensive approach to food security, creating board partnerships among key stakeholder groups and setting up mechanisms to coordinate a coherent agenda (Malabo Montpellier Panel, 2017).

The HLPE (2018, p. 43) defines multi-stakeholder partnerships (MSPs) as any collaborative arrangement among stakeholders from two or more different spheres of society (public sector, private sector and/or civil society), pooling their resources together, sharing risks and responsibilities in order to solve a common issue, to handle a conflict, to elaborate a shared vision, to realise a common objective, to manage a common resource and/or to ensure the protection, production or delivery of an outcome of collective and/or public interest.

In this context, stakeholders include the public sector; the private sector; and civil society. The HLPE (2018, p 42) defines these as:

- Public sector covers all forms of public organisations, including intergovernmental organisations at the global and regional levels, including UN agencies; international financial institutions and multilateral development banks; states, government agencies in different sectors (including health, nutrition, agriculture, environment, finance, economics, trade, justice); local authorities (at the subnational level); public universities; public research and development institutions; as well as other organisations, banks, companies or institutions with a public legal status;
- Private sector covers private individuals (including entrepreneurs, landowners, farmers, etc.); private companies (local, national and transnational) active at different stages of the food supply chain (e.g. production, storage and distribution, processing and packaging, retail and markets); commercial banks; cooperatives and other forms of organisations in the "social economy" with a private legal status; private foundations; other private organisations, institutions or federations – this category also includes publicly owned companies with a private legal status;
- Civil society gathers all the other non-state actors and non-profit NGOs created around shared values and objectives; this category includes: organisations created by sand/or working on behalf of specific groups; organisations representing, for instance, small food producers, consumers, workers, youth, women or indigenous peoples, humanitarian NGOs working on emergency situations or on long-term strategies; geographic, thematic, sectoral, cultural or religious organisations.

The HLPE (2018) asserts that multi-stakeholder partnerships hold much promise in contributing to the progressive realisation of the right to adequate food; improving the mobilisation, coordination and targeting of financing for food security and nutrition; strengthening transparency and accountability through effective governance and management principles; increasing the impact of policies and programmes through effective monitoring, evaluation and experience sharing and providing a framework for evaluating the effectiveness of partnerships.

14.2 Advantages and challenges of multi-stakeholder approaches versus traditional approaches

Multi-stakeholder partnerships hold a number of benefits and advantages for food security and nutrition. There is an increasing effort to document multi-stakeholder coordination in food security and nutrition. Although the scholarly evidence is still scanty regarding the study of the strategies and their outcomes (Candel, 2018), some state that multisectoral approaches are more effective in addressing malnutrition (Heaver, 2005). This provides a segway to begin to understand the potential benefits and challenges of such emerging institutional arrangements.

De Zeeuw and Dechsel (2015) and HLPE (2018) identified some of the benefits and advantages of multi-stakeholder coordinated approaches versus traditional approaches.

Some of the benefits for food security governance include that they:

- Enable better understanding of the problem from different angles of stakeholders
- Build consensus in decision process
- Improve knowledge generation process
- Improve implementation and sustainability
- Make governance more participatory
- Create environments for shared common goals and commitments

On the other hand, some question the extent to which multi-stakeholder coordination can work (Garrett et al., 2011). Studies that have discussed governance systems in food security (e.g., Harris et al., 2017; Kampman et al., 2017; Pomeroy-Stevens et al., 2016 as cited by Candel, 2018), provide insights into the difficulties of translating commitments into governance systems. AGRA (2018) and HLPE (2018) provide a clear set of challenges that governments face in sustaining multi-sector coordination, including that:

- Multi-sectoral coordination systems are created outside of the mainstream civil service system, which may create chasms with civil servants.
- The coordination mechanism may be driven by political agendas that may change with the political cycles.
- Multi-sectoral coordination mechanisms may be donor-driven, which creates dependency while it is still difficult to generate internal resources.
- Multi-sector coordination may experience reduced interest and commitment from the various stakeholders.
- Decisions taken in the multi-stakeholder sessions may not be binding and enforceable.
- Multi-sector coordination mechanisms outside of the mainstream civil service may be viewed as failure by governments

In general, institutions represent the rules of the game; including the clarification of roles and rights, coordination of collective action, management of transaction costs of integrating and coordinating the actions (Makhura et al., 2019). Ineffective organisational structures and power imbalances can have negative effects on food security (Babu and Blom, 2017). The HLPE (2018) illustrated how power asymmetries lead to lack of trust among partners or actors, while power imbalances among actors can fuel conflicts of interests. The HLPE (2016, 2017) also describes the rapid concentration of power in agriculture and food systems over the past decades in the hands of a few transnational corporations. Unequal resource endowments among partners is also a differential factor for the ability of partners to always be present and timely at meetings. Weaker stakeholders may have limited financial and human resources (time and expertise) to engage. The ability to engage could also be hampered by communication (Gaarde, 2017; Brem–Wilson, 2015), which is typically English for global meetings.

When the private sector and or civil society are involved in institutional bodies they often cannot make binding government decisions but serve on Advisory Bodies. However, the HLPE (2018) identified five main functions or domains of intervention where MSPs provide for roles beyond advisory and have been effective:

- MPSs engagement in *knowledge co-generation and capacity building* through the collection and sharing of information and experiences.
- The MSPs intervening in *advocacy* at the global, regional or national levels, raising awareness on major issues. They can also suggest possible pathways towards more sustainable food systems.
- MSPs in *setting of voluntary and market-based standards* to promote sustainable practices across agriculture and food systems.
- *Action-oriented* MSPs are involved in activities ranging from natural resource management and agricultural development to food processing and distribution.
- MSPs in *fundraising and resource mobilisation* can foster synergies and avoid fragmentation of efforts, contributing to better mobilisation, coordination and targeting of public and private funds for FSN.

14.3 Conceptualising an institutional architecture for food security in the context of multi-stakeholder partnerships

Coordination of food security efforts is challenging as it involves multiple sectors and partners that have different approaches, visions, and understandings of the problem (Garrett, Bassett, and Levinson 2011). The coordination of actors requires the establishment of an institution whose main function is to facilitate cooperation of actions and resources on a specific focus area.

Makhura et al. (2019) have proposed a framework for evaluating the implementation of these principles. The Inclusive Sustainable Partnerships for Development (ISP4D) Framework (Figure 14.1) illustrates a cascading effect when more stakeholders and coordination are included in line with the partnership and sustainability aspirations outlined above. The framework shows that multi-stakeholder coordination can take place at various levels. In the ISP4D model, multi-sectoral refers to sectors (represented

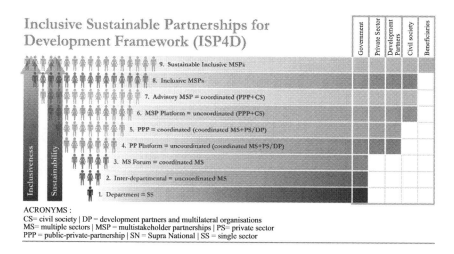

FIGURE 14.1 Inclusive Sustainable Partnerships for Development (ISP4D)
Source: Makhura et al., 2019

by departments) within government. Each department is tasked to deliver on a specific element. Every department has its own objective, goals and key priorities, where each sector focuses on its mandate without checking other sectors. The levels are presented below.

Level 1: Single Sector systems. The complexity of issues in the agriculture and food system call for institutional structures that transcend traditional Single Sector (SS) approaches. In many countries, food security is entrusted to the agriculture sector. Here, the institutional design is limited to the interrelationships and roles of divisions within the same department or sector. Institutional coordination is intra-sectoral (in other words within a specific department), and the rest of the stakeholders (including other departments) are likely viewed as clients to be served. Coordination may be simpler than in other models but may not be effective in delivering on comprehensive matters such as food security.

Level 2 and 3: Multi-sectoral (multi-departmental and inter-departmental) systems. Some countries' institutional designs reflect multi-sectoral elements that recognise food security as cross cutting. Multi-sectoralalism means different things to different people – either focusing on government only or sometimes including other sectors or stakeholders (AGRA, 2018). The multi-sectoral architecture can also be referred to as inter-departmental. More often, departments (or sectors) will operate in an uncoordinated way towards a common goal. In this environment, departments are concerned with their primary functions, while putting food security as just one of their strategic goals without formal coordination systems.

In cases where there is an overarching food security policy and a coordinated multi-sectoral environment, sectors tend to place food security as a primary focus area in which the sectoral focus area contributes. This urges departments to interact more closely and report on how their efforts contribute to the overall goal of food security. More formalised regular interactions will assist to monitor progress. Coordinated multi-sectoral systems are more likely to deliver on food security goals compared to uncoordinated systems. An uncoordinated system cannot result in more than a forum or platform – the equivalent of a talk shops – where the arrangements are informal and parties are not accountable to each other.

Normally, oversight of a multi-sectoral coordination system would involve a supra national and key line functionary (e.g. the Presidency or Office of the President). Even at subnational levels (say provincial and regional levels), these systems tend to have a higher-level coordination body. Successful coordination at the national level is more likely when the coordination body is chaired at the supra level.

Level 4 and 5: Government and private sector involvement. Coordination systems that are based on the involvement of government departments only may not be sustainable as they exclude other critical sectors in the food system. However, the government alone cannot achieve some priorities such as food security. Instead, governments reach out to the private sector through partnerships. These systems can be coordinated or uncoordinated. A coordinated partnership between government and the private sector may result in formalised medium term agreements on a project by project basis. These may include Public Private Partnerships (PPPs).

Level 6, 7, 8 and 9: Multi-stakeholder based Institutional Architectures. The PPP architecture assumes that target beneficiaries are passive recipients of interventions. However, as per the above HLPE definition of multi-stakeholder partnerships, civil society is a key stakeholder (HLPE, 2018).

The ISP4D framework illustrates that as inclusion increases, institutional sustainability also increases. The framework provides a visualisation and benchmark for the analysis of the level of inclusion of institutional arrangements for the coordination of food security efforts by governments.

However, an initial assessment of the coordination structures for 11 National Agriculture and Food Security Investment Plans in Africa (including the republics of Benin, Burkina Faso, Ghana, Guinea, Guinea-Bissau, Ivory Coast, Liberia, Malawi, Niger, and Nigeria and Togo) using this model showed that fewer than half the countries had supra-national, coordinated institutions (Makhura et al., 2019). Overall, the structures seemed to reflect a bias towards government, with lower inclusion of the private sector, civil society and beneficiaries (Makhura et al., 2019).

14.4 Assessing the adequacy of coordinated food security institutional systems

The HLPE (2018) identified two categories of criteria that can be used to assess the qualities of the MSPs, namely the results or outcome oriented qualities and the process qualities. A third criteria of "enabling environment" can be included for application to the multi-stakeholder coordinated institutional systems.

Results oriented qualities include the effectiveness and the impact that the institution can have on food security. *Effectiveness* denotes the extent to which a system delivers its expected outputs and immediate outcomes (HLPE, 2018). An effective institution will enable achievement of identified outputs that it is established for. These institutions are established to facilitate the implementation of food security initiatives and ensure the realisation of the benefits and advantages indicated earlier. The effectiveness of coordinating institutions may also entail addressing the challenges.

Process oriented criteria include inclusiveness, transparency, reflexivity, accountability and efficiency. Transparency is about all relevant stakeholders having open and easy access to the best available information (HLPE, 2018). The institutional rules should give participating stakeholders good access to critical information. Reflexivity is about the ability and capacity of the system to learn from its existence and adjust accordingly. A reflexive institute is likely to change and adapt over time. Accountability is the responsibility of representatives or a group (HLPE, 2018). Finally, efficiency is about making the most of the available resources.

Inclusiveness, defined as ensuring "that the voices of all relevant stakeholders – particularly those most affected by food insecurity are heard" (CFS, 2009), can strengthen the acceptability and legitimacy of decisions taken by a coordinating institution, address power asymmetries and promote equity (Dodds, 2015). Assessing inclusiveness in an institution raises the following questions (Hemmati, 2002; Vermeulen et al., 2008; Brouwer et al., 2016): Are all "relevant" stakeholders included? Who can participate in the discussions? Who takes the final decision?

Enabling criteria include policy and legislation; governance system and coordination. According to the UNDP (2006) having a conducive *policy and legislative* environment is critical for the success of multi-stakeholder partnership. If the appropriate policy and legislation framework is absent, the coordination process may not receive the necessary support from all stakeholders.

14.5 Conclusions

Multi-stakeholder partnerships are an emerging institutional mechanism in the coordination of food security. They hold much promise for:

- Contributing to the realisation of the right to adequate food
- Improving the mobilisation, coordination and targeting of financing for food security
- Strengthening transparency and accountability through effective governance and management principles
- Increasing the impact of policies and programmes through effective monitoring, evaluation and experience sharing

The question is whether these could be appropriate platforms to enable coordination of food security efforts. Makhura et al. (2019) state that there is still a need to determine if there has been a genuine shift to adopting multi-stakeholder partnership approaches to the coordination and management of food security. Doing so will help countries across the world to achieve inclusive development as set out in the SGDs. Adopting these approaches has potential to clarify roles and responsibilities, address imbalances of power and improve transparency and accountability for development efforts.

The ISP4D can be used to assess the level at which coordination mechanisms are multi-sectoral and multi-stakeholder. As such, there is a need to encourage more inclusive coordination mechanisms as they promise more benefits.

References

AAAA (Addis Ababa Action Agenda) (2015) 'Addis Ababa Action Agenda of the third international conference on financing for development', http://www.un.org/esa/ffd/wp content/uploads/2015/08/AAAA_Outcome.pdf.

AGRA (2018) 'Africa agriculture status report 2018: Catalysing government capacity to drive agricultural transformation', Issue no. 6, Alliance for a Green Revolution in Africa at Nairobi, Kenya.

Babu, S.C. and Blom, S. (2017) 'Strengthening and harmonizing food policy systems to achieve food security', Discussion paper no. 1607, IFPRI, Washington DC.

Brem-Wilson, J. (2015) 'Towards food sovereignty: Interrogating peasant voice in the United Nations Committee on World Food Security', *Journal of Peasant Studies*, vol 42, no 1, pp. 73–95.

Brouwer, J.H., Woodhill, A.J., Hemmati, M., Verhoosel, K.S. and van Vugt, S.M. (2016) *The MSP Guide: How to Design and Facilitate Multi-stakeholder Partnerships*. Practical Action Publishing Ltd, Wageningen.

Candel, J.J. (2018) 'Diagnosing integrated food security strategies', *NJAS-Wageningen Journal of Life Sciences*, vol 84, pp. 103–113.

CFS (Committee on World Food Security) (2009) 'Reform of the Committee on World Food Security', Final version. CFS. 35th Session, CFS, Rome.

Caron, P., y de Loma-Osorio, G.F., Nabarro, D., Hainzelin, E., Guillou, M., Andersen, I., Arnold, T., Astralaga, M., Beukeboom, M., Bickersteth, S. and Bwalya, M. (2018) 'Food systems for sustainable development: Proposals for a profound four-part transformation', *Agronomy for Sustainable Development*, vol 38, no. 4, pp. 41.

de Zeeuw, H. and Drechsel, P. (2015) *Cities and Agriculture: Developing Resilient Urban Food Systems*. Routledge, London and New York.

Dodds, F. (2015) 'Multi-stakeholder partnerships: Making them work for the Post-2015 Development Agenda', Global Research Institute, University of North Carolina, North Carolina.

Gaarde, I. (2017) *Peasants Negotiating a Global Policy Space: La Vía Campesina in the Committee on World Food Security*. Routledge, London and New York.

Garrett, J., Bassett, L. and Ntalicchio, M. (2011) *Working Multisectorally in Nutrition: Principles, Practices and Case Studies*. IFPRI, Washington DC.

Garrett, J., Bassett, L. and Levinsohn, J. (2011) 'Multisectoral approaches to nutrition: Rationale and historical perspective', in J. Garett, L. Bassett and M. Ntalicchio (eds) *Working Multisectorally in Nutrition: Principles, Practices and Case Studies*. IFPRI, Washington DC.

Harris, J., Drimie, S., Roopnaraine, T. and Covic, N. (2017) 'From coherence towards commitment: Changes and challenges in Zambia's nutrition policy environment', *Global Food Security*, vol 13, pp. 49–56.

Heaver, R. (2005) *Strengthnening Country Commitment to Human Development*. World Bank, Washington DC.

Hemmati, M. (2002) *Multi-stakeholder Processes for Governance and Sustainability: Beyond Deadlock and Conflict*. Earthscan, London.

HLPE (2016) 'Sustainable agricultural development for food security and nutrition: What roles for livestock?' Report by the HLPE, CFS, Rome.

HLPE (2017) 'Nutrition and food systems', Report no. 12, HLPE, Rome.

HLPE (2018) 'Multi-stakeholder partnerships to finance and improve food security and nutrition in the framework of the 2030 Agenda', Report no. 13, HLPE, Rome.

Kampman, H., Zongrone, A., Rawat, R. and Becquey, E. (2017) 'How Senegal created an enabling environment for nutrition: A story of change', *Global Food Security*, vol 13, pp. 57–65.

Malabo Montpellier Panel (MMP) (2017) 'Nourished: How Africa can build a future free from hunger and malnutrition', A Malabo Montpellier Report, MMP, Dakar, Senegal.

Makhura, M.N., Hendriks, S.L., Olivier, N.J.J., Mkandawire, E., Vilakazi, N. and Olivier, N.J.J. (2019) 'Are the NAIP II institutional architectures fit for purpose for achieving SDG 2 in Africa?', Feed the Future Innovation Lab for Food Security Research Paper no.115, Michigan State University, IFPRI and University of Pretoria, East Lansing, Washington DC and Pretoria.

OECD (2011) 'Busan Partnership for Effective Development Co-operation', Fourth high level forum on AID effectiveness, OECD at Busan.

Pattberg, P. and Widerberg, O. (2014) 'Transnational multi-stakeholder partnerships for sustainable development: Building blocks for success', Report no. R-14/31, IVM Institute for Environmental Studies at University of Amsterdam.

Pomeroy-Stevens, A., Shrestha, M.B., Biradavolu, M., Hachhethu, K., Houston, R., Sharma, I. and Wun, J. (2016) 'Prioritizing and funding Nepal's multisector nutrition plan', *Food and Nutrition Bulletin*, vol 37, no. 4, pp. 151–169.

UN (2015) *General Assembly Resolution 70/1*, http://www.un.org/ga/search/view_doc.asp?symbol=A/RES/70/1&Lang=E.

UNCED (1992) 'AGENDA 21', 'United Nations Conference on Environment & Development, 3–14 June 1992, United Nations, Rio de Janerio.

UNDP (2006) 'Multi-stakeholder engagement processes: A UNDP capacity development resource', Conference paper no. 7, UNDP, New York.

United Nations General Assembly (UNGA) (2015) *Resolution Adopted by the General Assembly on 25 September 2015: Transforming Our World: The 2030 Agenda for*, Seventieth session, Agenda items 15 and 116, UNGA, New York.

Vermeulen, S., Woodhill, A.J., Proctor, F., and Delnoye, R. (2008) *Chain-Wide Learning for Inclusive Agrifood Market Development: A Guide to Multi-stakeholder Processes for Linking Small-scale Producers to Modern Markets*. International Institute for Environment and Development, Wageningen.

15

GENDER AND FOOD SECURITY

Elizabeth Mkandawire

15.1   Introduction: what is gender?

Gender analysis is essential for development policy. It involves understanding the underlying causes of inequalities between men and women and integrating this understanding to the development of policies and programmes. The primary purpose of gender analysis is to achieve gender equality (Kabeer and Subrahmanian, 1996). Gender, defined as the roles and responsibilities socially allocated to men and women, considers the relationship and power dynamics between men and women (Moser, 2012). Gender analysis is vital for two reasons. First, gender dynamics can influence policy outcomes (Canada, 1998). For example, a policy may promote microfinancing programmes to empower women. However, if the policy does not consider women's limited control over household income, men may appropriate resources provided to women. Second, gender analysis is essential for ensuring that policies do not exacerbate but rather reduce inequalities between men and women (Canada, 1998). For example, women's economic participation is crucial for development, but policy design should consider women's other responsibilities, such as housework and care work to ensure that women are not overburdened.

The Sustainable Development Goals (SDGs) emphasise the importance of gender equality. While SDG 5 specifically focuses on gender, at least eight SDGs include gender and gender targets (UNGA, 2015). However, progress towards gender equality is slow because of inappropriate integration of gender in development policy. The integration of gender in all policies and at all levels of government has been a priority for many countries since the 1995 Beijing Fourth Conference on Women and the signing of the 1995 Beijing Declaration and Platform for Action (UN, 1995).

Before the conference, development practitioners applied the 'Women in Development' approach. While this approach was the first to recognise women's contribution to economic development, it did not consider the systematic reproduction of power relations that undermine women (Razavi and Miller, 1995). The 'Women and Development' approach also failed to consider women's reproductive roles and the constraints that women's socially prescribed responsibilities may have on their contribution towards economic development. The Beijing Fourth Conference on Women marked the shift from the 'Women in Development' approach to the 'Gender and Development' approach (Kabeer and Subrahmanian, 1996).

The 'Gender and Development' approach emphasises the relationship between men and women and the power dynamics that ensue because of socially prescribed gender roles (Moser, 2012). This approach requires understanding the institutionalised systems that privilege men and undermine women (Kabeer and Subrahmanian, 1996). Integrating 'gender in development' into policies and programmes is referred as gender mainstreaming (UN, 1995). The concept of gender mainstreaming was launched at the Beijing Fourth Conference on Women (UN, 1995). Gender mainstreaming involves assessing the implications of planned policy actions on men and women (UNESCO, 1997) and considering their needs in order to improve their socio-economic status (Kabeer and Subrahmanian, 1996).

Failure to adequately integrate gender into sectoral policies is one of the leading challenges of gender mainstreaming. While the Beijing Platform for Action provides guidelines for applying gender mainstreaming, these guidelines are not sector specific (Okali, 2011). Tools are needed to assist policy-makers in integrating gender into policies more adequately. However, no one tool can transverse across all sectors. Sector-specific tools are required.

15.2 Gender lenses

Gender analyses assist researchers, policy-makers and development practitioners in determining if a policy is gender-blind, gender-tepid or gender-responsive. These lenses ascertain whether policies reinforce or challenge inequalities. A policy is gender-blind when it fails to acknowledge gender norms, roles and relations that may negatively affect policy outcomes (Pederson et al., 2014). A gender-tepid policy integrates gender but does not challenge systematically embedded gender inequalities that disadvantage men and women (Mkandawire, 2018). A gender-responsive policy raises awareness, and directly influences and challenges institutionalised gender norms, roles and power relations between men and women (WHO, 2011).

15.3 Understanding gender and food security

This section focuses on the four components of food security and nutrition and discusses gender dynamics that may constrain stability and resilience, access, availability and nutrition. Globally, an estimated 60% of undernourished people are women and girls (De Schutter, 2013). Women's low social status and their limited access to resources exacerbate food insecurity. Improving women's education, access to resources and health has positive implications for food security and nutrition (Smith and Haddad, 2000; Quisumbing and Maluccio, 2003). However, gender power relations significantly influence the support women receive. While policies that target women have succeeded in reducing food insecurity (Smith and Haddad, 2000), progress toward reducing malnutrition is slow, and gender inequalities remain unchallenged. For example, several studies have suggested that there is a correlation between women's improved education and positive children's health outcomes (Dwyer and Bince, 1988; Hobcraft, 1993; Bicego and Boerma, 1993; Buvinic et al., 1992; Pitt et al., 2006; Duflo and Udry, 2004; Haddad et al., 1997; Quisumbing and Maluccio, 2003). However, socially prescribed ideals such as women bearing sole responsibility for childcare remain unchallenged. Also, men's role in childcare is undervalued. Efforts to support collaboration between men and women in reducing food insecurity and malnutrition could accelerate progress as well as advance gender equality.

15.3.1 Gender, stability and resilience

In situations of political, economic and social instability, women often experience significant challenges not only regarding accessing nutritious food but also concerning recovering from shocks. During emergency situations, women, girls and children are the most at risk. When food is in short supply, women and girls often reduce their food intake as a coping strategy. In some cases, women may be unable to access humanitarian services due to issues of mobility (Inter-Agency Standing Committee, 2006). Women who are pregnant or breastfeeding are most at risk because of their increased dietary requirements (Byrne and Baden, 1995). Gender dynamics may also increase risks for boys. For example, in a South Sundanese refugee camp in Northern Kenya, boys were separated from their families. Socio-cultural practices discouraging boys from cooking resulted in these boys being unable to prepare food for themselves (Inter-Agency Standing Committee, 2006). Policies should consider the gender norms surrounding instability and adopt contingency measures to ensure that households are not only able to cope but can recover from shocks and disasters.

15.3.2 Gender, access and availability

Women access food in three ways: producing food, purchasing food and social protection (De Schutter, 2013). Concerning availability, women who produce their food often face constraints in accessing agricultural inputs, technologies and extension services (Fletschner and Kenney, 2014). For example, in many sub-Saharan countries, women are discouraged from interacting with men to whom they are not related. However, many agricultural extension workers are male, limiting women's access to these services (Bezner Kerr, 2013). Consequently, women's productivity is reduced. Therefore, while women are responsible for producing food for household consumption (Moser, 2012), gender dynamics may constrain how much food they can make available.

Concerning access, women may have waged income that enables them to purchase food (De Schutter, 2013). However, in many cases, women have limited opportunities because of social norms that prevent them from pursuing income-generating activities (Moser, 2012). Society allocates responsibilities to men, women, boys and girls based on sex. In many low-income countries, society often expects women to take responsibility for housework, looking after children and the sick as well as farm work (Moser, 2012). While some men do participate in these activities, it is not typically considered the norm. Some men may face stigmatisation for engaging in work socially allocated to women (Mkandawire et al., 2018). As girls get older, they are expected to take on housework and care work, limiting their time to focus on school. Consequently, girls may drop out of school, reducing opportunities for formal employment when they get older (King and Winthrop, 2015). Similarly, housework and care work limit the time women have to pursue income-generating activities (Moser, 2012). Yet evidence suggests it is women who spend much of their income on food, education and healthcare (Meinzen-Dick et al., 2012).

Women may receive social support from government and other agencies who recognise the critical role that women play in household food security. Several social protection programmes have been established to support women's access to food. These include cash transfer programmes, public works programmes and asset transfer programmes (De Schutter, 2013). Such programmes need to account for the socio-cultural factors that limit women's decision-making and control of resources. While women may indeed have increased access to resources, they may not necessarily have the power to make decisions regarding how to use them. In many low-income countries, men remain the primary decision-makers in households (Richards et al., 2013). Gender-responsive policies not only mitigate such obstacles but take deliberate efforts to challenge such power dynamics.

15.3.3 Gender and nutrition

Gender inequality has significant implications for both men and women's nutrition and well-being. Women play a significant role in household nutrition because they are responsible for food production and preparation as discussed above. But women's diet also plays a vital role in reducing child undernutrition. Undernutrition begins as early as conception. Women who are undernourished are more likely to give birth to children with low birth weight (Opara et al., 2011). Girls who are well nourished before menarche tend to develop relatively faster than girls who are undernourished. Undernourished girls might not have fully developed by the time they become pregnant. Girls falling under this category may give birth to smaller babies because the foetus competes with the expectant mother for nutrients (United Nations General Assembly Special Session on Children, 2002). In low-income countries, undernutrition in women and girls is prevalent because of socio-cultural practices that compromise their nutrition. For example, in specific ethnic groups in Nigeria, men eat before women at mealtime. Hence women's dietary intake will depend on what food is leftover for them to consume. The remaining food might not be sufficient to meet their nutritional requirements, particularly during pregnancy (Chukuezi, 2010).

It is not only undernutrition that is gendered, gender dynamics also exacerbate obesity and non-communicable diseases. Globally, more women are obese compared to men. While there are biological factors that contribute to this predisposition, socio-cultural factors also play a significant role (Kanter and Caballero, 2012). For example, in some societies, it is unacceptable for women to exercise, especially in public spaces. Inactivity amongst women contributes to weight gain. Also, some cultures favour larger women as they considered a sign of prosperity. As a result, more women are overweight or obese and face increased health risks. Similarly, men are more predisposed to specific non-communicable disease than women (Garfield et al., 2008). For example, consuming excessive amounts of alcohol might be considered 'manly' in some societies, increasing men's chances of contracting diseases related to over-consumption of alcohol such as cardiovascular and digestive diseases (Shield et al., 2014). Such predispositions are often associated with socio-cultural factors that encourage misconceptions of masculinity.

The gender dynamics that exacerbate food insecurity are complex. While women do indeed face more challenges in accessing food, men too are constrained by gendered social expectations. It is not sufficient to merely focus on empowering women. Women play a critical role in food production and preparation, but the constraints that they face suggest an increased need to incorporate men as allies in food security and nutrition policy. Food security and nutrition policies should account for power relations between men and women, societal gender norms and the roles that perpetuate inequalities concerning access to food. Policy-makers should understand how these norms, relationships and roles are reproduced and ensure that policies do not perpetuate inequalities but instead challenge the systems that enforce them. The following section proposes some tools for helping policy-makers conduct gender assessments that would enable them to integrate gender more appropriately in food security and nutrition policies.

15.4 Suggested approaches to strengthen the integration of gender in food security policy

An assessment of tools for integrating gender in food security and nutrition policy was conducted. Several gender analysis tools exist. These include the WHO Gender Assessment Tool (WHO, 2011), the FAO gender mainstreaming in nutrition guidelines (FAO, 2011), Socio-Economic and Gender Analysis (SEAGA) (Bessuges et al., 2004), Guide for Conducting and Managing Gender Assessments in the Health Sector (Greene, 2013), the USAID Guide to Gender Integration and Analysis, Gender integration in Monitoring and Evaluation in agriculture toolkit (Mundial, 2005), and the Bill and Melinda Gates Gender Toolkits and Checklist. Many of these tools are not sector-specific and can apply to any policy. Some focus on specifically on agriculture, nutrition or health. The assessment found that there

Gender and food security 147

is a lack of tools for conducting gender analysis in food security and nutrition policy. Similarly, very few can determine if policies are gender-responsive, gender-tepid or gender blind. Two tools, in particular, were identified as relevant for assessing the integration of gender in food security and nutrition policy: the FAO gender mainstreaming in nutrition framework (FAO, 2011) and WHO gender assessment tool (WHO, 2011). These two specific tools are considered appropriate because the first provides guidance on the areas for improving the integration of gender in food security and nutrition policy. The second contains criteria for assessing if policies are gender-blind, gender-tepid or gender-responsive.

While the FAO framework focuses on gender in nutrition policy, the thematic areas apply to food security as well. The FAO framework proposes seven thematic areas that relate to gender, food security and nutrition, identified through an extensive review of international literature (FAO, 2011). Focusing on these priority areas can improve men and women's access to nutritious food. These seven priority areas are gender and nutrition in agriculture extension, income-generating activities and spending income on nutrition, local food culture and gender, nutrition and the life cycle, obesity, non-communicable diseases and nutrition, rights-based perspective related to gender and nutrition, targeting in nutrition (FAO, 2011).

The WHO gender assessment tool was developed for the health sector. However, the criteria used to assess a policy is transversal. The tool, validated through workshops in 23 WHO countries, contains 23 'yes' or 'no' questions. The number of affirmative responses and negative responses is tallied to determine the extent to which a policy or programme is gender-blind or gender-responsive. Some of the questions in the scorecard of this tool are repetitive and can be collapsed into one question. The most relevant questions from this tool are discussed below.

- Do the vision, goals or principles have an explicit commitment to promoting or achieving gender equality?

It is essential to understand if a policy prioritises gender. An explicit statement related to gender is necessary to establish if gender equality is an overarching objective of the policy. This commitment provides the benchmark for determining if the rest of the policy adheres to the gender goals that the policy promotes.

- Does the policy consider and include men and women's practical needs?

Practical needs refer to men and women's immediate needs (Moser, 2012; Kabeer and Subrahmanian, 1996). A policy should consider men and women's immediate requirements to enable them to access nutritious food. Women's micro-financing programmes are an example of a programme that addresses women's practical needs. Micro-financing programmes ensure that women have access to the income required to purchase nutritious food.

- Does the policy include men and women's strategic needs?

Strategic needs refer to men and women's requirements in order to improve their status and participation in society. Strategic needs involve identifying men's and women's requirements to ensure that they have equal opportunities to participate in the development process (Moser, 2012; (Kabeer and Subrahmanian, 1996). For example, increasing the number of days for paternity leave could improve men's participation in the first few months of children's lives and consequently raising their sense of responsibility towards women and children.

- Does the policy consider gender norms, roles and relations?

Gender norms are standards that society expects men and women to conform (Kabeer and Subrahmanian, 1996). Gender norms are institutionalised through sanctions and rewards. For example, if a man is engaging in women's work such as cooking, he might be mocked. But if a man is drinking excessively, he might be applauded. Gender roles are socially prescribed responsibilities that men and women are expected to perform based on their sex (Moser, 2012). For example, women are responsible for looking after children. Gender relations refer to the power dynamics between men and women (Kabeer, 2003). For example, in some low-income countries, men have sole control over resource allocation. Policymakers need to be aware of such gender dynamics to ensure that the intended policy outcomes are achieved. Policies that only target women without accounting for these dynamics are likely to be unsuccessful or result in unintended consequences.

- Does the policy avoid considering men and women as homogenous groups?

Policies should not consider men and women as one because they have different gender perspectives. Men and women's practical and strategic needs also differ (UN, 2002). Consequently, different policy actions required for men and women. It is critical to determine whether a policy considers men and women's needs as separate or as the same as this will influence policy outcomes. For example, a policy that only focuses on women's dietary requirements during pregnancy cannot claim to address the needs of the entire population.

- Does the policy clearly differentiate between sex and gender?

There is a difference between sex and gender. Sex is physiological; it pertains to whether a person is a man or a woman. Gender is sociological (Moser, 2012). Gender refers to the roles and responsibilities allocated to men and women because of their sex (Kabeer and Subrahmanian, 1996). A policy that does not distinguish between sex and gender is gender-blind because it fails to recognise that the social underpinnings that reinforce inequalities need to be addressed to improve gender inequality.

Both the FAO gender mainstreaming and nutrition framework and the WHO gender assessment tool can be applied separately in assessing food security and nutrition policy. However, to maximise the quality of the assessment, the two tools should ideally be combined. The integrated framework for gender analysis in nutrition policy is referred to in this chapter as the integrated framework. The tool is one of the options that development practitioners and researchers can use for assessing the integration of gender in food security and nutrition policy. It combines the FAO framework and the WHO gender assessment tool. The integrated framework presented in Table 15.1 below, aims to assist researchers and development practitioners in assessing policy documents and strategies to determine if gender is adequately integrated into food security and nutrition policies. The integrated framework includes the thematic areas proposed in the FAO framework as actions that can be taken to improve nutrition outcomes. These are referred to as policy instruments. The six questions from the WHO gender assessment tool discussed above are in the top row of (Table 15.1) (Mkandawire et al., 2018).

To apply the integrated framework a detailed policy chronology that documents international and national nutrition, political and gender events, conventions, declarations, commitments and policies should be developed. Presenting these events and documents together enables the user to understand what factors may have influenced the introduction of new policies or policy changes. The various policy instruments contained in the policy being assessed should then be identified. The first column in Table 15.1 lists eight policy instruments that food security and nutrition policies could and ideally should include. Table 15.1 presents some examples for each of these policy instruments. Each policy instrument is then interrogated against the list of questions in the top row of Table 15.1.

Once the assessment is complete, the results can then be interpreted to determine if the policy is gender-blind, gender-tepid or gender-responsive. If there are only a few ticks in the dark grey section, then the policy is gender-blind, suggesting that policy-maker's decisions were influenced by gender biases from within their frames of reference. If there are several ticks in this section, the policy is likely gender-responsive. If the majority of ticks are in the section shaded medium grey, then the policy is gender-tepid, suggesting that the policy makes attempts to address gender inequalities but does not address the structural inequalities that undermine men and women's access to nutritious food. It also suggests that policy-maker's personal experiences of gender may have influenced policy choices. If the majority of ticks is in the lighter shade of grey, then the policy is gender-blind, suggesting that policy-makers are aware of international commitments to gender and the importance of integrating gender but might not have the necessary capacity to incorporate gender adequately into the policy.

The empty boxes are considered gender gaps within the policy. Opportunities for improvement of the policy are reflected in the tool if a policy instrument has been selected, but each of the criteria in the top row has not been satisfied. The empty boxes suggest that policy-makers should review the design of the policy instrument and determine if all the factors that could result in adverse gender outcomes have been considered.

TABLE 15.1 Integrated framework for gender analysis in nutrition policy

Policy instruments	1. Do the vision, goals or principles have an explicit commitment to promoting or achieving gender equality?	2. Does the policy consider and include men and women's practical needs?	3. Does the policy include men and women's strategic needs?	4. Does the policy consider gender norms, roles and relations?	5. Does the policy avoid considering men and women as homogenous groups?	6. Does the policy clearly differentiate between sex and gender?
a.) Agricultural extension and nutrition	Commitment to promote equitable access to agriculture inputs, extension services and technologies	Creating a conducive environment for improving women's access to information	Supporting research and development of technologies that will reduce time spent farming	Promoting technologies that take into consideration the different farm work men and women are typically responsible for	Promote development of guidelines on the specific technological needs of different groups of women and men in agriculture e.g. young women and older men	Promote the redistribution of housework, care work and community work to free up women's time to pursue economic and other opportunities
b.) Local food culture and gender	Commitment to apply a community approach to addressing cultural and gender norms	Promote campaigns to address cultural taboos that undermine men, women and children's nutrition	Promote gender training for influential community leaders e.g. traditional leaders	Promoting men and women's cooking groups to promote sharing of household responsibilities	Promoting community based-learning to support changes in local food cultures that favour men at the expense of women	Promote awareness campaigns to sensitise community role models and leaders
c.) Nutrition and the life cycle	Commitment to address men and women's specific food and nutrition needs at different stages of the life cycle	Promoting school feeding programmes for secondary schools	Promote the development of standards for secondary school feeding programmes	Promoting the integration of gender norms and nutrition in the secondary school curriculum	Promoting specialised awareness campaigns targeted at adolescent girls and boys	Promote the inclusion of home economics as a compulsory subject for both boys and girls in the school curriculum

d.) Gender, obesity and non-communicable diseases	Commitment to improve men's access to health and nutrition services	Promote mobile clinics for men	Develop standards for men's health care check-up that include nutrition services	Create incentives to increase men's participation in nutrition awareness campaigns	Promote nutrition awareness campaigns for men at the different stages on the life cycle	Promote programming that creates a conducive environment for men's participation in nutrition activities
e.) Spending income on nutrition	Commitment related to improving joint decision-making and control over resources	Promote sensitisation of men on the benefits of gender equality and joint decision-making	Develop bylaws that requires the participation of both men and women	Prioritise the assessment of the anticipated gender outcomes of all nutrition interventions targeting women	Promote the development of nutrition programmes that target female and child-headed households	Promoting men's increased contribution toward spending on food.

Source: Adapted from Mkandawire, Hendriks and Mkandawire-Valhmu, 2017

The integrated framework can be used to influence policy in two ways: to compel policy-makers using international and national documents to fill gaps identified and to use the integrated framework to illustrate to policy-makers the gender gaps within the policy visually. First, the policy chronology indicates international, African, regional and national commitments. It also provides a list of national policies and strategies. Once the gaps have been identified, the international and domestic documents can be used to compel policy-makers to improve the policy. The chronology also enables users to determine if the policy aligns with other national documents. For example, the Malawi Growth and Development Strategy III explicitly states that one of the strategies for improving nutrition is to promote male involvement in maternal and child health, nutrition, childcare and household duties. If the Malawi Nutrition Policy does not have a policy instrument related to targeting, the Malawi Growth and Development Strategy III could be used to compel policy-makers to integrate this policy instrument.

Second, the integrated framework provides a visual representation of where the gaps in the policy lie. If there are glaring gaps regarding one policy instrument, then it is likely that gender analysis has not been conducted. The gaps can be used to encourage policy-makers to revise the policy and make deliberate efforts to conduct gender analysis.

15.5 Conclusion

The limited number of tools for conducting gender assessments in food security and nutrition policies suggests a need to stimulate demand for more rigorous sector-specific tools. While progress toward reducing food insecurity and malnutrition has been reported in the past few years, it is not sufficient for meeting international commitments such as the SDGs. Incorporating gender appropriately in food security and nutrition policies could accelerate progress toward achieving food security and nutrition commitments. But it could also accelerate progress toward gender equality.

References

Bessuges, P., Bloom, G., Fileccia, T., Graham, A. and Sisto, I. (2004) *Socio-Economic and Gender Analysis (SAEGA) for Emergency and Rehabilitation Programmes*. FAO and WFP, Rome.

Bezner Kerr, R. (2013) 'Seed struggles and food sovereignty in northern Malawi', *Journal of Peasant Studies*, vol 40, no. 3, pp. 867–897.

Bicego, G.T. and Boerma, J.T. (1993) 'Maternal education and child survival: A comparative study of survey data from 17 countries', *Social Science & Medicine*, vol 36, no. 9, pp. 1207–1227.

Buvinic, M., Valenzuela, J.P., Molina, T. and González, E. (1992) 'The fortunes of adolescent mothers and their children: The transmission of poverty in Santiago, Chile', *Population and Development Review*, vol 18, no. 2, pp. 269–297.

Byrne, B. and Baden, S. (1995) 'Gender, emergencies and humanitarian assistance', Report, European Commission Institute of Development Studies, Brussels.

Canada, Status of Women (1998) *Gender-based Analysis: A Guide for Policy-making*. Status of Women Canada, Ottowa.

Chukuezi, C. (2010) 'Socio-cultural factors associated with maternal mortality in Nigeria', *Research Journal of Social Sciences*, vol 1, no. 5, pp. 22–26.

De Schutter, O. (2013) 'Gender equality and food security: Women's empowerment as a tool against hunger', Report, Asian Development Bank, Mandaluyong City.

Duflo, E. and Udry, C. (2004) 'Intrahousehold resource allocation in Cote d'Ivoire: Social norms, separate accounts and consumption choices', Report, National Bureau of Economic Research, Cambridge.

Dwyer, D. H. and Bince, J. (1988) *A Home Divided: Women and income in the Third World*. Stanford University Press, Stanford.

FAO (2011) 'Nutrition and gender', Issue paper, FAO, Rome.

Fletschner, D. and Kenney, L. (2014) 'Rural women's access to financial services: credit, savings, and insurance', Working paper 1107 at FAO, Rome.

Garfield, C. F., Isacco, A. & Rogers, T. E. (2008) 'A review of men's health and masculinity', *American Journal of Lifestyle Medicine*, vol 2, no. 6, pp. 474–487.

Greene, M. (2013) *A Practical Guide for Managing and Conducting Gender Assessments in the Health Sector*. Population Reference Bureau, IDEA Project, Washington DC.

Haddad, L., Hoddinott, J. and Alderman, H. (1997) 'Intrahousehold resource allocation in developing countries: Models, methods and policies', Report no. 44, IFPRI, Washington DC.

Hobcraft, J. (1993) 'Women's education, child welfare and child survival: A review of the evidence'. *Health Transition Review*, vol 3, no. 2, pp. 159–175.

Inter-Agency Standing Committee (IASC). (2006) *Women, Girls, Boys and Men: Different Needs-Equal Opportunities*. IASC, New York.

Kabeer, N. (2003) *Gender Mainstreaming in Poverty Eradication and the Millennium Development Goals: A handbook for policy-makers and other stakeholders*. Commonwealth Secretariat and International Development Research Center, London and Ottowa.

Kabeer, N. and Subrahmanian, R. (1996) *Institutions, Relations and Outcomes: Framework and tools for gender-aware planning*. Institute of Development Studies, Brighton.

Kanter, R. and Caballero, B. (2012) 'Global gender disparities in obesity: A review', *Advances in Nutrition*, vol 3, no. 4, pp. 491–498.

King, E. and Winthrop, R. (2015) 'Today's challenges for girls' education', Working paper 90, Brookings Institution, Washington DC.

Meinzen-Dick, R., Behrman, J., Menon, P. and Quisumbing, A. (2012) 'Gender: A key dimension linking agricultural programs to improved nutrition and health', in S.A.P.L. Fan (ed) *Reshaping Agriculture for Nutrition and Health*. IFPRI, Washington DC.

Mkandawire, E. (2018) *Interpretations of Gender and Implications for Policy: A case study of Malawi's Nutrition policymaking process*. PhD thesis. University of Pretoria, Pretoria.

Mkandawire, E., Hendriks, S.L. and Mkandawire-Vahlmu, L. (2018) 'A gender assessment of Malawi's National Nutrition Policy and Strategic Plan 2007–2012', *Development Policy Review*, vol 36, no. 2, pp. 634–656.

Moser, C. (2012) *Gender Planning and Development: Theory, practice and training*. Routledge, London.

Mundial, B. (2005) *Gender Issues in Monitoring and Evaluation in Rural Development: A tool kit*. World Bank, Washington DC.

Okali, C. (2011) 'Achieving transformative change for rural women's empowerment', Expert paper, UN Women, Accra.

Opara, J.A., Adebola, H.E., Oguzor, N.S. and Abere, S.A. (2011) 'Malnutrition during pregnancy among child bearing mothers in Mbaitolu of South-Eastern Nigeria', *Advances in Biological Research*, vol 5, no. 2, pp.111–115.

Pederson, A., Greaves, L. and Poole, N. (2014) 'Gender-transformative health promotion for women: a framework for action', *Health Promotion International*, vol 30, no. 1, pp. 140–150.

Pitt, M.M., Khandker, S.R. and Cartwright, J. (2006) 'Empowering women with micro finance: Evidence from Bangladesh', *Economic Development and Cultural Change*, vol 54, no. 4, pp. 791–831.

Quisumbing, A.R. and Maluccio, J.A. (2003) 'Resources at marriage and intrahousehold allocation: Evidence from Bangladesh, Ethiopia, Indonesia, and South Africa', *Oxford Bulletin of Economics and Statistics*, vol 65, no. 3, pp. 283–327.

Razavi, S. and Miller, C. (1995) *From WID to GAD: Conceptual shifts in the women and development discourse*. United Nations Research Institute for Social Development, Geneva.

Richards, E., Theobald, S., George, A., Kim, J.C., Rudert, C., Jehan, K. and Tolhurst, R. (2013) 'Going beyond the surface: Gendered intra-household bargaining as a social determinant of child health and nutrition in low and middle income countries', *Social Science & Medicine*, vol 95, pp. 24–33.

Shield, K.D., Parry, C. and Rehm, J. (2014) 'Chronic diseases and conditions related to alcohol use', *Alcohol Research: Current reviews*, vol 35, no. 2, pp. 155–171.

Smith, L.C. and Haddad, L.J. (2000) 'Explaining child malnutrition in developing countries: A cross-country analysis', IFPRI, Washington DC.

UN (1995) 'Beijing declaration and platform for action', Fourth world conference on women, 1995, UN, New York.

United Nations General Assembly Special Session on Children. (2002) 'A world fit for children', May 2002, UN, New York.

UN (2002) *Gender Mainstreaming: An Overview*. UN, New York.

UN Educational, Scientific and Cultural Organisation (UNESCO) (1997) 'Gender main-streaming', Report, Division for Advancement of Women, UN Department of Economic and Social Affairs, New York.

UN General Assembly (UNGA) (2015) 'Transforming our world: The 2030 agenda for sustainable development', Resolution adopted by the General Assembly at New York

World Health Organisation (WHO) (2011) *Gender Mainstreaming for Health Managers: A Practical Approach*. WHO, Geneva.

16

INCLUSION AND ENGAGEMENT WITH INDIGENOUS PEOPLES

Carol Kalafatic

16.1 Introduction

There is strong interest and rationale for development practitioners and policy makers to seek engagement with Indigenous Peoples (IPs), particularly in this time of global food, water, and climate crisis. For these collaborations to be effective, it is important to understand that IPs are distinct from other Peoples/groupings (e.g., the rural poor, small farmers).

16.2 Indigenous Peoples: who are they?

Indigenous Peoples (IPs) as a whole are distinct from others for historical, cultural and other reasons. Their interdependent relationships with their specific environments is the basis for their respective identities, ways of life, livelihoods and food systems. Also, their unique relationships to the countries/ States in which they live centres mainly on self-determination as a right that entitles IPs to co-exist with others living within those States while deciding their own pathways and priorities for economic, social and cultural development.

Instead of a universally accepted definition of "Indigenous Peoples", which might not encompass their diversity, a working definition is used internationally as a practical basis for engagement with IPs. Its list of the key characteristics that IPs share globally is based on consensus developed through decades of IPs' and others' advocacy, as well as through extensive studies. It provides universal but general background on the ways in which IPs (who in some contexts are known as, e.g., Tribal, Hill or Highland Peoples; First Nations, etc.), are historically, culturally and socio-politically distinct from others particularly in relation to lands, territories and natural resources. In combination with international legal instruments that protect IPs' rights, it is a starting point for international organisations, national and other-level governments, legal experts, development practitioners and others to engage with IPs in the development of policies in food security and other sectors that affect IPs (UNPFII, 2004). However, to be effective, engagement also needs to be guided by frameworks that include, e.g., allocation of the time necessary to build respectful relationships with IPs at local level, and adherence to IPs' specific cultural protocols.

WORKING DEFINITION OF INDIGENOUS PEOPLES AND CHARACTERISTICS MOST SHARED BY THEM

Indigenous Peoples:

- Have historical continuity with societies developed within their territories prior to invasion and colonisation
- Live within/maintain links to their ancestral territories
- Self-identify, and are recognised by other groups or by State authorities as distinct collectivities
- Want to remain culturally, geographically and institutionally distinct from dominant society
- Were once fully independent Peoples, and then were colonised
- Retain and want to keep retaining their own:

  - Forms of social organisation, governance and customary law
  - Strong collective ties to ancestral territories
  - Distinct languages and other cultural features

- Have a unique relationship to their lands, territories and natural resources, which:

  - Includes cultural, spiritual, economic, and political dimensions as well as responsibilities
  - Includes an inter-generational aspect crucial to IPs' continued existence as Peoples, in accordance with their own cultural patterns, social institutions and legal systems
  - Is fundamentally collective (under international law IPs have collective rights)
- Have a relationship to states which centres on self-determination
- Face trans-boundary challenges in the form of State borders, policies/conflicts limiting access to their habitats and natural resources, etc.

16.3 Indigenous Peoples' role in biocultural diversity and associated knowledge systems

IPs are extraordinarily diverse, comprising about 5,000 distinct Peoples (Claudia, 2008). According to conservative estimates, worldwide there are over 370 million Indigenous individuals, which is a small percentage of overall population but represents over 75% of the world's approximately 6,000 cultures in 90 countries (Oviedo et al., 2000; Schnuttgen et al., 2007). This extraordinary diversity is a result of thousands of years of IPs' co-evolution with their specific environments. It is no accident that about 80% of the world's remaining biodiversity is found within IPs' territories; there is a fundamental interdependence between the many plant, animal and other species, and the culturally-based knowledge systems and resource management practices of the IPs within these "hot spots" of biodiversity (Nabhan, 2016; RAFI, 1999; Toledo, 2001; WRI and World Bank, 2005).

As the originators and custodians of millennial agricultural systems, IPs are estimated to have cultivated 65% of the crop varieties that are eaten throughout the world (Clayton Brascoupe – Traditional Native American Farmers Association 2008, personal communication, 6 April). Through an interconnected web of IPs' own systems and institutions (e.g., bands, clans, cooperation groups, assemblies, councils and other customary governance structures/systems that are specific to each People or community), and their customary use of resources, (including shifting cultivation), many IPs continue to shape and sustainably manage an extraordinary range of agricultural systems and landscapes (Gadgil et al., 1993; Ostrom, 2010; Roy, 2012; HLPE, 2017a; Robinson et al., 2018). These and other components of their ways of life sustain their food systems *and* their ability to continue their dynamic conservation of the vast majority of the world's biodiversity.

AGRICULTURAL SYSTEMS AND LANDSCAPES SHAPED AND MANAGED BY INDIGENOUS PEOPLES

The 800 year-old "Kihamba" system in the United Republic of Tanzania is one of many agroforestry systems in Africa that rely on the traditional knowledge systems of Indigenous Peoples and local communities. Covering 120,000 hectares of Mount Kilimanjaro's southern slopes, it provides livelihoods for approximately one million people – one of the largest rural populations in the continent. Its multi-layered vegetation structure maximises land use, produces a large variety of foods year round, generates income through wood and cash-crops production, and provides fundamental ecosystem services well beyond the areas where it is practiced (e.g., through carbon storage, and by playing a major role in ensuring that Mount Kilimanjaro remains a "water tower" for the whole region).

Near Pisaq, throughout more than 12,000 hectares in the southern Andean region in Peru, is the Potato Park. It is a community conservation area where, based on complex, millennial knowledge systems and practices, several Quechua

> communities grow a majority of the over 4,000 known varieties of Native potato in the world and are the lead decision-makers in their collaborations with others. The Park prioritises local indigenous institutions, values, governance, as well as customary law. As a protected agroecological area, the park is considered fundamental to the region's biodiversity (HLPE, 2017b; Argumedo, 2008).

16.4 Indigenous Peoples at "the" table and at their own tables

IPs' vital role in sustainable development is well recognised. Due largely to their millennial knowledge systems, practices and institutions, they are essential actors in food production and in the stewardship of biodiversity (Trosper, 2009). IPs increasingly draw on the former, and on the genetic diversity of their seeds and animals, as sources of their communities' climate resilience – even as climate change threatens that very diversity (Thrupp, 2000).

As actors in achieving food security and in developing related policies, IPs apply and draw from their knowledge systems. These systems depend on and sustain biological diversity, and are contingent on IPs' ability to enjoy their human rights and collective rights – including rights of access to and use of their lands, territories (including water), and natural resources (HLPE, 2015)

IPs' knowledge systems result from living daily life or "lived knowledge," reinforced by generations of experience and intelligent, practical reasoning for individual and collective survival (Barnhardt, 2005; Pimbert, 2017). IPs' knowledge systems emerge from and function in local contexts, relying on interconnected *in-situ* systems, institutions and productive resources that are unique to each IPs' community/other locality (Ostrom, 2010; Oskal et al., 2009)

IPs' traditional agroecological practices and landscape management practices are a basis for their food systems and food security. Several of these practices are among those recognised by the UN Food and Agriculture Organisation (FAO) as "Globally Important Agricultural Heritage Systems" (GIAHS). IPs have developed and sustained their GIAHS over millennia, reflecting their knowledge systems, cultures, and place-based relationships with their local ecosystems (HLPE, 2017b; Boerma and Koohafkan, 2004). GIAHS should be dynamically protected and supported for their fundamental value to IPs themselves, and for their significance to all of humanity.

16.5 The distinct body of international law and legal framework that pertains to IPs

IPs are not mere stakeholders, they are rights-holders with inherent and collective rights to the lands, territories and natural resources (including productive resources, such as seeds) that they have customarily occupied, owned or used (IASG, 2014). IPs have a fundamental dependence on the latter for their food security and livelihoods, and for their cultural continuity and identity.

Engagement with Indigenous Peoples   159

The international legal framework for the recognition and protection of IPs' rights includes: ILO Convention 107; ILO Convention 169; Agenda 21 and Rio Declaration (UNCED); The Convention on Biological Diversity, particularly Articles 8(j) and 10(c); UN Convention to Combat Desertification; the Vienna Declaration and Programme of Action-World Conference on Human Rights; and the UN Declaration on the Rights of Indigenous Peoples.

16.6 Understanding food insecurity among IPs

Due often to long-term impacts of colonisation and IPs' political marginalisation, as well as to dispossession or degradation of their lands, territories and other productive resources that sustain IPs (e.g., by socio-political forces that erode IPs' governance, by imposed development activities of mining and other extractive industries, by industrial agriculture, and by land grabs for mono-crop plantations), many IPs are considered to be among the most economically disadvantaged (UNDESA, 2009; UNGA, 2005; IASG, 2014; HLPE, 2015). These and other circumstances, such as influx of certain industrial foods into communities, make IPs vulnerable to food insecurity and poor nutritional status (Kuhnlein et al., 2009). Other negative consequences include the erosion of genetic diversity of IPs' seeds, and migration of IPs to urban areas where they often face severe discrimination and alienation, economic hardship, malnutrition, and chronic diseases such as diabetes (Claudia, 2008; Kuhnlein et al., 2009)

IPs food security and subsistence livelihoods are also harmed by imposed conservation schemes that ignore the needs of IPs who, for example, rely on pastoral systems that support healthy ecosystems and complement wildlife conservation (Niamir-Fuller et al., 2012). In addition, many IPs in remote areas who want to broaden distribution of their foods lack access to markets.

While the majority of IPs live in *economic* poverty and are among the most vulnerable social groups in terms of food and livelihood security, and health, they maintain a wealth of knowledge systems and practices that play an essential role in the management of natural resources and the stewardship of biodiversity. Their cultural wealth is a source of IPs' world views, ethics, spiritual practices, knowledge, governance systems, and identities, as well as being central to sustainable development (IASG, 2014).

The majority of IPs are marginalised from meaningful participation in policy-making processes about development in all sectors that affect them (Ooft, 2006). In addition, collaborative research and natural resource management that attempts to combine IPs' science (built on their knowledge systems) and "western" science, often create bureaucracies that duplicate unequal power relations or institutionalise IPs' disenfranchisement (Cajete, 2000; Nadasdy, 2005; Spak, 2005).

The right of self-determination, which encompasses the right of all peoples to freely pursue their economic, social and cultural development, is at the core of the UN Declaration on the Rights of Indigenous Peoples (UNDRIP) and other instruments of international law and standard setting. Self-determination is the cornerstone for engagement with IPs, whose own priorities and criteria for well-being and development with identity must be respected and supported.

The right to adequate food, and the corollary rights of Food Security and Food Sovereignty, cut across many sectors and disciplines. The food security of IPs, in particular, calls for transdisciplinary approaches that prioritise IPs as actors (HLPE, 2014; Pimbert, 2017).

The culturally based foods that IPs grow, herd, hunt, fish, and gather play a significant role in IPs livelihoods, existence and well-being. IPs' food systems sustain and are sustained by intangible cultural components (e.g., IPs' stories, languages, ceremonies, value systems, spiritual practices, and knowledge systems) (Indigenous Peoples' Consultation, 2015; IASG, 2014; Claudia, 2008). In turn, the fulfilment of IPs' cultural rights and food security are inter-twined:

> Food sovereignty is the right of Peoples to define their own policies and strategies for sustainable production, distribution, and consumption of food, with respect for their own cultures and their own systems of managing natural resources and rural areas, and is considered to be a precondition for Food Security.
>
> *(Indigenous Peoples' Consultation, 2015)*

In IPs' conception of food sovereignty, their traditional foods (including subsistence foods) and food systems are: an assertion of self-determination; a source of collective identity and well-being; and vital to sustaining inter-generational relationships through collective food practices. The cultural dimensions of their food systems are fundamentally linked to *place* (specific land/territory) and to the vitality of songs, dances, language, and IPs knowledge systems (Kuhnlein et al., 2009).

IPs continue to assert their right to subsistence, which is ensconced in the International Covenant on Civil and Political Rights and the International Covenant on Economic, Social and Cultural Rights – two binding, international Treaties that state in Article 1 in common, "In no case may a people be deprived of its means of subsistence" (UNGA, 2015; UNGA, 1966).

16.7 Ways forward

Development with identity, or self-determined development, provides respect for sociocultural context. It is a principle whereby development processes should not threaten or harm peoples' sociocultural expressions, values and traditions (FAO, 2008). IPs' own concepts of well-being and collective identity depend on the continuation of their traditions/customs and the well-being of their lands, territories and natural resources. Food security must therefore prioritise these values and address the needs and aspirations of IPs.

The integrity of IPs food systems is one of the primary indicators of IPs' well-being. To address the missing, fourth pillar of sustainable development, IPs and their organisations (and this author) in collaboration with FAO, developed a set of "Cultural indicators of IPs' food and agroecological systems" (e.g., right of access to and use of traditional lands and territories; change in consumption and preparation of traditional foods and medicines, and their associated ceremonial uses; use of languages associated with traditional food systems, etc.) (Woodley et al., 2006).

It is important to understanding gaps in the DGs. IPs were not enabled to participate meaningfully in the development of the Sustainable Development Goals (SDGs), and are missing from them. The SDGs lack a focus on diversity and context specificity. They don't allow a culturally based conception of poverty, and as a development roadmap, could end up being harmful to IPs.

One possible way to contribute to mitigation of SDG gaps in relation to IPs' food security is to support IPs in their application of their own development metrics (including the above Cultural Indicators, which group indicators under Structural, Process and Results categories), and to respect those metrics as valid in all stages of development activities, including but not limited to conceptualisation, implementation, evaluation and assessment.

16.8 Suggested principles and approaches to strengthen food security

In addition to the ethical and legal imperatives to work with IPs, there is a practical imperative to do so. IPs have an existential "self-interest" in biodiversity conservation (Berkes et al., 1994). Eagerness to collaborate with IPs has increased due to the severe global crises related to food, water and climate change. Many IPs are at the frontlines of impacts from these crises (e.g., in the eight countries that are within the Arctic, or on the small islands or low-lying river-dependent communities in other regions). Climate change is an extreme stressor to IPs, many of whose ways of life and food systems – particularly those including subsistence foods – depend on fragile ecosystems within their lands and territories.

Development practitioners and others have collaborated on natural resource management that incorporates IPs' knowledge systems. Since the millennium, several UN agencies and other institutions have established specific, formal policies to guide their engagement with IPs (e.g., FAO, IFAD, UNDP). As a broad framework in support of respectful and effective engagement with IPs for desired food security outcomes, below are general approaches urging development practitioners, policy makers and scholars to:

- Undertake a trans-sectoral and trans-disciplinary approach regarding IPs, being sure to value qualitative evidence as much as quantitative evidence
- Apply a Human Rights Based Approach (HRBA) to understanding and engaging with IPs, for its own ethical and legal imperative and because it would likely result in co-benefits (e.g., IPs' own food security and the protection of biodiversity). HRBA is a framework that integrates international human rights and dignity into human development plans and processes. It aims to empower rights holders and to improve the ability and accountability of duty bearers to respect, protect and fulfil those rights.

- Recognise and respect the rights of IPs, using the UNDRIP as the minimum international standard for the protection and promotion of the rights of IPs (see Section 16.9).
- Understand and address the unequal power relations between "western" science (which enjoys privilege) and the empirical science within IP's knowledge systems; in designing collaborations, determine together: whose value system(s) and cultural standard(s) will guide the decision making process? (Grey and Patel, 2015; Kalafatic, 2013; Koohafkan and Cruz, 2011; Peters, 2003)
- Question assumptions about food security solutions (e.g., cooperatives), as they may be embedded in perspectives/values that are not appropriate for all cultural contexts
- Strengthen their own institutional environments and capacities to be informed about and engage with IPs
- Respect and support IPs' own customary institutions, as well as their own research and methodologies (e.g., the use of prophecies/other oral histories and information coding traditions, as in the Potato Park – a Quechua community conservation area near Pisaq, Peru) and their *in situ* conservation of agrobiodiversity in their pursuit of food security and development with identity, or self-determined development (Smith, 2013; Pimbert, 2017)
- Support IPs' communication systems and initiatives for their own horizontal exchange of knowledge, technologies and skills-strengthening among themselves and with non-IPs, if they choose (Pimbert, 2017).
- Respect and promote the inter-dependence of biological and cultural diversity, in part by supporting IPs own place-based and culturally-grounded knowledge systems, practices, and the adaptive strategies/technologies that IPs draw from that heritage (e.g., the use of zaï pits to restore/improve soils, the increase in mobility of pastoralists to cope with escalating desertification due to climate change, etc.) (Vermeulen and Dinesh, 2016)
- Support and enable the full and effective participation of IPs in all stages (from conceptualization/design to monitoring and evaluation) of research and policy making on food security and other development activities that could affect them, emphasising a trans-sectoral and transdisciplinary approach (HLPE, 2015)
- Recognise that culture and local context matter for IPs (Gavin et al., 2015). Therefore, it's crucial to accept that development with identity is paramount, and that food sovereignty – with its emphasis on the cultural appropriateness of food systems – is a pre-requisite for IPs' food security and central to IPs' realisation of the Right to Adequate Food (Knuth, 2009). Also, food sovereignty would afford better results in agroecological approaches to food security (e.g., by keeping seeds in Peoples' hands and protecting local varieties).

16.9 Suggested tools

In 2007, the UN General Assembly adopted the milestone **UN Declaration on the Rights of Indigenous Peoples** (UNDRIP), which is the minimum international standard for the protection and promotion of the rights of IPs, meaning that current and future laws, policies, and programs regarding or affecting IPs will need to be consistent with it. It is the only UN rights declaration that was drafted with the participation of the rights-holders themselves (i.e., IPs).

The UN Charter, the International Covenant on Economic, Social and Cultural Rights (ICESCR) and the International Covenant on Civil and Political Rights (ICCPR) affirm the fundamental importance of the **Right of Self-Determination** of all peoples. Article 1 in common of the two Covenants states, "All people have the right of self-determination. By virtue of that right they freely determine their political status and freely pursue their economic, social and cultural development". The Human Rights Committee and the Committee on Economic, Social and Cultural Rights (the two monitoring bodies for the International Covenants) have applied the right of self-determination to IPs.

The international standards framework calls for **Free Prior and Informed Consent (FPIC)**, which can be summarised as meaningful consultation, and the explicit and un-coerced consent of IPs, on the basis of IPs' review of culturally appropriate and thorough information *well prior* to any legislative/administrative decisions, projects or other measures that will likely affect IPs or their lands, territories, resources or livelihoods. The right of self-determination underlies FPIC. FPIC should incorporate the participation of IPs' traditional/customary authorities based on local, cultural protocols. As a right, and as a pragmatic principle that supports sustainability and conflict prevention, FPIC should be intrinsic to any engagement with IPs.

FPIC has become a formal part of, e.g., the International Fund for Agricultural Development's work with IPs, the UN FAO's formal guidelines for all FAO field operations, the Convention on Biological Diversity – Akwé: Kon Guidelines, and the UN Development Group Guidelines for country-level planning and programming. There should be support for capacity building among IPs about FPIC, and for the sharing of experiences and lessons learned for improving FPIC processes.

IPs' cultural protocols are culturally specific rules that guide the appropriate conduct and processes for communication, research, collaboration, and other forms of engagement with IPs or entry into their lands and territories. These protocols are often specific to each of their many communities, as they generate from and support their local governance systems and rights priorities.

Cultural indicators of IPs' food and agroecological systems are practical metrics developed by IPs in collaboration with FAO. They aim to help IPs monitor the multi-dimensional impacts that development activities have on their particular food systems and well-being, and to guide policy makers and development practitioners in their understanding and respect for culture as a pillar in the continued well-being of IPs and their food systems.

164 Carol Kalafatic

References

Argumedo, A. 2008. 'The Potato Park, Peru: Conserving agrobiodiversity in an Andean indigenous biocultural heritage area', in T. Amend, J. Brown, A. Kothari, A. Phillips, S. Stolton (eds) *Protected Landscapes and Agrobiodiversity Values. Vol 1*. International Union for the Conservation of Nature and Deutsche Gesellschaft für Internationale Zusammenarbeit (GTZ), Heidelberg

Barnhardt, R. (2005) 'Indigenous knowledge systems and Alaska Native ways of knowing', *Anthropology and Education Quarterly*, vol 36, no. 1, pp. 8–23.

Berkes, F., Folke, C. and Gadgil, M. 1994. 'Traditional ecological knowledge, biodiversity, resilience and sustainability', in C.A. Pweeings, K.G. Maler, C. Folke, C.S. Holling and B.O. Jansson (eds) *Biodiversity Conservation*. Springer. Dordrecht, pp. 269–287.

Boerma, D. and Koohafkan, P. (2004) 'Local knowledge systems and the management of dryland agro-ecosystems: some principles for an approach', Globally Important Agricultural Heritage Systems (GIAHS) Background document, FAO, Rome.

Cajete, G. (2000) *Native Science: Natural Laws of Interdependence*. Clear Light Publishers, Santa Fe.

Claudia, S. (2008). *The Role of Indigenous Peoples in Biodiversity Conservation*. World Bank, Washington DC.

FAO (2008) *Conservation and Adaptive Management of GIAHS*. FAO, Rome.

Gadgil, M., Berkes, F. and Folke, C. (1993) 'Indigenous knowledge for biodiversity conservation', *Ambio*, vol 22, no. 2, pp. 151–156.

Gavin, M. C., Mccarter, J., Mead, A., Berkes, F., Stepp, J. R., Peterson, D. and Tang, R. (2015) 'Defining biocultural approaches to conservation', *Trends in Ecology and Evolution*, vol 30, no. 3, pp. 140–145.

Grey, S. and Patel, R. (2015) 'Food sovereignty as decolonization: Some contributions from indigenous movements to food system and development politics', *Agriculture and Human Values*, vol 32, no. 3, pp. 431–444.

HLPE (2014) 'Note on critical and emerging issues for food security and nutrition' Prepared for the Committee on World Food Security (CFS), Rome.

HLPE (2015) 'Water for food security and nutrition', Report no 9, CFS, Rome.

HLPE (2017a) 'Sustainable forestry for food security and nutrition', Report no. 11, CFS, Rome.

HLPE (2017b) 'Nutrition and food systems', Report no. 11, CFS, Rome.

Indigenous Peoples' Consultation on the Right to Food (2002), 'Declaration of Atitlán'. Atitlán, Panajachel, Sololá, Guatemala, April 17–19.

Inter Agency Support Group (IASG) (2014) *Thematic Paper on Lands, Territories and Resources*. IASG, New York.

Kalafatic, C. (2013) 'Indigenous knowledge and sustainability: Strengthening collaborations and closing local-global gaps through a restorative economy of respect' in E. Simmons (ed.) *Indigenous Earth: Praxis and Transformation*. Theytus Books, Penticton.

Knuth, L. (2009) *The Right to Adequate Food and Indigenous Peoples: How Can the Right to Food Benefit Indigenous Peoples?*. FAO, Rome.

Koohafkan, P. and Cruz, M.J.D. (2011) 'Conservation and adaptive management of globally important agricultural heritage systems (GIAHS)', *Journal of Resources and Ecology*, vol 2, no. 1, pp. 22–28.

Kuhnlein, H.V., Erasmus, B. and Spigelski, D. (2009) *Indigenous Peoples' Food Systems: The Many Dimensions of Culture, Diversity and Environment for Nutrition and Health*. FAO, Rome.

Nabhan, G.P. (2016) *Enduring Seeds: Native American Agriculture and Wild Plant Conservation*. University of Arizona Press, Arizona.

Nadasdy, P. (2005) 'The anti-politics of TEK: The institutionalization of co-management discourse and practice', *Anthropologica*, vol 47, no. 2, pp. 215–232.

Niamir-Fuller, M., Kerven, C., Reid, R. and Milner-Gulland, E. (2012) 'Co-existence of wildlife and pastoralism on extensive rangelands: competition or compatibility?', *Pastoralism*, vol 2, no. 8, pp. 1–14.

Ooft, M. (2006) *United Nations Development Programme (UNDP) and Indigenous Peoples: Towards Effective Partnerships for Human Rights and Development*. UNDP, New York.

Oskal, A., Turi, J. M., Mathiesen, S. D. and Burgess, P. (2009) *EALÁT. Reindeer Herders Voice: Reindeer Herding, Traditional Knowledge and Adaptation to Climate Change and Loss of Grazing Lands*. International Centre for Reindeer Husbandry, Kautokeino.

Ostrom, E. (2010) 'Beyond markets and states: Polycentric governance of complex economic systems', *American Economic Review*, vol 100, no. 3, pp. 641–672.

Oviedo, G., Larsen, P.B. and Maffi, L.(2000) *Indigenous and Traditional Peoples of the World and Ecoregion Conservation: An Integrated Approach to Conserving the World's Biological and Cultural Diversity*, World Wide Fund For Nature (WWF), Gland.

Peters, E.J. (2003) 'Views of traditional ecological knowledge in co-management bodies in Nunavik, Quebec', *Polar Record*, vol 39, no. 1, pp. 49–60.

Pimbert, M.P. (2017) 'Democratizing knowledge and ways of knowing for food sovereignty, agroecology and biocultural diversity', in M.P. Pimbert (ed.) *Food Sovereignty, Agroecology and Biocultural Diversity*. Routledge, London.

Rural Advancement Foundation International (RAFI) (1999) 'Creators and conservers of biodiversity map', Annual report, RAFI, Pittsboro.

Robinson, M., De Souza, J. G., Maezumi, S. Y., Cárdenas, M., Pessenda, L., Prufer, K., Corteletti, R., Scunderlick, D., Mayle, F.E. and Blasis, P. (2018) 'Uncoupling human and climate drivers of late Holocene vegetation change in southern Brazil', *Scientific Reports*, vol 8, no. 7800, pp. 1–10.

Roy, D. (2012) 'Study on shifting cultivation and the socio-cultural integrity of Indigenous Peoples', Note by the secretariat, UN, New York.

Schnuttgen, S., Vacheron, F. and Martell, M. (2007) *UNESCO and Indigenous Peoples' Partnership to Promote Cultural Diversity*. UNESCO, New York.

Smith, L.T. (2013) *Decolonizing Methodologies: Research and indigenous peoples*. Zed Books Ltd, London.

Spak, S. (2005) 'The position of Indigenous knowledge in Canadian co-management organisations', *Anthropologica*, vol 47, no. 2, pp. 233–246.

Thrupp, L.A. (2000) 'Linking agricultural biodiversity and food security: The valuable role of agrobiodiversity for sustainable agriculture', *International Affairs*, vol 76, no. 2, pp. 283–297.

Toledo, V.M. (2001) 'Indigenous peoples and biodiversity',in S. Levin (ed) *Encyclopedia of Biodiversity*. Academic Press, Massachusetts, pp451–463.

Trosper, R. (2009) *Resilience, Reciprocity and Ecological Economics: Northwest Coast sustainability*. Routledge, London.

UN Department of Economic and Social Affairs (UNDESA) (2009) *State of the World's Indegenous Peoples*. UN, New York.

United Nations Permanent Forum on Indigenous Issues (UNPFII) (2004) 'The concept of indigenous peoples', Background paper for the workshop on data collection and disaggregation for indigenous peoples. UNFPII, New York.

UN General Assembly (UNGA) (1966) 'International Covenant on Economic, Social and Cultural Rights', Treaty Series, vol 993, UN, New York.

UN General Assembly UNGA (2015) 'International Covenant on Civil and Political Rights', Treaty Series, vol. 999, UN, New York.

UN General Assembly UNGA (2005) 'Right to Food', Interim Report of the Human Rights Council's Special Rapporteur on the Right to Food, UN, New York.

Vermeulen, S. J. and Dinesh, D. (2016) 'Measures for climate change adaptation in agriculture. Opportunities for climate action in agricultural systems', Breif, CGIAR, Wageningen.

Woodley, E., Crowley, E., De Pryck, J.D. and Carmen, A. (2006) 'Cultural indicators of Indigenous Peoples' food and agro-ecological systems', Paper jointly commissioned by FAO and the International Indian Treaty Council (IITC), with support from the Government of Norway and, indirectly, from the Christensen Fund. FAO, Rome.

World Resource Institute (WRI) in collaboration with United Nations Development Programme, United Nations Environment Programme, and World Bank (2005) *World Resources Report 2005: The Wealth of the Poor – Managing Ecosystems to Fight Poverty*. WRI, Washington DC.

PART III

Measurement and information systems

17

MEASURING FOOD INSECURITY

Carlo Cafiero

17.1 Introduction

In the current prevailing definition of food security, access to food is the pivotal aspect: food security is said to exist not simply if enough food is available, but when all people, at all times have *access* to sufficient safe and nutritious food for an active and healthy life (World Food Summit, 1996). In terms of data, evidence and monitoring, this has implied – at least since Sen's seminal work on poverty and famine (Sen, 1982) – a focus shift in food security assessments from the macro to the micro level and from questions of availability and supply to those of distribution and access (Maxwell, 1996; Jones *et al.*, 2013; Hendriks, 2016; Coates, 2015).

Often, the "household" or "individual" qualifiers are added to the expression "food security", to stress the tension between traditional measures of the adequacy of food supplies (FAO, 1975), and the fact that the ability to access food is an attribute of individuals. To determine whether access to food is "adequate" requires not only that there is sufficient availability, but also that the *distribution* of food across individuals or households is considered. To avoid confusion, this chapter proposes that the expression "food security" may still be applied at different levels and in different ways, as encompassing aspects ranging from adequacy of food supplies to absence of various forms of malnutrition, but that the term "food insecurity" – as used here – be interpreted and used with reference to individuals or small groups of individuals (such as households) to indicate a condition of inability to access food.

In this sense, food insecurity is clearly a measurable construct in terms of its *severity*. Individuals and households can be described as "more" or "less" food insecure than others, depending on the severity of their condition, and communities or populations can be evaluated in terms of the prevalence of individuals suffering from food insecurity, at given levels of severity. Classifications of households in groups of "mild", "moderate" and "severe" food insecurity classes, and the related estimates of the prevalence of food insecurity have long been used in food security assessments. However, before concluding that they are actually "measuring" food insecurity, two problems must be addressed that are still evident in recent discussions around food security indicators.

On the one hand, the complexity of the food insecurity problem and of the interconnections between the determinants and causes of food insecurity has presented challenges for the very definition of what is meant by "severity of food insecurity". Qualitative assessments based on triangulation of evidence and consensus building, such as the Integrated Food Security Phase Classification (IPC), discussed elsewhere in this book, have adopted definitions that point to different levels of severity, but which are not interpretable properly as "measures". On the other hand, recognising the "power of numbers" that accompanies quantification and measurement (as epitomised by the famous quote "If you can't measure it, you can't improve it" attributed to Peter Drucker) there have been many examples of *apparent quantification* through the construction of indexes, scores, or counts, that are often treated as if they were valid measures, even though no evidence exists that they are such (Cafiero *et al.,* 2014).

To contribute to a better-informed discussion, this chapter presents data and analytic approaches that can be used to actually *measure* the severity of food insecurity and to create *valid* food insecurity indicators. As recently pointed out by Frongillo *et al.* (2018), the validity issue and the related concept of reliability must take centre stage, when discussing indicators. Reliability is the result of the combination of two aspects (accuracy and precision) among which there may be trade-off so that no measure can ever be considered 100% reliable. As the validity of an indicator must always be discussed in relation to its intended use, the indicators most often currently used in food security assessments will be reviewed here with the objective of providing a reasoned guide to their choice, depending on the context in which the assessment is conducted.

This chapter draws on, integrates and extends recent reviews by Jones *et al.* (2013), Leroy *et al.* (2015) and Coates (2015), including a discussion of the innovations that have occurred in this field since 2015, as presented by Sassi (2018). However, this chapter also makes a much more explicit reference to the formal *statistical* properties of the indicators and to the implications that such properties should have on their use to inform decision making. These considerations have received little attention in food security discussions; perhaps because the most recent progress in the area of statistical measurement in the social sciences, especially as applied to food insecurity, has not yet permeated the profession. One main point made in this chapter is that, when choosing which indicator to use, considerations of *timeliness, cost effectiveness* and, especially, *ease of application* have dominated the choice thus far. Often, indicators have been selected and used without asking whether they possess the minimal set of properties needed to establish their *validity* and *reliability*, which should be fundamental aspects guiding the choice (Cafiero *et al.,* 2014; Coates, 2015).

The chapter is organised as follows. Section 1 briefly deals with the availability element of food security and draws on Cafiero (2013). Section 17.2 introduces and discusses the concepts of validity and reliability as referred to in this chapter. By presenting a definition of validity as conceptually distinct from reliability, the discussion here differs in the way in which these concepts have been discussed by food security analysts to date (for example, by Frongillo, 1999; Coates, 2004 or in Leroy *et al.*, 2015). Sections 17.3 and 17.4 present existing indicators based, respectively, on food consumption (Section 17.3) and food insecurity experiences (Section 17.44) data, discussing the respective merits and drawbacks in terms of validity, reliability, cost effectiveness and timeliness. The discussion in Section 17.3, in particular, highlights the interplay between conceptual/theoretical and practical/empirical considerations to be made when defining an indicator of the adequacy of food consumption. It shows, for example, how determining the adequacy of dietary energy consumption at individual, household and population levels is not as trivial as it may intuitively appear and why it calls for the need to embed sufficient statistical sophistication in the analyses to avoid dangerous, but easy to make, mistakes in drawing conclusions from available data. Section 17.4 presents the opportunity to introduce the concept of *latent trait measurement* as addressed by Item Response Theory (IRT) (an area being rapidly established as "the" way to conduct proper measurement in the social sciences). See, for example, the discussion in Bond and Fox, 2015), and to illustrate how it has been applied to food insecurity measurement (see also Nord (2014).

Section 17.5 provides a summary to facilitate a comparative assessment of the indicators of food access discussed in the chapter that may be used to guide the selection of the most appropriate indicator in each of a number of possible analytic contexts, ranging from emergency assessments, to policy and program evaluation, to long term, structural monitoring.

17.2 Food availability assessments

The two main sources of food availability data that are global in scope are FAO's Food Balance Sheets (FBS), and the Production, Supply and Demand Online system maintained by the Foreign Agricultural Service of the United States Department of Agriculture (USDA see https://apps.fas.usda.gov/psdonline/app/index.html). Both databases provide estimates of annual production, trade and utilization of agricultural commodities at the level of single countries and territories (Cafiero, 2013). By compiling complete accounts of supply and utilization of food commodities, both systems provide an assessment of food available for human consumption, in the country as a whole, in a specific year.

17.2.1 FAO food balance sheets

FAO's FBS (see http://www.fao.org/faostat/en/#data/FBS for the publicly available data) seek to present a comprehensive picture of the pattern of a country's

172 Carlo Cafiero

food supply during a specified reference period. Conceptually, a FBS shows, for each food item (i.e. each primary commodity and a number of processed commodities potentially available for human consumption), the source of supply and its utilisation. The supply available during a period is derived from the total quantity of foodstuffs produced in a country added to the total quantity imported and adjusted for any change in stocks that may have occurred since the beginning of the reference period. On the utilization side, an account is made of the quantities exported, fed to livestock, used as seed stock, processed for non-food uses, and lost during storage and transportation.

Subtracting all other uses from the total supply, the quantities available for human consumption at the retail level are obtained as a balance. The per capita supply of each food item available for human consumption is then obtained by dividing the respective quantity by the related data on the population actually consuming it. Data on per caput food supplies are expressed in terms of quantity and – by applying appropriate food composition factors for all primary and processed products – also in terms of energy, protein and fat content.

The FAO currently compiles balance sheets for about 180 countries throughout the world and on a large number of primary food commodity and food items. Of course, the amount of data needed to complete them is huge, and not all of it is available through official sources. For that reason, both official and unofficial data available in the Statistics Division and other Units concerned in FAO are used. In addition, a large number of missing data points are estimated by FAO on the basis of agricultural and household surveys and other information, as well as on technical expertise available in house.

Ideally, the basic data required for the preparation of food balance sheets should be obtained from the same source. In principle, each country should have a comprehensive agricultural and food statistical system, recording all current information relating to each component of the food balance sheet. Definitions of the data series should correspond to those of the food balance sheet concepts and the information available should be consistent, at least with respect to measurement unit and time reference period. However, in practice, despite considerable technical assistance efforts made by the FAO and other organisations, an ideal statistical system does not exist in many countries, and the problems of harmonisation of standards and definitions still constrain full cross country comparison. Even in the few, mainly developed, countries with sophisticated reporting procedures for agricultural statistics, the available data do not always meet all criteria.

As a result, the basic data used come from a variety of sources and the quality and coverage vary considerably among countries and commodities. Production and trade data are part of the ongoing national official statistics. They are based either on direct enquiries or records, or are estimated by Government agencies and reported upon request. Where available, information on stock changes comes from marketing authorities, the processing industry or from farmer stock surveys. Information on industrial uses is obtained from industrial/manufacturing censuses/surveys. Feed and seeding rates are obtained from cost of production surveys or are estimated by the Government agencies concerned. Losses occurring in industrial processing are also obtained from manufacturing surveys.

Since they are obtained from different sources, the basic data may reveal inconsistencies. Inconsistencies may be due to different definitions of the basic concepts; to different time reference and estimation or to missing data. Adjustments and imputations are thus necessary in order to maintain a sufficient degree of consistency, completeness and reliability of the resulting food balances.

1.2.2. Reliability of FBS

Assessing the reliability of FBS data is not easy. There are many considerations to be made, and no generally valid conclusion can be drawn for all countries and commodities.

Conceptual problems frequently arise with respect to coverage/representativeness of the basic data. For example:

- Production statistics are mostly confined to commercialised major food crops only. Non-commercial or subsistence production (i.e. home produce and food obtained from hunting, fishing and gathering by households for their own consumption), are usually not included in official statistics and are very difficult to estimate. This might be an appreciable part of total production in some countries.
- Manufacturing surveys may cover only industrial establishments of larger size, missing small-scale producers.
- Information on commercial stocks may be available from official or marketing authorities, factories, wholesalers and retailers, but inventories of catering establishments, institutions and households may not be available.
- Information on waste in industrial processing may be available, but waste/ losses during storage, transportation or on quantities intentionally discarded for the purpose of price control or epidemic disease control may not be available.

In all these cases, even though the basic data are reliable, some adjustments are required to adapt the basic data to food balance sheets concepts/coverage. Of greater concern, is the incompleteness and inaccuracy of basic data; even when gathered from official sources. For example:

- Production statistics may not be available for all commodities and, where available, they are not always reliable. This may be because patterns of production and utilization of some crops in developing countries may be rather complex, making it difficult to estimate the actual production. The estimation of production for some crops is further complicated because they are continuously harvested or harvested or irregular intervals over a long period of time (e.g. cassava and certain fruits and vegetables).
- Certain kinds of food may not be covered by food balance sheets because they are not included in national production statistics. For example meat from

174 Carlo Cafiero

game, wild animals and insects may be excluded for this reason. In many developing countries, this meat may form a substantial part of the consumption of animal protein. Also, major food crops may be grown in mix-planted fields of bewildering complexity, eluding the possibility of accurate production assessments by governmental officers.

The reliability of official production data may also be questionable. They may be underestimated when based on farmers' reporting as farmers may equate production with tax collection. On the other hand, reliable information on pre-harvest food grain losses caused by pests and diseases are not usually available, making assessments based on planted areas rather imprecise.

In most countries, import and export data may be accurate but in some countries there may be significant amounts of unrecorded trade across national boundaries. Moreover, import and export transactions may not receive equal attention from the customs administration as taxes or quantitative controls are generally concentrated on import items rather than exports. As a consequence, the reliability of export data may be questionable.

One common problem is that the availability of basic data on the feed, seed and industrial/manufacture use components of food crops are rather limited. Seeding rates for crops are fairly well established in most countries, but when the quantities fed to animals have to be estimated, many aspects must be considered. Feeding practices vary from country to country according to the quantity and quality of pastures, the degree to which rearing is intensive, the prices of feedstuffs, etc. In addition, the quality of grain and other feedstuffs fed to livestock may vary from one year to the next. Cost of production and manufacturing surveys, which are the appropriate sources of such data, have not been regularly conducted in most developing countries. Even where surveys are conducted, their coverage is usually limited (e.g. cost of production surveys cover only a few major crops or do not cover livestock commodities, etc.).

Another crucial aspect for the relevance of FBS data for food security analysis is that official information on stock changes and losses/waste during storage and transportation are often virtually non-existent or, at best, only fractional in coverage, e.g. commercial stocks of some commodities may occasionally be available from official sources or marketing authorities.

Even if reliable figures on the total amount of stock held by governments and large private enterprises would be available, stocks held by small farmers and households during the reference period may not be covered.

To give a complete account of the food supply, all potentially edible commodities should be taken into account, regardless of whether they are actually eaten or used for non- food purposes. The definition of a complete list of potentially edible commodities does present virtually insurmountable difficulties – both conceptual and statistical. For practical purposes, therefore, a pragmatic list of commodities has typically been adopted. Consequently, the reliability of the balances may be very different across items for the same country.

The estimate of the total population is also a part of the official statistics.

The per capita estimate of each food commodity is obtained by dividing the estimate for food available for human consumption by the total population consuming it during the reference period. However, for many countries, the total population estimates may refer to the de jure population, i.e., the official legally resident population only. Thus, non-resident population, such as illegal immigrants, tourists, refugees, and foreign diplomatic personnel and their dependents, foreign armed forces, etc., are not included. This omission may constitute a considerable portion in some countries.

There are also problems related to the time-reference period used in preparing food balance sheets. Several 12-month periods, such as July/June, October/September, April/March, have been proposed and applied. However, none of these periods satisfactorily and uniformly covers the production of all agricultural commodities, their trade and domestic utilization. It can be assumed that there is no single 12-month period that is fully suitable for recording supply and utilization for all products. The decision of taking the calendar year time-reference period (January–December) has been made mostly for accounting purposes, but may have consequences in the determination, for example, of the levels of stock variations.

All these problems raise concern on the reliability of the detailed information that is provided through a typical FBS, some of which seem not to have been recognised if the data is to be used to inform sophisticated analysis, for example in the nutritional value of the diet.

17.2.3 Uses of FBS data

The main use of the annual FBSs, tabulated regularly over a period of years, is to show the trends in the overall national food supply; reveal changes that may have taken place in the types of food available for consumption; reveal the extent to which the food supply of the country as a whole is adequate in relation to nutritional requirement and compare these trends across countries. Observed trends are also useful in developing projections of future food supply, setting targets for agricultural production and trade; for establishing relationships between national food supplies and various other dimensions of food security and development, as well as for evaluating national food policies.

Arguably, FAO FBSs provide the best assessment of food supply worldwide – a fundamental basis for policy analysis and decision-making for food security. For this reason, international organisations, governments, planners and researchers view them as a very important tool in determining whether a nation as a whole is moving towards adequate food supply. The FAO, in particular, has been using the average per capita caloric availability derived from FBS as an estimate of the mean food consumption for the assessment of undernourishment, a use that has not been exempt from criticisms (see Section 17.4.1 below).

Another useful indicator that can be derived from FBS data is the comparison of the quantities of food available for human consumption with those imported (the

176 Carlo Cafiero

food import dependency ratio), indicating the extent to which a country depends upon food imports. Similarly, the amount of food crops that is used for feeding livestock, in relation to total crop production indicates the degree to which primary food resources are used to produce animal feed. This is useful information for analysing livestock policies or patterns of agriculture.

These are all very important uses, which justifies the maintenance and continued improvement of the FBS System by FAO. It is important, however, to point also to what FBS data is not and what information they do not contain. For example, they do not give any indication of the differences that may exist in the diet consumed by different individuals or population groups, e.g. people of different socio-economic groups, ecological zones or geographical areas within a country. Neither do they provide information on seasonal variations in the total food supply. To obtain a complete picture of the distribution of the national food supply at various times of the year, across regions and among different groups of the population, different kinds of data would be needed. The best source of this is certainly food consumption surveys of the population.

In fact, the two sets of data – those from aggregate supply and those from consumption surveys – are complementary in many respects. There are, in fact, commodities for which a production estimate could best be based on estimated consumption as obtained from food consumption surveys rather than from official production statistics. However, there are commodities for which production, trade and utilization statistics could give a better nationwide consumption estimate than the data derived from food consumption surveys. Data obtained through household and food consumption surveys are often the preferred source of food consumption estimates to conduct analyses of covariates of the food consumption, as they provide also information on the people who are purchasing and eating the food, a type of information that is not available from food balance sheets.

Another warning should be raised on the use of FBS to provide information on specific components of the food supply. Even though the list of items covered is long, the information provided at the level of each individual item is likely to be less reliable than the one provided on aggregates such as the total calories. There are reasons to believe that the latter is much more reliable than other aggregates, such as the supply of micronutrients such as minerals and vitamins. Generally, FBSs are constructed for primary crops, livestock and fish commodities up to the first stage of processing in the case of crops and to the second (and sometimes the third) stage of processing in the case of livestock and fish products. The reason for the restriction on the higher stages of processing is the difficulty in obtaining data for all the varied forms of processed products and, even more difficult, in tracing the components of the processed composite products. Reliable quantities of food availability can be estimated only at the level of primary commodities (say "wheat" or "bananas") with no possibility of knowing whether, say, wheat is made available to consumers as refined flour or whole grains or if it is enriched or not. While these may make little difference in estimating the average caloric content (to the extent that the proper nutrient conversion factor is use) it become much more problematic in estimating contents of micronutrients such as minerals and vitamins.

17.3 Validity and reliability of food insecurity measures: theoretical and empirical considerations

The value of an indicator of access to food depends on the extent to which it can reveal if and where there may problems in accessing food and which members of a population are facing this food insecurity. What is adequate food access, and at which point inadequacy requires intervention, can be normatively defined in different ways, depending on the context, so there is no question that different indicators may be preferred in different situations. It is obvious, for example, that in gathering evidence needed to guide emergency interventions, rapid assessments are needed to detect life-threatening conditions in time. More lengthy, sophisticated tools, capable of providing a more nuanced view of the severity of the food insecurity condition of households or individuals, would be less helpful due to the time they take to be applied. Nevertheless, the choice should always be of indicators that are proven to be *valid* and founded on a careful assessment of trade-offs existing between *reliability* and *practical feasibility* (Cafiero *et al.*, 2014).

As pointed out by Cafiero *et al.* (2014), a review of the literature on food security indicators of the last few decades reveals that, generally, limited attention has been devoted to the formal properties of *validity* and *reliability* of the indicators most commonly used in this domain, a gap that this chapter aims to contribute towards filling. Here, I assume that a measure is *valid* only if its values reflect the characteristics (magnitude) of what it is intended to measure. This implies that the numbers used as "measures" are in a strict relation with the magnitude of the attribute they are intended to measure. Apart from possible "noise" or "disturbances", the readings produced by the measurement tool should change if, and only if, there is a change in the class, rank, relative or absolute magnitude of the attribute being measured. *Reliability*, in turn, is the result of the combination of direction, magnitude and frequency of measurement errors that may be induced by everything other than the magnitude of the attribute of interest.

The problem with measuring food insecurity (understood as people's specific inability to access food) is that there is no other way to measure it and therefore there is no "gold standard", as pointed out by many others who have discussed the issue (Jones *et al.*, 2013; Coates, 2015). This implies that comparisons of the values of the food insecurity measure against measures of other attributes such as poverty or malnutrition – a practice referred to as "concurrent validation" – cannot be considered a proper way to "validate", unless one is willing to lose the distinction that makes food insecurity a construct of its own. There is no level of correlation between, say, poverty and food insecurity, or between food insecurity and malnutrition, that can be used as reference to conclude for validity. Concurrent validation can, at best, provide qualitative indications that the measure of food insecurity puts the households where one would expect them to be, based on the indirect information available on the other dimensions of social and physical wellbeing.

178 Carlo Cafiero

The lack of a gold standard is a problem shared by many areas of human and social sciences, which makes measurement in these domains a distinctively different proposition than as used in the realm of physical of biological sciences. Fortunately, recent methods developed to measure so-called "latent traits" have provided a solution. However, they require that, to speak of a measure, two conditions should hold:

a   The attribute being measured (i.e., the "measurand") is unambiguously described;
b   A model is defined that links the values of the observable data to the magnitude of the attribute being measured.

As the measurand is unobservable, the model in (b) can only be set in terms of the probability to observe what we observe, given the magnitude of the attribute. Then, it is possible to assess formally the properties of *validity* and *reliability* of the measures obtained as the results from applying the model to the available data and assessing the extent to which the data fit the model.

A comprehensive treatment of measurement theory and of the implications for defining measures in the social science realm is way beyond the scope of this chapter. The interested reader is referred to the three-volume series edited by Krantz *et al.* (2006), Suppes *et al.* (2006) and Luce *et al.* (2006). For a specific discussion of fundamental measurement in the social sciences, see Bond and Fox (2015).

Almost all household food insecurity indicators reviewed in the rest of this chapter are expressed as numerical variables, and almost always a clearly defined protocol is available to compute those variables in practice. However, while numbers can always be used to represent variables, not all numeric variables can be considered *measures*. What remains quite ambiguous is the definition of the measurand, without which any discussion of validity and reliability risk being ambiguous and futile.

These considerations may seem obvious, but they are rather telling, if used to reveal how loosely the term "measurement" is currently used in most food security assessments worldwide, and how questionable the conclusions are in terms of the "validity" of food security indicators. In many cases, the attribute being measured has not been specified narrowly enough to be uniquely determined, or no discussion is conducted on the possibility that the value of the indicator may change independently from changes in the attribute being measured. Recognising the possible presence of "noise" in the numbers used as measure (that is, of a residual uncertainty regarding the magnitude of the attribute being measured) is important, as it allows for distinguishing the issue of *validity* from that of *reliability*. In this sense, the validity question asks whether, when using an indicator to measure a certain attribute, one does it "right"; the reliability question, on the other hand, asks if one does it "well".

Statisticians are very aware of noise and residual uncertainty, what are called "measurement errors". Unfortunately, most manuals on food security assessment methodologies (see, for example, WFP, 2008, or Maxwell and Caldwell, 2008), while usually sufficiently detailed regarding how to construct the variables proposed as indicators, include only cursory discussion on, and no formal treatment of, possible measurement errors. The fact that in the social sciences, the lack of a gold standard measure for essentially unobservable (i.e., *latent*) attributes, makes such a discussion particularly difficult should not be an excuse to neglect a serious consideration of how to assess, and possibly address, measurement errors when proposing an indicator.

The main lesson derived from the application of statistical inference principles to food insecurity measurement, is that the only legitimate conclusions we can draw are those framed in terms of *probability*. When we say that a household or an individual is food insecure, based on observable data, what we truly express is only our belief regarding the (hopefully high) likelihood that the statement is true, conditional on the available evidence. If there is substantial residual uncertainty around the measures, use of the indicator at household or individual level requires greater attention. A careful survey design and the proper implementation of the data collection methods may help to reduce the presence of systematic errors and to guarantee sufficiently reliable measures of the *prevalence* of food insecurity in the reference population. However, the use of the indicator to single out the food insecure households or individuals should still be avoided, as misclassification due to measurement errors would be very likely.

In the following sections, some of the most common indicators based on food consumption and on food insecurity experiences will be described with reference to whether the two conditions needed to consider them as measures (that is, the unambiguous definition of the "measurand" and the specification model that links the measure to the data) are fulfilled. A discussion on validity and reliability considerations is included, to be contrasted with considerations related to cost and practical feasibility.

17.4 Indicators of access to food based on food consumption data

The first and most obvious way to think about monitoring whether people have access to adequate food, has focused on collecting and analysing evidence on food *consumption*. Intuitively, as noted also by at least one well-known voice in the development field, monitoring whether access to food is adequate should be easy: it would suffice to "take a sample of individuals that is representative of the population and determine how many are not eating enough" (Gates, 2013, p. 32). Yet, determining if someone is eating enough is not as simple as it looks, as there are subtle considerations to be made when defining the two terms of the equation: the measure of food consumption and the threshold used to establish adequacy.

17.4.1 Measuring food consumption

In addition to provide nutrients, the consumption of food by humans serves also other individual and, most importantly, social functions. These considerations make it clear that how to aggregate quantities of different food items in a meaningful

180 Carlo Cafiero

measure depends on which aspect of food consumption one is interested in, and that this entails a decision about the *operational definition* of food consumption whose adequacy is being measured.

The most obvious choice – namely, to treat food simply as the source of energy needed to sustain life – is too narrow to be able to capture the full spectrum of food consumption adequacy, neglecting, for example, aspects of the quality of the diet that determine its overall nutritional value. The consideration has led, for example, to the definition of different constructs related to *quality* of the diet, usually associated with the *diversity* or qualitative composition of the diet rather than with actual quantities of single nutrients.

Another important aspect linked to the operational definition of food consumption that gets embedded in an indicator is the fact that daily food consumption – no matter how defined – can vary within rather broad ranges, without necessarily implying detectable negative consequences. This means that any assessment of adequacy should be based on food consumption observed over a sufficiently long period, to be able to distinguish between *occasional* and *habitual* consumption. What really matters is the adequacy of the latter, even though often we can only observe the former. This leads to an important feature of food consumption adequacy assessments, namely, that they *can only be conducted in probabilistic terms*. Even if we were interested in assessing the adequacy of food consumption of a single individual, for which we have repeated observations of daily food consumption, the assessment will be conditional on the analyst's ability to correctly estimate the level of habitual food consumption from observations of occasional food consumption. As this will necessarily imply a certain degree of uncertainty, the resulting measure of adequacy (even if defined in nominal terms, as a binary variable) will be de-facto expressed in terms of its probability distribution.

17.4.2 Choice of threshold

Once the issue of how to express food consumption has been solved, one still needs to operationalise the second term of the equation, namely the threshold used in establishing its adequacy (or inadequacy). This is also a non-trivial issue. To illustrate, we focus on the definition of food consumption in terms of its dietary energy or of nutrient content (as opposed, for example, of monetary values). The first consideration is that human dietary energy (and most nutrient) requirements are not fixed but depend, in obvious and not so obvious ways, on the sex, age, body mass, physical activity level and other physiological characteristics of the individual. In establishing recommended intake levels, nutritionists take care to explain that they refer to specific groups of individuals (e.g., "adult men, engaged in moderate physical activity", or "women of reproductive age", and so on) and for good reasons: what is adequate for one person may not be adequate for another.

Not knowing the specific characteristics of a given individual following the dietary guidelines, recommended levels of energy and/or nutrients are set by taking into consideration the distribution of requirements within the reference group of individuals and balancing the risks associated with both possible insufficient and excessive intakes. Whenever there is no harm in possible slight excess consumption of a nutrient, for example, the recommended intake level is set close to the maximum of the range of normal requirements for the group, so that the probability of inadequate consumption, when following the recommended intake, is minimised. When instead there is potential harm from either excess or insufficient consumption (as it is the case for dietary energy or iron) the recommended level of intake is set at the average requirement. This makes sense, as it is unknown which *specific* individual will follow the guidelines, and the probability of promoting inadequate consumption is minimised by suggesting consuming amounts equal to the average. Notice, however, that this does not imply that every member of the group consuming less than the recommended level will be consuming insufficient amounts, or that every member of the group consuming more than the recommended level, will be having excessive consumption. If the range of requirements within the group is wide, there may be a significant number of individuals who consume less or more than the average, but for whom intake is perfectly adequate.

This has the important consequence that when the objective of an empirical analysis is to establish the percentage of individuals in a group with inadequate intake, *the thresholds to be used to establish insufficient or excessive intake must be conceptually distinct from the recommended intake levels*, and be close to, respectively, the lower and the upper end of the range of requirements.

With these considerations in mind, we can now discuss some of the most commonly used indicators of access to food, based on food consumption data. In the following sections, each indicator will be only briefly described, as a full treatment would exceed the scope of this chapter. References are provided in each case, for more in-depth descriptions of each indicator.

17.4.3 Adequacy of nutrient intake from the analysis of individual dietary intake survey data

When data from individual dietary intake surveys are available, indicators of the risk of inadequacy of nutrient intake in a population are computed by calculating the *probability of inadequate intake*. The two methods to obtain the estimate, described as the "probability approach" and the "EAR cut point method" (National Research Council, 1986; Carriquiry, 1999; Gibson, 2005) are based on a comparison of the distribution of *usual* nutrient intake levels with the distribution of nutrient requirements in the same population group. As no information is usually available on the usual intake and the requirements of each individual in the sample, the methods cannot be used to identify the actual individuals who are at risk of inadequacy, but only to determine the proportion of the population at risk. Both methods require that a reliable estimate of the usual daily intake level is available for each individual in a representative sample of the population and that the distribution of nutrient requirements across members of the same population is known. See Gibson (2005) for a comprehensive treatment of this topic.

182 Carlo Cafiero

Then, *assuming that intakes and requirements are independent* (that is, that the estimated usual intake level for an individual does not carry information on that same individual requirement), the estimated probability of inadequacy in the population is obtained by first computing the probability of inadequacy associated with the usual intake level of each individual in the sample, and then averaging them up over the sample.

$$PoI = \sum_{i=1}^{N} w_i \times PoI_i = \sum_{i=1}^{N} \left(w_i \times \left(1 - \int_{-\infty}^{x_i} f(r)dr \right) \right)$$

Where: EAR is the estimated average requirement for the group, w_i are sampling weights and x_i the estimates of usual intake for each individual in the sample, and $f(r)$ denotes the probability density function of requirements in the population group. When $f(r)$ is symmetric, the formula reduces to:

$$PoI = \sum_{i=i}^{N} (w_i \times I\{x_i < EAR\})$$

Where $I\{x_i < EAR\}$ is an indicator function taking the value one, if $x_i < EAR$, and zero otherwise. This simply amounts to counting the (weighted) number of cases in the sample for which usual intake is estimated to be below the EAR.

There is no doubt regarding the validity of these indicators, as the specific attribute being measured (i.e., the *risk* of nutrient intake inadequacy in the population) and the normative basis on which to base the assessment (i.e., human nutrient requirements as defined by nutrition experts) are very clearly described. Reliability, on the other hand, strongly depends on the quality of individual dietary intake data and on the accurate design of the survey used to collect them (see the discussion in Chapters 4–7 of Gibson, 2005). Given the many possible sources of both random and systematic measurement errors, collecting sufficiently precise individual dietary intake data is a costly endeavour, requiring skilled enumerators, which contributes to explaining the relative paucity and low frequency of available large scale, nationally representative datasets. The Global Individual Food consumption data Tool (GIFT) initiative (www.fao.org/gift-individual-food-consumption/) provides an assessment of existing individual food consumption data sets available worldwide.

For the formulas described above to be correct, usual intakes and requirement must be statistically independent (an assumption that does not apply to dietary energy, as there are many reasons why individual dietary energy consumption is expected to be correlated with individual's dietary energy requirement). This has led nutritionists to advise against the application of these indicators to measure the inadequacy of dietary energy consumption (see Carriquiry, 1999 and Gibson, 2005, Section 8.3). We will return on this point in the following section when discussing the use of food consumption data collected with household surveys.

17.4.4 Adequacy of dietary energy consumption from the analysis of household survey data

The scarcity of large-scale individual dietary intake surveys, particularly in the developing world, has led to the identification of alternative sources of food consumption data for food security assessments. In many countries, the main sources of food consumption data in the population are household consumption surveys (HCS) often designed to inform poverty assessments and living conditions studies (FAO, 1977, 1908, 1981, 1983, 1988, 1993a, 1993b). These surveys provide information on the food that households acquire for their own consumption, over a certain reference period, through recording expenditures on and, often, quantities of different food items, which can be used to derive some food security indicators (Sibrian, 2008; Moltedo *et al.* 2014). Although there is often no explicit indication of whether the food acquired by a household is actually consumed by its members, the quantities of, or expenditures on each food item can be converted into the equivalent dietary energy and nutrient content, summed-up and divided by the number of days in the reference period and by the number of household members to obtain rough estimates of the *average, per capita, apparent daily consumption* in each surveyed household (q_i). The distribution of q_i across households is, then, used to derive indicators on the adequacy of food consumption in the population.

17.4.4.1 The "2100 kcal" approach

Over the years, many researchers and institutions have proposed using household survey data to assess the proportion of the population with food consumption inadequacy. In most cases, they have done it by suggesting a rather naïve approach, in which the estimate is obtained as the proportion of households which report average, per caput, apparent daily dietary energy consumption below a given threshold often set at 2100 kcal (Smith, Alderman, and Aduayom, 2006; Smith and Subandoro, 2007). We identify these methods as based on the "2100 kcal" approach because in choosing the threshold, reference is often made to the average dietary energy requirement (or recommended daily dietary energy intake level) for individuals of a certain group (such as the 2100 kcal), which 'would cover the energy needs of a "typical" population, assuming standard population distribution, body size, ambient temperature, pre-emergency nutritional status and a light physical activity level of 55% above basal metabolic rate for males and 56% for females (UNHCR/WFP, 1997).

There are two fundamental problems with such an approach, which are likely to generate significantly biased estimates of the actual prevalence of dietary energy inadequacy in a population. The first, as already noted, is that in estimating the percentage of individuals in a group that have insufficient intake, one has to refer to the lower end of the range of requirements that can be applied to that group, and not to the average. The reason is that, by referring to the average, one neglects the fact that there may be individuals who should not be counted among the

184 Carlo Cafiero

"undernourished", even if they report food consumption lower than the average requirement because those are people with lower than average requirements. The presumption that "misclassification errors" resulting from referring to the average might cancel out (as there may also be some among those with consumption larger than requirements, who are actually undernourished) is misleading, as it fails to recognise that the probability of inadequate consumption is a decreasing function of dietary energy consumption levels and therefore it is higher for those on the left than for those on the right of any of any threshold.

The second problem is that estimating the average, per capita, daily dietary energy consumption level in each household from a household consumption survey generates a rather noisy proxy of the average habitual daily energy consumption. If not treated, measurement errors will inflate the variance of the estimated distribution of habitual consumption, and therefore increase the probability mass under the left tail of the distribution, overestimating inadequacy, irrespective of where the threshold is set (see Wiesmann *et al.*, 2009, p.13).

From this discussion, it should be evident that indicators constructed as the percentage of households reporting per capita apparent dietary energy consumption below recommended levels of dietary energy intake lack substantive validity as indicators of dietary energy consumption inadequacy. Even if, in some cases, the estimates obtained seem plausible (as the estimates presented in Smith *et al.*, 2006 for 12 countries in Sub-Saharan Africa), they do so because of two mistakes somehow counterbalancing each other. The overestimation induced by referring to the average requirement as a threshold is somewhat counterbalanced by the underestimation due to applying requirements for light physical activity only, an operational assumption that might be read as implying that people are only entitled to amounts of food that would permit minimal levels of activity.

The problems with the principles behind this type of indicator remained unnoticed except for cases in which the availability of relatively long time series of assessments for the same population has made it evident that the indicator failed to reflect the progress known to have been achieved over the years. For example, a report on MDG progress in Indonesia (Alisjahbana, 2012), reported that, based on data from the SUSENAS (the country's large-scale annual household living standard measurement survey) the percentage of households reporting average dietary energy consumption below 2000 kcal had fallen from 64.21% in 1990 to 60.03% in 2011, a reduction of only 6.7% its initial value, over 21 years. At the same time, the percentage of children under five years of age who are underweight had been reduced by more than 42%, from 31.0% in 1989, to 17.9 in 2010.

17.4.4.2 The FAO approach

These incorrect methods of using food consumption data from household surveys to generate dietary energy inadequacy estimates gained popularity, even while another method, more solidly based on theoretical and empirical considerations, had been available for several years. FAO introduced estimates of the prevalence of undernourishment (PoU) in the world in 1974 and sketched the essence of how the estimates could be obtained using household survey data (FAO, 1975, see the Annex to Chapter 3). The method has been constantly refined and applied by FAO to produce PoU estimates, generating, *inter alia*, the figures used as a reference to set the very first global target to reduce hunger in the world at the World Food Summit in 1996, and Target 1C of the Millennium Development Goals. More recently, the PoU has been included in the list of official indicators for the SDGs, specifically under Target 2.1. (For a detailed description of the method as applied by FAO, see FAO 1996, Appendix 3 and the series of *The State of Food Insecurity in the World* reports from 2011 to 2015).

The FAO method addresses both the problem related to the correlation between dietary energy consumption and requirements (which prevents the application of the probability approach to the analysis of dietary energy adequacy from individual dietary intake data) and the "noise" in food consumption data from household surveys. It achieves this by relying on a statistical model to represent the distribution of habitual daily dietary energy consumption for the *average individual* as a statistical device used to represent the population in both dimensions of dietary energy consumption and dietary energy requirements. In essence, it recognises that even in a perfectly fed population, there would be variability in the levels of habitual dietary energy consumption, reflecting differences in requirements mainly associated with differences in body mass, even among healthy individuals of the same sex and age class. As values of the Body Mass Index (BMI) ranging from 19 to 25 cannot be deemed unhealthy, one must recognise that, even for an individual of given sex, age, height and physical activity level, dietary energy requirements may vary, depending on her or his "ideal" (and unobservable) BMI. This implies that *individual energy requirements must always be defined over a range*, extending from a minimum to a maximum, which can be computed based on the sex, age, and height of the individual. In moving from individuals to a population, a range of requirements can also be computed for the "average" individual representing the entire population, by averaging the specific minima and maxima across the different population groups in terms of sex, age, and – if the available information allows it – physical activity levels.

In formal terms, once an estimate of the probability density function for habitual daily dietary energy consumption for the average individual, $f(x)$, has been obtained (from the household survey data and/or any other suitable source of information on food consumption in the population), the prevalence of undernourishment is computed as

$$PoU = \int_{-\infty}^{MDER} f(x)dx$$

where MDER is the lower bound of the range of requirements for the average individual in the population.

The *validity* of the PoU indicator stands on the careful considerations of the nutritional principles used in informing its definition. That alone, however, cannot guarantee

186 Carlo Cafiero

that the *reliability* of the estimates is sufficiently high, especially when the assessment is conducted at disaggregated levels and has to rely on small samples to estimate the parameters of the $f(x)$ distribution (particularly its coefficient of variation), or when insufficient data is available to characterise the relevant population in terms of sex, age, height and physical activity levels.

FAO typically reports PoU estimates at the national level only and as three-year moving averages, to reduce the potential impact of errors in estimating the annual average dietary energy consumption level from FBSs. Even though the availability of household surveys collecting food consumption data has increased considerably over the last few decades, there are still many questions regarding the possibility to obtain from them sufficiently precise estimates of habitual dietary energy consumption. More research needs to be conducted to evaluate the direction and extent of bias induced by low quality food consumption data (Smith, Dupriez and Troubat, 2014) and to suggest methods to address the most relevant issues (FAO and the World Bank, 2018). This is particularly relevant if the analyses are intended to provide assessments for subnational population groups.

17.4.5 Indicators of dietary diversity based on individual food consumption data

In part because of the difficulty and the time needed to collect sufficiently reliable quantitative individual food consumption data, and in part because of the fact that the nutritional value of a diet depends not only on the adequacy of consumption of single nutrients, but also on their combination, nutritionists have long explored the possibility of defining indicators based on the concept of *dietary diversity*. Dietary diversity explores the consumption of foods belonging to different food groups. For a detailed treatment, see Kennedy *et al.* (2010a) and, more recently, FAO and FHI360 (2016).

The rationale for such indicators is that the risk for a variety of micronutrient deficiencies is high when consuming low-quality diets, made up of only few items (Arimond *et al.*, 2010) and that young children and women of reproductive age are particularly susceptible to such risks. These considerations led to the development of a Minimum Dietary Diversity indicator for Children aged 6–23 months (MDD-C) (WHO, 2006) and later to the Women's Dietary Diversity Score (WDDS), to be used for women of reproductive age (Arimond *et al.* 2010; Kennedy *et al.* 2010a). Recently, the WDDS has been replaced by the Minimum Dietary Diversity for Women (MDD-W) indicator (FAO and FHI 360, 2016).

WDDS was originally defined as the number of different food groups represented in the list of food items that women reported having consumed in the past 24 hours (FAO, 2013). Based on a list of nine different food groups, the score would range from 0 to 9. It was originally meant to be treated as a *quantitative* measure, which could be used to identify individuals with different degrees of dietary quality. However, attempts at validating the WDDS as an invariant measure of dietary quality have failed, as it has proven impossible to find a consistent set of WDDS thresholds to identify classes of dietary quality across different population groups.

It seems clear now that the proper way to interpret individual dietary diversity scores is as indicators of dietary quality meant to reflect one key dimension of diet quality: micronutrient adequacy. The definition of the indicator must include the list of food groups considered and the threshold used to classify respondents into just two classes of individuals with "low" or "minimally adequate" dietary diversity. In defining the MDD-W (definition of food groups and associated threshold) the criterion has been to identify the combination that would best predict the mean probability of adequacy computed with reference to 11 micronutrients, across nine datasets which included sufficiently reliable nutrient intake data from women in reproductive age from Bangladesh, Burkina Faso, Mali, Mozambique, Philippines and Uganda (Martin-Prével *et al.*, 2015). The conclusion is that MDD-W can be considered a valid indicator to compute the percentage of women of reproductive age in a population with "low" dietary diversity, meaning that they are expected to have larger than average probability of suffering from micronutrient deficiencies. The indicator is computed by counting the proportion of cases with a score of less than 5.

However, a careful reading of the validation study reveals that the criteria to judge "reasonable" association with the mean probability of inadequacy were generous and that the strengths of the MDD-W indicators are not its measurement properties. While it can be used as a proxy to capture overall micronutrient adequacy in national and subnational assessments – including to compare with previous assessments in the same populations (so long as survey timing accounts for seasonality) – the indicator should not be used to screen individuals for selection for interventions, nor to identify individuals at risk for poor intakes. (FAO and FHI360, 2016). Very similar considerations can be made for the Minimum Dietary Diversity Indicator for infants and young children (WHO, 2006).

17.4.6 Indicators of dietary diversity at the household level

Although the concept of diversity as an indicator of dietary quality logically applies to the diets of individuals, indicators of dietary diversity at household level have also been proposed as generic indicators of "food security" (Hoddinott and Yohannes, 2002). The main motivation was to find ways to obtain information on the household's ability to access food in a relatively easy and inexpensive way, as an alternative to conducting more complete food consumption studies. In an initial validation study, using linear regression techniques, the number of unique food items reported as having been consumed in the household over a certain reference period was tested as a predictor of other indicators obtained from the data collected in the same survey. The reference indicators were:

- household, per capita, total consumption expenditure (a measure of real income, arguably one of the determinants, but a rather indirect way of capturing the ability to access food) and
- household, per capita, dietary energy availability (as described above, a poor proxy of actual dietary energy intake of household members), the latter also divided into two components, as derived from staples and non-staples.

The results showed that the number of unique food items were consistently associated with the households' proxy of real income, and somehow associated with total dietary energy consumption, but again, these results do not provide solid evidence that dietary diversity scores might constitute a valid *measure* of access to food. The authors considered their results as evidence that household dietary diversity could be used as a proxy for dietary energy consumption. However, there is a concrete possibility that the fact that "increases in dietary diversity are associated with increases in the number of calories consumed from non-staples", is simply a consequence of how the variables included in the analysis were computed (Hoddinott and Yohannes, 2002, p. 22).

In the type of surveys used for the analysis, short food item lists may miss some of the food items consumed; it is then easy to predict that the more disaggregated the food list is, the more likely is that: (a) reported total dietary energy consumption would increase; and (b) relatively more of the reported consumption would come from non-staples. This might explain the consistent, statistically significant, yet *weak* correlation found between the two variables. Unfortunately, the number of food items included in the food items list in each of the surveys was not controlled for in the regression analyses.

Despite this, attempts at operationalising the concept of household dietary diversity into food security indicators have progressed and crystallised around two main products: The Household Dietary Diversity Score (HDDS) (Kennedy *et al.* 2010b) and the Food Consumption Score (FCS) (WFP, 2008), which have been applied in practice and used in food security assessments for several years now. The HDDS is a simple count of the number of food groups reported being consumed in the household in the previous 24 hours, while the FCS is a weighted sum of the frequency of consumption (how many days in the week) of different food groups reported at the household level.

One might have hoped that the benefit from having these simplified indicators would be to have many more datasets available and that many more validation studies would have been published. Unfortunately, this is not the case. Although there is mention of validation studies of the HDDS or the FCS in the manuals that FANTA and WFP provide for their use, an insufficient number of validation studies has been documented to allow an assessment of how robust the conclusions on validity are.

Reported evidence of validity (see for example WFP, 2008) still amounts to mentioning statistically significant, positive, but quite low correlations (in the order of 0.3) between, for example, the FCS and the per capita apparent dietary energy consumption levels of the same households. (See for example Table 6 in Kennedy *et al.* 2010b.) Almost invariably, a careful reading of the conclusions points to issues with using either the HDDS or the FCS alone as proxy measures of the ability of households to access food (Kennedy *et al.* 2010b; Lovon and Mathiassen, 2014), and suggest that they be best used in conjunction with other indicators when conducting food security assessments.

The lack of solid evidence on the validity of HDDS and FCS as food consumption measures is not surprising. The main problem when attempting validation of the HDDS and FCS is the ambiguity regarding what exactly they are meant to capture. On the one hand, reference to dietary diversity would suggest that they are measures of *dietary quality*. As they refer to food consumption at the household, not at the individual level, they cannot take into account both possible differences in the individual diets created by intra-household allocation of food and the fact that the actual dietary quality is conditional on the requirements of the specific household members. On the other hand, as already commented on, the positive, statistically significant, but low correlation that HDDS/FCS scores show with measures of dietary energy consumption, are insufficient to claim that they are good proxies for quantitative measures of household level food consumption.

In addition to not having a basis for evaluating their "absolute" validity, there is another quite serious concern regarding the use of HDDS and FCS in assessments intended to provide actionable evidence for intervention. Contrary to indicators based on quantitative measures of food consumption or self-reported food insecurity experiences (see below) there is no formal basis nor any empirical procedure through which the *reliability* of the classification they generate could be assessed. As there is no reference against which measurement errors could be evaluated, the analyst must take it as an act of faith that the value of the score obtained for each household is an unbiased measure of whatever it is that it is measuring, and that large measurement errors are rare.

Furthermore, while it is often suggested to treat these scores as continuous numerical variables (see for example WFP, 2008, pp. 8, 13 and 20), it should be evident that they are not, being at most discrete, *ordinal* measures. Compare this, for example, with the prevailing practice to report the "average" FCS in a group. Even if treated as a continuous variable, it is obvious that the FCS in highly non-linear, making the average a non-robust indicator of central tendency.

In conclusion, the only reasonable explanation for the popularity of the use of these indicators as proxy indicators of food consumption (or of food insecurity) must be found in the relative, apparent simplicity of their use, as neither validity nor sufficient reliability of the measures they provide for each specific application has been established yet.

17.5 Indicators of access to food based on self-reported behaviours and experiences

At the same time as dietary diversity started to be explored as the basis for compiling food security indicators, a different approach was also being pursued, based on the idea that food insecurity is characterised by experiences that people face, or behaviours (strategies) they engage in, that are quite typical and recurrent, so that, by observing them, one may infer on the presence and severity of the food insecurity condition.

Pioneering examples of these approaches are found in Radimer *et al.* (1990; 1992) and have been reviewed by Frongillo (1999). The seminal work by Radimer was a

190 Carlo Cafiero

qualitative study, based on interviews with women in upstate New York, which revealed the dimensions of their experience of food insecurity. Questions were developed (using the women's words) to capture those dimensions and used to form a quantitative survey instrument which was tested and validated (Campbell, 1991; Radimer *et al.* 1992). The findings from many other studies in the United States and several other countries have since shown how data on the self-reported occurrence of typical experiences contain sufficient consistent information to inform a measure of the severity of the underlying food insecurity condition.

A different stream of research focused on recording the frequency in which different strategies that were used by urban households when faced with short term insufficiency of foods (Maxwell, 1996).

The common thread in all these applications is the idea that the *severity* of the food insecurity condition (an unobservable variable) can be linked to observable facts. By observing these "symptoms", an analyst may deduce the presence and severity of the condition. While the concept has remained at the level of an intuition in the development of the *Coping Strategy Index* (CSI) and its variations, it was effectively translated into a proper measurement tool with the development of what has become the family of *experience-based food security measurement scales* (EBFS).

17.5.1 Coping strategies: CSI and rCSI

The CSI is a weighted count of responses given to the question "In the past 7 days, if there have been times when you did not have enough food or money to buy food, how often has your household had to: ..." followed by a predetermined (and context specific) list of possible strategies. More recently, the CSI appears to be computed using answers to questions based on a 30 days recall period.

Although described by its proponents as a *"measure of food insecurity"*, on the presumption that *"the higher the score, the greater the food insecurity"* (Maxwell and Caldwell, 2008, p.12), and by reviewers as *"a methodologically more sophisticated approach to identifying the food insecure by quantifying what previously had produced only qualitative results"* (Coates, 2004, p. 3), its development is what I termed before as "apparent" quantification. The reasons are given below.

Computing the CSI amounts to calculating a weighted count of the adopted coping strategies, chosen from the predetermined list. The weights are the product of the frequency of reporting (over the last seven days) and a severity weight obtained by determining the number (N) of possible severity levels (with a minimum of 3) assigning each coping strategy to one severity category, and assigning them a score from 1 to N (see Maxwell and Caldwell, 2008).

Even though the resulting variable is an integer number, possibly ranging from 0 to $7 \times N$, the statement that "the higher the score, the greater the food insecurity" (which would qualify it at least as a measure defined on an *ordinal* scale), is never formally demonstrated, but simply assumed. Moreover, as with the HDDS and FCS, it is not very clear what the operational definition of "food insecurity" embedded in it is. As we saw, Maxwell and Caldwell present it as a "measure of food insecurity", others – perhaps more adequately – describe it as a "direct measure of [households'] vulnerability" (Anderson, 2011). One obvious problem with this is the fact that the questions are asked conditional on there have been times, during the (usually short) reference period, when the respondent did not have enough food or money to buy food, which may have been the result of specific "shocks". This implies that the score provides evidence of a current, possibly occasional, condition that reflects a combination of two elements – the severity of the shock and the coping ability of the respondent – that are not separately identified.

The main evidence that is provided to support the validity of the CSI as a food security measure is the correlation with other indirect indicators of asset ownership, poverty or food consumption. As already stated, what is relevant to establish validity here is the *magnitude* of the correlation, not simply the results of tests of the null hypothesis that the correlation is zero. Maxwell *et al.* (1999) report "statistically significant", but practically irrelevant, values of correlation ranging from –0.220 to 0.181 for four versions of the CSI against measures of apparent daily caloric consumption, shares of food expenditure, or child anthropometry Z-scores. This means that, even in the most positive scenario, CSI explains only about 4% of the variance in these other dimensions of food insecurity as captured by the reference indicators. That is too little to even claim concurrent validity.

Other problems with using the CSI as a generally valid measure of food insecurity are the need for contextualising it and the fact that values of the CSI cannot be compared across time and space. Even though attempts have been made at deriving a more comparable reduced version of the index, called the Comparative (or Reduced) Coping Strategy Index (rCSI), based on a specific set of strategies/behaviours and with a universal set of severity weightings for each behaviour (Maxwell and Caldwell, 2008, p. 17), there is still no convincing published evidence that classifications based on the CSI or the rCSI, using a set of standard thresholds would indeed be comparable when the data is collected at different times of the year, or in different communities affected by different types of shocks.

17.5.2 Experience-based food security measurement scales (EBFS)

17.5.2.1 The US HFSSM and the Rasch model

The first example of a proper, complete, experience-based food insecurity measurement scale (EBFS) is the US Household Food Security Survey Module (US HFSSM). Building on the theoretical ground-breaking work of Kathy Radimer and colleagues at Cornell University (Radimer *et al.* 1990; 1992) and of the Community Childhood Hunger Identification Project (CCHIP) (Wehler *et al.* 1992) an 18-item module was developed and applied through the Current Population Survey in 1995. It has been

192 Carlo Cafiero

used annually since 1997, as the official tool to monitor food insecurity in the US. See Carlson, Andrews and Bickel (1999) for a discussion of the development of the indicator.

While survey questions aimed at obtaining self-reported information on food insecurity experiences had been long used in population surveys, for the first time the evidence provided was scrutinised through the lenses of a formal statistical measurement model to measure food insecurity in the US in 1995 (Hamilton *et al.*, 1997). Rather than simply *assuming* that an affirmative answer to a question about the occurrence of an experience believed to reflect food insecurity implies *being food insecure*, the application of the Rasch model to these data framed the problem in probabilistic terms. While a complete treatment of the Rasch model is beyond the scope of this chapter, the comprehensive treatments can be studied from Fischer and Molenaar (2002) and Bond and Fox (2015).

The severity of the food insecurity condition of the respondent was treated as a latent trait, which could be measured along a continuous scale. The probability that a respondent (i), located at a certain level a_i on the scale, would report an experience (j) that implied a severity level of b_j on the same scale, was modeled as an increasing function of the distance $(a_i - b_j)$. In other words, the only assumptions made were that (a) the chances that a respondent would report having experienced a certain condition increased with the severity level of his or her own condition, and that (b) severe conditions were less likely to be reported and, therefore, less frequently reported than relatively milder ones in any sample of respondents. Everything else – namely, the severity level associated with each item and whether the information contained in the responses were sufficiently reliable to provide a useful measure – was left to the empirical validation derived from application of a statistical model to the data.

While there is relatively little difference in how data are collected, compared to indicators such as the HDDS, the FCS and the CSI, the difference in the way in which they are treated to obtain a measure is striking in many respects. With EBFS based on Rasch modelling, the analyst is not obliged to make prior assumptions on how the items are scored and hope that nothing went wrong when collecting the data (Molenaar, 1995, p.4). Given the assumptions embedded in the Rasch model, the values of the parameters a_i (the severity measures we aim at) and b_j (which are linked to the weights to be attached to each item) can be computed as the solution to a likelihood maximisation problem and, what matters the most, the reliability of such parameters' estimate, be formally assessed. For this reason, and contrary to the choice made by Coates (2015), coping strategy indexes and experience-based food security measurement scales should be recognised as belonging to different "generations" of food insecurity indicators (Barrett, 2010).

One of the Rasch model's most striking results, namely that, if the model's assumptions are met, the "raw score" (that is, the simple sum of affirmative responses) is a proper ordinal measure of the severity of food insecurity, helped to popularise the approach. Scoring HFSSM data must have appeared incredibly simple to the practitioners: you simply count the number of "yes" answers provided and classify

Measuring food insecurity **193**

respondents into classes, based on the count. This has likely contributed to the successful development and use of adaptations of the US HFSSM in many other countries and contexts (see following sections). As in the US, the results of the analyses of data collected with these scales have been featured in high-visibility national reports in Canada, Brazil and Mexico, and used by governmental institutions to monitor food security and nutrition programs, such as the Supplementary Nutrition Assistance Program (SNAP) in the US and the Zero Hunger Strategy in Brazil.

However, three aspects may somehow have been overlooked in popularising the use of EBS in contexts different from the US:

i   that the sufficiency of the raw score to estimate respondent's parameters is only guaranteed if the data fit the Rasch model's assumption of conditional independence and equal discrimination of the items (see Nord, 2014) for a discussion of these technical aspects)

ii that respondents' parameters are not "exact" measures of the severity level assigned to the individual or the household, and

iii that the numeric scale resulting from estimation of the Rasch model, on which the severity parameters are denominated, is only an *interval* scale, with no natural zero and that, therefore, the actual numbers associated with them are not directly comparable across applications.

These observations have relevance for how data should be analysed and results interpreted (se discussed in a later section).

Over the years, the HFSSM has been subject to very deep scrutiny, culminating in a report from the National Research Council (2006) and a comprehensive assessment of the proposals for potential technical improvement of the measure (Nord, 2012). The reading of these reports fundamentally confirms the validity and aptness of use of the HFSSM and similarly conceived tools for large-scale monitoring of household food insecurity.

17.5.2.2. Latin American EBFSs

Following the applications of the HFSSM in the USA, a group of academics from public health engaged in validating the use of EBFS in Latin America, leading to the development of the *Escala Brasileira de Insegurança Alimentar* (EBIA) the *Escala Latinoamericana y Caribeña de Seguridad Alimentaria* (ELCSA) and the *Escala Mexicana de Seguridad Alimentaria* (EMSA) (Segall-Corrêa *et al.*, 2012; CONEVAL), grouped here under the same rubric, given the very large similarities among them. In all cases, items from the US HFSSM were translated in Portuguese or Spanish and separately adapted for use and validated in Venezuela (Lorenzana and Sanjur, 1999), Brazil (Perez-Escamilla *et al.*, 2005), Colombia (Alvarez *et al.*, 2006) and other countries in Latin America. The results were scales that include 12 to 16 items, used to identify food insecure households and to classify them into the

194 Carlo Cafiero

classes of 'mild', 'moderate' and 'severe' food insecurity, based on pre-determined thresholds in terms of the reported raw score.

Over the years, many studies have provided evidence of the validity of the EBS used in Latin America, determined by following the criteria listed in Segall-Corrêa *et al.* (2012, chapters III and IV). However, limited attention has been devoted to the need to recalibrate the severity thresholds used for classification before comparing classifications obtained in a different population. Even if analysts using these scales refer to similarly labelled classes of food insecurity (e.g., "mild", "moderate" and "severe"), the raw score-based thresholds used to define the classes do not necessarily correspond to the same severity level in the various applications. This is because the Rasch model only generates estimates of the *relative* severity of the items on a scale whose "zero" point is unidentified. Moreover, how broadly items' severity levels are spread along the numeric scale is somehow specific to each application, as it depends on how informative the actual sample happened to be. The bottom line is that before comparing the numbers obtained in different applications, they need to be transformed so that they are expressed on the same metric. In other words it is necessary to make sure that numbers are denominated in the same *reference scale* before comparing them.

17.5.3. HFIAS and HHS

As the Latin American scales were being developed, the US HFSSM was being adapted for international use by USAID, resulting in the development of the Household Food Insecurity Access Scale (HFIAS) by the Food and Nutrition Technical Assistance (FANTA) Project (Coates *et al.* 2007). The HFIAS is a 9-item EBS, in which questions are asked with a 30-day reference period, admitting a "yes" or "no" answer. If the answer is "yes", a follow-up question asks whether the experienced occurred "rarely", "sometimes" or "often". Even though the scale was developed by making explicit reference to the HFSSM and is presented as 'an adaptation of the approach used to estimate the prevalence of food insecurity in the United States (U.S.) annually' (Coates *et al.,* 2007, p. 1), the guidelines provided by FANTA make only passing reference to Rasch model-based validation as a necessary step to obtain an interval-measurement scale (see Knueppel *et al.* 2009 for an alternative, non-Rasch-based validation study of the HFIAS as used in Tanzania).

According to the FANTA manual, each item is assigned a score of 0, 1, 2 or 3, depending on whether the answer is, respectively, "no", "rarely", "sometimes" and "often". The resulting numeric variable, ranging from 0 to 27, is described as 'a continuous measure of the degree of food insecurity (access) in the household in the past four weeks (30 days)' (Coates *et al.,* 2007, p. 17). This is not the case, however, as the score, while numeric, is certainly not continuous as it can only take *discrete* values. Moreover, it must be considered, at most, an *ordinal* measure. This means for example that to take averages or to apply other mathematical operations that presume an *interval* measure to the HFIAS score should be avoided.

A few years after the HFIAS was presented, a carefully conducted study (Deitchler *et al.* 2010) addressed the issues of its validity and cross-culture comparability. Rigorous Rasch model-based analyses were conducted to assess the *internal validity* of the HFIAS data collected in six surveys conducted in five countries (two surveys in Mozambique and one each in Malawi, Kenya, South Africa and Palestine). Pairwise comparison of the relative position of the different items along the severity scale in each pair of applications was used to establish cross-culture comparability. While several combinations of items showed sufficient internal validity to ensure consistent measurement of the latent trait in each of the applications, some of the items in some of the applications were found to not pass the infit-based tests of equal discrimination (see Nord, 2014), leading to the conclusion that the HFIAS, as originally proposed, was not always internally valid. Moreover, the authors concluded that only the three most severe of the nine HFIAS items revealed sufficient stability of their severity position along the scale across all applications. The results led to the proposal of the Household Hunger Scale (HHS) as an internally valid and cross-culturally robust measurement scale of severe food insecurity only (Ballard *et al.* 2011).

17.5.4. The Food Insecurity Experience Scale

By 2012, the cumulated published evidence on the use of EBS had amply demonstrated the validity of a food insecurity measurement approach based on self-reported experiences and shown how it could be successfully implemented in a very wide range of settings. In addition to being the only type of food insecurity indicators for which the question of (internal) validity could be established, EBS possessed all the characteristics needed for a relatively inexpensive, yet sufficiently reliable survey-based instrument for measuring household or individual food insecurity. These considerations led the Statistics Division at FAO to set-up the "Voices of the Hungry" project (www.fao.org/in-action/voices-of-the-hungry), intended to explore the possibility of applying the same simple EBS questionnaire throughout the world and produce internationally comparable estimates of the prevalence of food insecurity at different levels of severity. The Food Insecurity Experience Scale (FIES) was designed as an adaptation of questions included in the HFSSM, ELCSA and HFIAS, intended for global use. Lessons learned from the attempts made with the ELCSA and the HFIAS were carefully taken into account when proposing a scale that admitted binary responses ("yes" or "no") to the adult individual- or household-referenced items.

These choices were key to keep the instrument internally valid and simple, yet sufficiently broad to be able to scan a wide range of severity, so that it could be used to measure food insecurity in a way that would be relevant for every country in the world, wealthy as well as poor. Eight items derived from the HFSSM/ELCSA were used to define the FIES survey module. The module was then adapted for application through the Gallup World Poll (https://www. gallup.com/178667/gallup-world-poll-work.aspx,) which provided a unique opportunity to administer it globally, in a consistent way. The adaptation consisted of the framing of the questions at the individual level, to be consistent with the design of the Gallop World Poll as an individual rather than a household survey, and involved the translation of the questions into the hundreds of languages and dialects used.

The results from analysis of the data collected in 146 countries in 2014 (FAO, 2016) were so robust as to lead FAO, WFP and IFAD to include a FIES-based indicator in the list of indicators proposed to monitor Target 2.1 of the newly established 2030 Agenda for Sustainable Development.

The combination of four innovations embedded in the FIES method of collecting and analysing the data make it a significant improvement over other existing applications of EBS. The first one is that, by focusing on binary responses ("yes" or "no") instead of graded frequency ("never", "sometimes", "often", "always"), it clearly defines the latent trait being measured as the *severity* of the food insecurity condition, distinguishing it from the related, but different, issue of its *frequency* or *persistence*. This is important, as one of the likely reasons why the least severe HFIAS items did not pass the Rasch-based validation tests (Deitchler *et al.*, 2010) is because the HFIAS tries to capture both severity and frequency, which do not necessarily collapse easily on a one-dimensional scale. Perhaps the analysis of HFIAS data suggests that being frequently exposed to a relatively mild condition and being rarely exposed to a more serious one are two different things. In other words, severity and frequency should be assessed as two separate dimensions of the food insecurity experience, for example by conducting more frequent surveys in the same community, using an EBS with a short reference period.

The second innovation is the fundamental importance given to the statistical validation of the data through the Rasch model-based analysis, as a precondition to determining how items are scored. Rather than imposing *a-priori* assumptions about the contribution of each item to the severity measure, with the FIES, items are only used if they are proven to be productive for measurement. In doing so, the FIES method recognises from the outset that:

a   The relative position that each item occupies on the severity scale is not imposed *a priori*, but it is rather the result of the data analysis, and
b   Raw-score based classifications are not to be assumed directly comparable across applications.

Correct application of fundamental measurement principles underlying the Rasch model (Bond and Fox, 2015; Engelhard Jr., 2013) allows to distinguish between the items' and respondents' parameters. One can still have comparable respondent measures, even if the items (questions) used for the assessment are not perfectly equivalent (see the literature on scale equating, for example in von Davier, 2011).

The third innovation, developed with the US HFSSM, but not extended to the HFIAS, the ELCSA or the EBIA, that accompanies the FIES relates to the precision of latent trait measurement. Reference to the respondent's parameters and the associated standard errors, makes it possible to formally embed in the analysis considerations related to the extent of measurement errors (National Research Council, 2006; Nord, 2012, Chapter 5), that is, the unavoidable residual uncertainty that exists around an individual measure derived from only eight pieces of discrete information. Latent trait measures, in this context, are recognised as being inherently probabilistic, and so raw scores are recognised as providing only an average of the actual severity levels of the respondents. The group of respondents with the same raw score are characterised by varying severity levels that cluster around the value of the estimated parameter, but that may deviate from it, as reflected in the standard error of estimation. Assuming a distribution of "true" severity levels around the mean, it is possible to assign a *probability of being food insecure*, at any level of severity to each raw score. In this way, one is not forced to classify only based on raw scores, but thresholds can be set at any level of severity along a continuous scale.

A combination of the above considerations is at the heart of the fourth and likely most significant innovation brought about by the FIES development: namely, the possibility of:

a   Creating a *global reference scale*, against which measures of the severity of household or individual food insecurity obtained with most EBS survey modules can be calibrated
b   Setting thresholds on the global reference scale, and
c   Computing estimates of the prevalence of food insecurity at the same ranges of severity, in every country or population group where the FIES or similar EBS are applied.

Details of this are provided in FAO (2016) and Cafiero *et al.* (2018). It is because of these features that the FIES has been endorsed as the basis for compiling one of the indicators included in the SDG global monitoring framework.

17.6 A taxonomy of household food insecurity indicators

The preceding Sections 17.4 to 17.5 revealed how several indicators have been proposed in the literature on food security assessment and used in practice, as a means to monitor the food insecurity status of households. This section compares them in terms of the properties that are likely to be the most relevant in the various possible contexts in which food security measures may be needed, to guide the selection of the indicators for specific uses. The three possible contexts considered here are: emergency assessments, monitoring and evaluation of interventions intended to promote food security, and large scale monitoring programs such as for the food security targets of the SDGs. The underlying rationale in the proposed classification is that trade-offs exist among the various properties that need to be taken into consideration when deciding on which indicator to use. While for emergency assessments, often conducted in difficult situations, *timeliness* and *ease of application* can become determinant factors, producing indicators for research purpose will require instead that much more careful consideration is given to issues of *validity* and *reliability*.

198 Carlo Cafiero

Based on the considerations made in the preceding sections, Table 17.1 lists 13 different indicators, divided among those based on food consumption data and those based on self-reported experiences. For each indicator, an evaluation (from very negative, represented by three minus signs, to very positive, with three plus signs) is given in terms of the validity (i.e., the ability to capture the construct for which the indicator is defined), reliability (the combination of precision and accuracy of the measure it produces), cross-country comparability, timeliness and ease of application. All judgements are based on an assumption regarding the use of data how it is typically collected and the level of available statistical and analytic skills that can be reasonably expected in practical situations.

17.6.1 Food consumption data-based indicators

Food consumption data are ideally collected at the individual, rather than at the household level. The ability to reliably assess the adequacy of food consumption in both quantitative and qualitative terms, in fact, relies on the possibility to characterise individual diets. *Individual dietary intake data*, though, are costly to collect and, therefore, relatively rare. As a result, related indicators of the adequacy of individual food consumption are not suited to emergency assessments or for large scale, annual assessments as required for SDG monitoring. Their use is mostly limited to the important functions of research and of monitoring and evaluation of specific programs and interventions intended to improve diets.

Household-level food consumption (not intake) *data* are much more frequently and widely available. This is why they have been used to conduct assessments in all the three contexts considered here, though none of the indicators we list can be considered appropriate to all three tasks. Adequacy of caloric consumption at the population level, based on the approach developed by FAO, is used for SDG monitoring, in continuity with the tradition that FAO had in using it to monitor the MDG hunger target. The possibility to extend the approach to research and to monitor and evaluation of specific food security programs depends on the possibility of obtaining sufficiently reliable estimates at disaggregated, sub-national population level, something for which more research and possibly better data is required. Simplified approaches to food consumption data collection, such as those on which HDDS and FCS are based, simply lack the validity and reliability needed to be used for research, monitoring and evaluation. Their use is relevant only for rapid assessments in emergency contexts.

17.6.2 Self-reported experience-based indicators

Among the indicators based on self-reported coping and experiences, the FIES-based ones present the potential to be used in all three contexts, provided appropriate data are collected.

TABLE 17.1 Properties and potential appropriate use of food security indicators

Indicator	Validity	Reliability	Cross-country comparability	Timelines	Ease of application	Emergency assessments	Monitoring and evaluation and research	SDG monitoring
Food consumption based								
Individual level								
Adequacy of nutrient intake (individual dietary intake data)	+ + +	+	+ +	- - -	- - - -	NO	YES	NO
MDD-W	+ +	+ +	+ +	+ + +	+ + +	YES	YES	NO
Household level								
Adequacy of dietary energy consumption (household level)								
2100 kcal method	- - -	n.a.		- - -	+ +	NO	NO	NO
PoU method	+ +	-	+ +	- - -	+ +	NO	?	YES
FCS (as a proxy of energy)	?	- - -	- -	+ + +	+ + +	YES	NO	NO
Household Dietary Diversity								
HDDS	?	- -	+	+ + +	+ + +	YES	NO	NO
FCS (as a measure of diversity)	?	- - -	- -	+ + +	+ + +	YES	NO	NO
Experience-based								
Coping Strategies								
CSI	?	- -	- - -	+ +	+ +	YES	NO	NO
rCSI	?	- - -	+	+ + +	+ +	YES	NO	NO
Experience-Based Measurement Scales								

Indicator	Validity	Reliability	Cross-country comparability	Timelines	Ease of application	Emergency assessments	Monitoring and evaluation and research	SDG monitoring
US HFSSM	+ + +	+ + +	n.a.	+ +	+ +	NO	YES	YES★
HFIAS	+ +	+	–	+ + +	+ + +	?	YES	NO
HHS	+ +	+ +	+	+ + +	+ + +	YES	NO	NO
EBIA/ELCSA/EMSA	+ + +	+ +	+ +	+ + +	+ + +	?	YES	YES★
FIES	+ + +	+ + +	+ + +	+ + +	+	?	YES	YES

★ Providing appropriate classifications are used.

The FIES role in the monitoring of the SDG Target 2.1 has been formally established with the inclusion – as indicator 2.1.2 in the list of official SDG indicators by the UN Statistical Commission – of the "prevalence of moderate and severe food insecurity in the population based on the FIES".

The analytic procedure for scale calibration developed with the FIES also allows for the use of HFSSM and EBIA/ELCSA/EMSA data to inform SDG indicator 2.1.2.

Similarly, the potential use of FIES-based indicators for research and for monitoring and evaluation is confirmed by the growing number of research papers being published and by the inclusion of the FIES in the monitoring and evaluation toolkits of important programs in food security and nutrition intervention, such as the Global Agriculture and Food Security Program (GAFSP) and Feed the Future, the US Government's Global Hunger and Food Security Initiative. As for its use in the context of rapid, emergency assessments such as those conducted by the Integrated Food Security Phase classification initiative (IPC), the ease of data collection with the FIES module is a definitive benefit, although research is still ongoing regarding the need for specific adaptations of the module to capture current experiences in emergency contexts. In these contexts, the HHS, CSI and rCSI have proven useful and will likely continue to be used, particularly in Africa and Asia, but – similarly to FCS – their interpretation as proper measures has significant theoretical limitations.

17.7 Conclusions

This review has demonstrated how different approaches have been taken to define indicators of household food insecurity. It also highlighted how sufficient attention has not always been given to the *validity* of the indicator as a proper *measure* of the underlying construct and the reliability of the measures produced in practical situations.

Except for individual dietary intake assessments and experience-based food security scales, studies of the proposed indicators have focused mostly on *external* validation through an analysis of the associations/correlation with the evidence provided by other indicators, often providing statistically significant, albeit not very high levels that are insufficient to establish their validity. The economy of resource use, timeliness and ease of application, rather than statistical validity, seem to have been the major elements determining the popularity of the use of those indicators in the past decade. The group of EBS, and the FIES in particular, emerges as the most promising one in terms of methodological rigour, ease of application and cross-country comparability, to suggest that their use will greatly expand in the near future.

References

Alisjahbana, A.S. (2012) *Report on the Achievement of the Millennium Development Goals in Indonesia, 2011.* Ministry of National Development Planning, Indonesia.

Anderson, E.S. (2011) *Coping Strategies Index (SCI) Development: Construction of SCI Survey Tools for Use in the West Bank and Gaza Strip. Technical report*. CARE, Gaza.

Arimond, M., Wiesmann, D., Becquey, E., Carriquiry, A., Daniels, M.C., Deitchler, M., Fanou-Fogny, N., Joseph, M.L., Kennedy, G., Martin-Prevel, Y. and Torheim, L.E. (2010) 'Simple food group diversity indicators predict micronutrient adequacy of women's diets in 5 diverse, resource-poor settings', *The Journal of Nutrition*, vol *140*, no. 11, pp. 2059–2069.

Ballard, T., Coates, J., Swindale, A. and Deitchler, M. (2011) *Household Hunger Scale: Indicator Definition and Measurement Guide*. FANTA, Washington DC.

Barrett, C. (2010) 'Measuring food security', *Science*, vol327, no. 5967, pp. 825–828doi: doi:10.1126/science.1182768

Bickel, G., Nord, M., Price, C., Hamilton, W. and Cook, J. (2000) *Guide to Measuring Household Food Security*. USDA, Washington DC.

Bond, T.G. and Fox, C.M. (2015) *Applying the Rasch Model: Fundamental Measurement in the Human Sciences*. Lawrence Erlbaum Associates, London.

Cafiero, C., Melgar-Quiñonez, H.R., Ballard, T.J. and Kepple, A.W. (2014) 'Validity and reliability of food security measures', *Annals of the New York Academy of Sciences*, vol 1331, no. 1, pp. 230–248.

Cafiero, C., Viviani, S. and Nord, M. (2018) 'Food security measurement in a global context: The food insecurity experience scale', *Measurement*, vol 116, pp. 146–152.

Cafiero, C. (2013) 'What do we really know about food security?', National Bureau of Economic Research (NBER) working paper no. 1886, NBER, Massachusetts.

Campbell, C.C. (1991) 'Food insecurity: A nutritional outcome or a predictor variable?', *The Journal of Nutrition*, vol 121, no. 3, pp. 408–415.

Carriquiry, A.L. (1999) 'Assessing the prevalence of nutrient inadequacy', *Public Health Nutrition*, vol 2, no. 1, pp. 23–34.

Carlson, S.J., Andrews, M.S., and Bickel, G.W.(1999). 'Measuring food insecurity and hunger in the United States: Development of a national benchmark measure and prevalence estimates', *The Journal of Nutrition*, vol129, no. 2, pp. 510–516. doi: doi:10.1093/ jn/129.2.510s

Coates, J., Swindale, A. and Bilinsky, P. (2007) 'Household food insecurity access scale (HFIAS) for measurement of household food access: Indicator guide', Version 3, FANTA, Washington DC.

Coates, J. (2004) *Experience and Expression of Food Insecurity across Cultures: Practical Implications for Valid Measurements*. FANTA, Washington DC.

Coates, J. (2015) 'Measuring food insecurity', in L. Ivers (ed) *Food Insecurity and Public Health*. CRC Press, Boca Raton.

Chaparro, C., Oot, L. and Sethuraman, K. (2014) *Overview of the Nutrition Situation in Seven Countries in Southeast Asia*. Report, FANTA, Washington DC.

De La Elcsa, C.C. (2012) *Escala Latinoamericana y caribena de seguridad alimentaria (ELCSA): Manual de uso y aplicaciones*. FAO, Rome.

Deitchler, M., Ballard, T., Swindale, A. and Coates, J. (2010) *Validation of a Measure of Household Hunger for Cross-Cultural Use*. FANTA, Washington DC.

Engelhard, G. (2013) *Invariant Measurement: Using Rasch models in the Social, Behavioral, and Health Sciences*. Routledge, New York.

FAO (1975) *The State of Food and Agriculture 1974*. FAO, Rome.

FAO (1977) 'Review of food consumption surveys – 1977: Food and nutrition papers no. 1', FAO, Rome.

FAO (1980) 'Analysis of food and nutrition survey data for developing countries', FAO, Rome.

FAO (1983) 'Review of Food Consumption Surveys – 1981, 1983', Food and nutrition papers no. 27. FAO, Rome.

FAO (1988) 'Review of food consumption surveys – 1988: Household food consumption by economic groups', Food and nutrition paper no. 44, FAO, Rome.

FAO (1993a) 'Compendium of food consumption statistics from household surveys in developing countries: Asia', Economic and social development paper no. 116/1, FAO, Rome.

FAO (1993b) 'Compendium of food consumption statistics from household surveys in developing countries: Africa, Latin America and Oceania', Economic and social development paper 116/2, FAO, Rome.

FAO (1996) *The Sixth World Food Survey*. FAO, Rome.

FAO and FHI360 (2016) 'Minimum dietary diversity for women: A guide for measurement', FAO, Rome.

FAO and The World Bank (2018) *Food Data Collection in Household Consumption and Expenditure Surveys. Guidelines for Low- and Middle-Income Countries*. Rome. http://www.fao.org/3/CA1561EN/ca1561en.pdf

Fischer, G.H. and Molenaar, I.W. (2012) *Rasch Models: Foundations, Recent Developments, and Applications*. Springer-Verlag, New York.

Frongillo Jr, E.A. (1999) 'Validation of measures of food insecurity and hunger', *The Journal of Nutrition*, vol 129, no. 2, pp. 506–509.

Frongillo, E.A., Baranowski, T., Subar, A.F., Tooze, J.A. and Kirkpatrick, S.I. (2018) 'Establishing validity and cross-contact equivalence of measures and indicators', *Journal of the Academy of Nutrition and Dietetics*, vol 118, pp. 1–14.

Gates, B. (2013) *Development Asia - Beyond the MDGs*. Asian Development Bank, Mandaluyong. Available at:https://www.adb.org/sites/default/files/publication/31131/devasia15.pdf

Gibson, R.S. (2005) *Principles of Nutritional Assessment*. Oxford University Press, Oxford.

Habicht, J.P., Yarbrough, C. and Martorell, R. (1979) 'Anthropometric Field Methods: Criteria for selection', in E. Jelliffe and D. Jelliffe (eds) *Nutrition and Growth*. Springer-Verlag, Boston.

Haddad, L., Achadi, E., Bendech, M.A., Ahuja, A., Bhatia, K., Bhutta, Z., Blössner, M., Borghi, E., Colecraft, E., De Onis, M. and Eriksen, K. (2015) 'The Global Nutrition Report 2014: Actions and accountability to accelerate the world's progress on nutrition', *The Journal of Nutrition*, vol 145, no. 4, pp. 663–671.

Hamilton, W.L., Cook, J.C., Thompson, W.W., Buron, L.F., Frongillo, E.A., Jr. Olson, C.M. and Wehler, C. (1997) 'Household food security in the United States in 1995', Report of the food security measurement project, USDA, Alexandria.

Hendriks, S.L. (2016) 'The food security continuum: A novel tool for understanding food insecurity as a range of experiences', *Food Security*, vol 7, no. 3, pp. 609–619.

Hoddinott, J. and Yohannes, Y. (2002) 'Dietary diversity as a household food security indicator:', FANTA, Washington DC.

Jones, A.D., Ngure, F.M., Pelto, G. and Young, S.L. (2013) ' What are we measuring when we measure food security? A compendium and review of current metrics', *Advances in Nutrition*, vol 4, no. 5, pp. 481–505.

Kennedy, G., Ballard, T. and Dop, M.C. (2010a) 'Guidelines for measuring household and individual dietary diversity', FAO, Rome.

Kennedy, G., Berardo, A., Papavero, C., Horjus, P., Ballard, T., Dop, M., Delbaere, J. and Brouwer, I.D. (2010b) 'Proxy measures of household food consumption for food security assessment and surveillance: Comparison of the household dietary diversity and food consumption scores', *Public Health Nutrition*, vol 13, no. 12, pp. 2010–2018.

Knueppel, D., Demment, M. and Kaiser, L. (2010) 'Validation of the household food insecurity access scale in rural Tanzania', *Public Health Nutrition*, vol 13, no. 3, pp. 360–370.

Krantz, D. H., Suppes, P. and Luce, R. D. (2006) *Additive and Polynomial Representations*. Dover Publications, New York.

Leroy, J.L., Ruel, M., Frongillo, E.A., Harris, J. and Ballard, T.J. (2015) 'Measuring the food access dimension of food security: A critical review and mapping of indicators', *Food and Nutrition Bulletin*, vol 36, no. 2, pp167–195.

Lovon, M. & Mathiassen, A. (2014) 'Are the world food programme's food consumption groups a good proxy for energy deficiency?', *Food Security*, vol 6, no. 4, pp. 461–470.

Luce, D., Krantz, D. H., Suppes, P.and Tversky, A.(2006) *Foundations of Measurement: Representation, Aziomatization, and Invariance*. Dover Publications, New York.

Martin-Prével, Y., Allemand, P., Wiesmann, D., Arimond, M., Ballard, T., Deitchler, M., Dop, M-C., Kennedy, G., Lee, W.T.K.and Moursi, M.(2015) *Moving Forward. On Choosing a Standard Operational Indicator of Women's Dietary Diversity*. FAO, Rome. Available at: http://www.fao.org/3/a-i4942e.pdf

Maxwell, D. and Caldwell, R. (2008) 'The coping strategies index: Field methods manual', CARE, Atlanta.

Maxwell, D.G. (1996) 'Measuring food insecurity: The frequency and severity of "coping strategies"', *Food Policy*, vol 21, no. 3, pp. 291–303.

Maxwell, D., Ahiadeke, C., Levin, C., Armar-Klemesu, M., Zakariah, S.and Lamptey, G.M. (1999). 'Alternative food-security indicators: revisiting the frequency and severity of 'coping strategies', *Food Policy*, vol. 24, pp. 411–429.

Molenaar, I.W. (1995) 'Some background for Item Response Theory and the Rasch Model', in G. Fischer and A.L. Molenaar (eds) *Rasch Models: Foundations, Recent Developments, and Applications*. Springer-Verlag, New York.

Moltedo, A., Troubat, N., Lokshin, M. and Sajaia, Z. (2014) *Streamlined Analysis with ADePT Software: Analyzing Food Security Using Household Survey Data*. The World Bank, Washington DC.

NRC (National Research Council) (1986) *Nutrient Adequacy: Assessment Using food consumption surveys*. National Academies Press, Washington DC.

NRC (National Research Council) (2006) *Food Insecurity and Hunger in the United States: An Assessment of the Measure*. National Academies Press, Washington DC.

Nord, M. (2012) 'Assessing potential technical enhancements to the US household food security measures', Technical bulletin no. TB-1936, USDA, Washington DC.

Nord, M. (2014) 'Introduction to item response theory applied to food security measurement: Basic concepts, parameters and statistics', Technical Paper, FAO, Rome.

Radimer, K.L., Olson, C.M., Greene, J.C., Campbell, C.C. and Habicht, J.P. (1992) 'Understanding hunger and developing indicators to assess it in women and children', *Journal of Nutrition Education*, vol 24, no, 1, pp. 36–44.

Radimer, K.L., Olson, C.M and Campbell, C.C. (1990) 'Development of indicators to access hunger', *The Journal of Nutrition*', vol 120, no. 11, pp. 1544–1548.

Read, C. (1909) *Logic: Deductive and Inductive*. A. Moring Ltd, London.

Sassi, M. (2018) *Understanding Food Insecurity: Key features, indicators, and response design*. Springer-Verlag, Berlin.

Sen, A. (1982). *Poverty and Famines: An essay on entitlement and deprivation*. Oxford University Press, Oxford.

Sibrian, R. (2008). *Deriving Food Security Information from National Household Budget Surveys: Experiences, Achievements, Challenges*. FAO, Rome.

Smith, L. C., Alderman, H. and Aduayom, D. (2006) 'Food insecurity in Sub-Saharan Africa: New estimates from household expenditure surveys', Report no. 46, IFPRI, Washington DC.

Smith, L.C and Subandoro, A. (2007) *Measuring Food Security Using Household Expenditure Surveys*. IFPRI, Washington DC.

Smith, L.C., Dupriez, O and Troubat, N. (2014) 'Assessment of the reliability and relevance of the food data collected in national household consumption and expenditure surveys', IHSN working paper no. 8, International Household Survey Network, Rome.

Von Davier, A. (2011) *Statistical Models for Test Equating, Scaling and Linking*. Springer, New York.

Wehler, C. A., Scott, R. I., and Anderson, J. J.(1992). 'The community childhood hunger identification project: A model of domestic hunger—Demonstration project in Seattle, Washington', *Journal of Nutrition Education*, vol24, no. 1, pp. 29–35. doi:doi:10.1016/s0022-3182(12)80135-x

Wiesmann, D., Bassett, L., Benson, T. and Hoddinott, J. (2008) 'Validation of food frequency and dietary diversity as proxy indicators of household food security', Report submitted to World Food Programme, IFPRI, Washington DC.

WFP (World Food Programme) (2008) 'Food consumption analysis: Calculation and use of the food consumption score in food security analysis', Technical guidance sheet, WFP, Rome.

UNHCR (United Nations High Commission for the Refugees) and WFP (1997) 'WFP/UNHCR guidelines for estimating food and nutritional needs in emergencies', UNHCR, Geneva. Available at:https://www.unhcr.org/3b9cbef7a.pdf

WHO (2006) *Indicators for Assessing Infant and Young Child Feeding Practices, Part I: Definitions*. WHO, Geneva.

World Food Summit (1996) 'World Food Summit Plan of Action'. Available at: http://www.fao.org/3/w3613e/w3613e00.htm

18

THE INTEGRATED PHASE CLASSIFICATION APPROACH AS AN EXAMPLE OF COMPREHENSIVE SYSTEM APPROACHES

Jannie Armstrong, Leila Oliveira, Kaija Korpi-Salmela and Jose Lopez[1]

18.1 Introduction

No single indicator can provide a comprehensive overview of food insecurity. Because food security is a complex, multifaceted phenomenon, it requires consideration of a range of indicators to determine the severity and magnitude of the situation, to in turn provide meaningful information to decision makers. This chapter introduces the Integrated Food Security Phase Classification (IPC), a standardised global approach for the classification of acute and chronic food insecurity based on a concurrent analysis of data drawn from multiple sectors.

First established in 2006, the IPC represents a harmonised approach to food security analysis. By 2018, some 15 organisations and 33 countries were using the IPC, with multiple countries conducting regular and sequential cycles of analysis. Data, findings and analysis from IPC analysis is routinely used in global flagship reports on food insecurity (FAO, 2017), provides the mainstay of the Global Report on Food Crises (FSIN, 2017), and was the basis for drawing global attention to major food crises in Somalia, South Sudan, Syria and Yemen in 2017.

Food security analysis is inherently challenging involving multiple data sources, methodologies, varying types of hazards, different livelihood systems and stakeholder institutions. As Jones et al. (2013, p. 481), put it, 'a sufficiently large number of terms have been used in discussions of food security to cause difficulties in identifying what, exactly, is being discussed, measured, or intervened upon'. Given the difficulty of providing a 'complete' analysis, the IPC provides a systematic, standardised approach to classifying the nature and severity of food insecurity, which does not rely on any single indicator, but rather on a consensus-driven, systematised approach which examines all relevant data available.

Rather than 'pushing' technical data to decision-makers in granular detail, the IPC is demand-driven and is aimed at decision support for policymakers, recognising that in almost all food security decision-making contexts; data and evidence gaps exist. Therefore, the approach of the IPC is to make the best use of what evidence is available, doing so rigorously and transparently. This requires a classification system that is generic enough to be used in a vast array of food security situations, disaster types and livelihood systems; simple enough to be practical in the field and understood by multiple stakeholders and rigorous enough to meet international standards (IPC Global Partners 2012).

In broad terms, the IPC seeks to answer six questions about the scale and magnitude of food insecurity:

- How severe is the situation?
- Where are the food-insecure populations?
- Who is food insecure?
- How many are food insecure?
- Why are people food insecure?
- When will people be food insecure?

The IPC approach consists of a consensus-driven process involving key stakeholders at the national level coming together to generate a 'big picture' overview of the overall food security context and its projected evolution to answer these questions based on the best evidence available. This process is broken down into a sequence of four functions, with specific protocols (in turn broken down into tools and procedures) to guide the planning and implementation of an IPC analysis. The four functions include:

- Building Technical Consensus
- Classifying Severity and Identifying key drivers
- Communicating for Action
- Quality Assurance.

This chapter focuses on two specific tools: the Analytical Framework and the Reference Table. These two tools provide a clear illustration as to (a) how analysis is drawn from the range of indicators presented in previous chapters, and (b) provide a clearly articulated point of entry for food security analyses for early-stage researchers.

It should be noted that these two tools in and of themselves are an incomplete representation of the IPC approach as a whole, and that fuller understanding of the conceptual underpinnings of the IPC approach (including meta-analysis, convergence of evidence and the interface between acute and chronic food insecurity as well as acute malnutrition) require further elaboration.

This chapter limits itself to consideration of the reference tables for acute food insecurity, not chronic food insecurity, for which subject-specific tools have been developed (IPC Global Partners 2015). Finally, while much of what follows has been drawn from the IPC Technical Manual 2.0, interested readers are referred to the ipcinfo.org website where a greater range of detail on all of these issues is available.

18.2 IPC Analytical Framework

The IPC Analytical Framework (Figure 18.1) provides an overview of how food security outcomes come to exist, what factors have caused the situation, and provides the basis for measuring the scale and magnitude of the situation (see the six questions listed above).

The Analytical Framework guides the classification of areas and populations based on the extant body of evidence. The IPC Analytical Framework provides a model to explain and situate individual data within a larger conceptual whole.

Taking the household as its spatial frame of reference, the IPC Analytical Framework draws together causal logic, schematic structures and concepts from four commonly accepted conceptual frameworks for food security, nutrition, and livelihoods analysis, reaffirming food security as a multisectoral, multidimensional concept:

- Risk = f (Hazard, Vulnerability) (White and Haas, 1975; Turner et al., 2003)
- Sustainable Livelihoods Framework (Frankenberger, 1992), Save the Children Fund (SCF, 2000; DfID, 1999).
- The four dimensions of food security: availability, access, utilization, and stability (FAO, 2008)
- The UNICEF Conceptual Framework on undernutrition (UNICEF, 1990).

The overall IPC classification of acute food insecurity is based on the entire body of food security evidence, which is divided into food security outcomes and food security contributing factors. Care should be taken to distinguish between

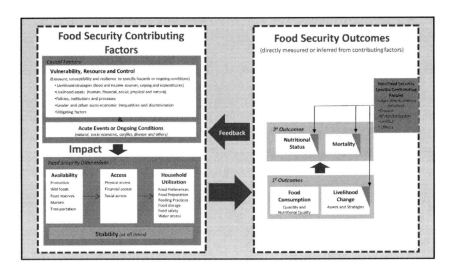

FIGURE 18.1 IPC's analytical framework
Source: IPC Global Partners (2012)

'area' and 'population' level classification, a distinction which will become clearer in the presentation of Reference Tables that follows.

18.2.1 Food security outcomes

Starting the bottom right of the framework figure, phase classification at the area level is done based on outcomes, including most primary outcomes (food consumption and livelihood change) and supported by secondary outcomes (nutritional status and mortality). IPC analysis is carried out concerning international standards (or thresholds) for these outcomes.

Based on the indicator levels/thresholds presented in the Reference Tables, how an indicator level corresponds to a phase can be determined. Because food security outcomes are comparable irrespective of livelihood, ethnic, socio-economic and other contextual factors, this provides the IPC with a basis for comparability across contexts, rendering the IPC approach applicable and comparable across all countries and regions.

For all four outcomes, only food consumption (including both dietary quantity and quality) is exclusively an outcome of food security. The other three outcomes (livelihood change, nutrition and mortality) can all have non-food-security-specific contributing factors (including health, disease, water, sanitation, access to social services, etc.). In the Analytical Framework, these are visually represented by the grey shading in the top right quadrant.

18.2.2. Food security contributing factors

In the top left quadrant of the Analytical Framework, the Food Security Contributing Factors are divided into two components: causal factors and food decurity dimensions.

18.2.3. Causal factors

Vulnerability is a term with multiple definitions and variable usage across development contexts (Dilley and Boudreau, 2001), but which broadly applies to a person, household or community's exposure to shocks (covariant or idiosyncratic), and the ability to withstand the impact of such shocks. Consistent with the Risk= f (hazard, vulnerability) framework, causal factors include vulnerability elements and hazard elements. In this framework, vulnerability is conceptually understood in relation to exposure (does the hazard event affect a population, and to what degree?), susceptibility (in what ways does the hazard event affect the livelihood of a population, and to what degree?), and resilience (what is the population's coping capacity?).

Consistent with the Sustainable Livelihoods Approach, vulnerability can be analytically understood in terms of:

- Livelihood Strategies – an analysis of the pattern and amounts of food sources, income sources and expenditure patterns of households;

- Livelihood Assets – a structural analysis of the five capitals required for sustaining a household's livelihood (i.e. human, financial, social, physical and natural capital).
- Policies, Institutions and Processes – consideration of the social, political and economic factors which support (or do not support) household livelihoods.

Although the frame of reference for the Analytical Framework is the household level, food security will also be directly or indirectly affected by acute events or ongoing conditions at the macro-level, such as natural disasters (drought, flood, tsunami, etc.), socio-economic changes (market price volatility, etc.), conflict (war, civil unrest, etc.), disease (HIV/AIDS, cholera, malaria, etc.) and other events/conditions. The analyst is expected to consider such events as they directly or indirectly pertain to food security.

18.2.4 Food security dimensions

The interactions of causal factors (including acute/chronic events and vulnerability) have direct impacts on the four food security dimensions: availability, access, utilization and stability. These dimensions intersect with one another: food must be available, households must have access to it, and it must be utilised appropriately, and the whole system must be stable.

The combined effect of the interaction among contributing factors (including causal factors and food security dimensions) is a positive or negative change in food security outcomes. Those changes are reflected in food security outcomes, which in turn then lead to further subsequent changes in the food security context.

18.3 Classifying severity and causes: reference tables for area and household group classification

With the Analytical Framework well understood, the IPC Reference Tables provide the analyst with the means to convert the logical through-flows represented in the Analytical Framework into context-specific data which allows for phase classification, indicating the severity and magnitude of the food security situation.

18.3.1 Key parameters for classification

The IPC classifies severity of acute food insecurity into five phases based on common reference indicators:

- Phase 1 – No Acute Food Insecurity
- Phase 2 – Stressed
- Phase 3 – Crisis
- Phase 4 – Emergency
- Phase 5 – Famine/Catastrophe.

Given the seriousness of its political and humanitarian implications, classification of famine is subject to a separate, specific set of decision points and protocols which are not fully treated in this chapter (IPC Global Steering Committee 2016).

Classifications are applied to two-time frames: current and projected. The future projection is based on the most likely scenario. Multiple projection periods are possible if this serves the needs of decision-makers. The classification of acute food insecurity primarily informs short-term responses and interventions are focusing on decreasing food gaps, and thus saving lives and protecting livelihoods, generating immediately measurable results over a maximum 12 month time period.

For acute food insecurity, the IPC has two units of classification: (i) area-based (i.e. the overall population within a given area); and (ii) household group-based (i.e. groups of households with similar food security outcomes, categorised by factors such as wealth, social affiliations and livelihoods). The minimum standard for IPC analysis is area-based classification. A population within a given geographic area is distributed across the five IPC Phases based on the severity of food insecurity at the overall population level. The Phase for area classification is based on the '20 per cent' rule: the area is classified in the most severe Phase which applies to at least 20 per cent of the population. When possible, IPC analysts are encouraged to provide more detailed analysis by also focusing the analysis and the classification on specific Household Groups as per data availability and needs for decision-making. The 20 per cent rule also provides the basis for mapping of the results.

Evidence in support of the classification is captured in the IPC Analysis Worksheets, including an assessment of the reliability of the evidence and overall confidence in the analysis. Classification at the area level can only take place if Minimum Quality standards are met: in IPC Manual 2.0, these are described as 'at least one piece of reliable evidence (direct or indirect) for any of the food security outcomes + at least four pieces of reliable evidence from different contributing factor and outcome elements)' (IPC Global Partners, 2012, p. 29).

18.3.2 Reference Tables

The Reference Tables (Figures 18.2 and 18.3) provide a general description, reference outcomes and priority response objectives for five phases of acute food insecurity at the household level. As with the area table, reference indicators are organised according to the IPC Analytical Framework.

The IPC Acute Reference Tables are divided into two mutually supporting tables: Reference Table for Area Classification, and Reference Table for Household Group Classification. The reason for this delineation is the different units of data collection: data included the Household Group Reference Table is relevant at the level of the individual and households, for which cut-offs are established, whereas data in the Area reference tables are relevant for the entire geographic area.

Purpose: To guide short term strategic objectives linked to medium and long-term objectives that address underlying causes and chronic food insecurity
Usage: Classification is based on convergence of evidence of current or projected most likely conditions, including effects of humanitarian assistance.

		Phase 1 Minimal	Phase 2 Stressed	Phase 3 Crisis	Phase 4 Emergency	Phase 5 Famine
Phase Name and Description		*More than four in five households (HHs) are able to meet essential food and non-food needs without engaging in atypical, unsustainable strategies to access food and income, including any reliance on humanitarian assistance*	*Even with any humanitarian assistance at least one in five HHs in the area have the following or worse:* *Minimally adequate food consumption but are unable to afford some essential non food expenditures without engaging in irreversible coping strategies.*	*Even with any humanitarian assistance at least one in five HHs in the area have the following or worse:* *Food consumption gaps with high or above usual acute malnutrition* *OR* *Are marginally able to meet minimum food needs only with accelerated depletion of livelihood assets that will lead to food consumption gaps*	*Even with any humanitarian assistance at least one in five HHs in the area have the following or worse:* *Large food consumption gaps resulting in very high acute malnutrition and excess mortality* *OR* *Extreme loss of livelihood assets that will lead to food consumption gaps in the short term.*	*Even with any humanitarian assistance at least one in five HHs in the area have an extreme lack of food and other basic needs where starvation, death, and destitution are evident.* *(Evidence for all three criteria of food consumption, wasting, and CDR is required to classify Famine.)*
Priority Response Objectives		Action required to Build Resilience and for Disaster Risk Reduction	Action required for Disaster Risk Reduction and to Protect Livelihoods	**Urgent Action Required to:** ➜		
				Protect livelihoods, reduce food consumption gaps, and reduce acute malnutrition	Save lives and livelihoods	Prevent widespread mortality and total collapse of livelihoods
Area Outcomes (directly measured or inferred)	**Food Consumption and Livelihood Change**	More than 80% of households in the area are able to meet basic food needs without engaging in atypical strategies to access food and income, and livelihoods are sustainable	Based on the IPC Household Group Reference Table, at least 20% of the households in the area are in phase 2 or worse	Based on the IPC Household Group Reference Table, at least 20% of the households in the area are in phase 3 or worse	Based on the IPC Household Group Reference Table, at least 20% of the households in the area are in phase 4 or worse	Based on the IPC Household Group Reference Table, at least 20% of the households in the area are in phase 5
	Nutritional status	**Acute Malnutrition:** <5% **BMI <18.5 Prevalence:** <10%	**Acute Malnutrition:** 5–10%, **BMI <18.5 Prevalence:** 10–20%	**Acute Malnutrition:** 10–15% OR > usual and increasing **BMI <18.5 Prevalence:** 20–40%, 1.5 x greater than reference	**Acute Malnutrition:** 15–30%; OR > usual and increasing **BMI <18.5 Prevalence:** >40%	**Acute Malnutrition:** >30% **BMI <18.5 Prevalence:** far >40%
	Mortality	**CDR:** <0.5/10,000/day **U5DR:** ≤1/10,000/day	**CDR:** <0.5/10,000/day **U5DR:** ≤1/10,000/day	**CDR:** 0.5–1/10,000/day **U5DR:** 1–2/10,000/day	**CDR:** 1–2/10,000/day OR >2x reference **U5DR:** 2–4/10,000/day	**CDR:** >2/10,000/day **U5DR:** >/10,000/day

*For both nutrition and mortality area outcomes. household food consumption deficits must be an explanatory factor in order for that evidence to be used in support of a Phase classification. For example, elevated malnutrition due to disease outbreak or lack of health access—if it is determ1ned to not be related to food consumption deficits—shou ld not be used as evidence for an IPC classification. Similarly, excess mortality rates due to, murder or conflict - if they are not related to food consumption deficits--should not be used as evidence for a Phase classification. For Acute Malnutrition, the IPC thresholds are based on % of children under 5 years that are below 2 standard deviations of weight for height or presence of oedema. BMI is an acronym for Body Mass Index. CDR is Crude Death Rate. U5DR is Under 5 Death Rate.

FIGURE 18.2 The IPC Acute Food insecurity table for area classification
Source: IPC Global Partners (2012)

		Phase 1 None	Phase 2 Stressed	Phase 3 Crisis	Phase 4 Emergency	Phase 5 Catastrophe
Phase Name and Description		HH group is able to meet essential food and non-food needs without engaging in atypical, unsustainable strategies to access food and income, including any reliance on humanitarian assistance.	Even with any humanitarian assistance: • HH group has minimally adequate food consumption but is unable to afford some essential non-food expenditures without engaging in irreversible coping strategies	Even with any humanitarian assistance: • HH group has food consumption gaps with high or above usual acute malnutrition; OR • HH group is marginally able to meet minimum food needs only with accelerated depletion of livelihood assets that will lead to food consumption gaps.	Even with any humanitarian assistance: • HH group has large food consumption gaps resulting in very high acute malnutrition and excess mortality; OR • HH group has extreme loss of livelihood assets that will lead to large food consumption gaps in the short term.	Even with any humanitarian assistance: • HH group has an extreme lack of food and/or other basic needs even with full employment of coping strategies. Starvation, death, and destitution are evident.
Priority Response Objectives		Action required to Build Resilience and for Disaster Risk Reduction	Action required for Disaster Risk Reduction and to Protect Livelihoods	**Urgent Action Required to:** ───────────────────►		
				Protect livelihoods, reduce food consumption gaps, and reduce acute malnutrition	Save lives and livelihoods	Prevent widespread death and total collapse of livelihoods
Household Outcomes (directly measured or inferred)	**Food Consumption*** (quantity and nutritional quality)	**Quantity:** adequate (2,100Kcal pp/day); stable **HDDS:** no recent deterioration and >=4 food groups (based on 12 food groups) **FCS:** "acceptable consumption"; stable **HHS:** "none" (0) **CSI:** = reference, stable **HEA:** No "Livelihood Protection Deficit"	**Quantity:** minimally adequate (2,100kcal pp/day) **HDDS:** recent deterioration of HDDS (loss of 1 food group from typical based on 12 food groups) **FCS:** "acceptable consumption (but deteriorating) **HHS:** "slight" (1) **CSI:** = reference, but unstable **HEA:** "small or moderate Livelihood Protection Deficit"	**Quantity:** food gap; below 2,100 kcal pp/day OR 2,100 kcal pp/day via asset stripping **HDDS:** severe recent deterioration of HDDS (loss of 2 food groups from typical based on 12 food groups) **FCS:** "borderline" consumption **HHS:** "moderate" (2-3) **CSI:** > reference and increasing **HEA:** Substantial "Livelihood Protection Deficit" OR small "survival Deficit" of <20%	**Quantity:** large food gap; much below 2,100 kcal pp/day **HDDS:** <4 out of 12 food groups **FCS:** "poor" consumption **HHS:** "server" (4-6) **CSI:** Significantly > reference **HEA:** "Survival Deficit" >20% but <50% with reversible coping considered	**Quantity:** extreme food gap **HDDS:** 1–2 out of 12 food groups **FCS:** [below] "poor" consumption **HHS:** "server" (6) **CSI:** far > reference **HEA:** "Survival Deficit" >50% with reversible coping considered
	Livelihood Change (assets and strategies)	Sustainable livelihood strategies and assets	**Livelihood:** Stressed strategies and assets; reduced ability to invest in livelihoods **Coping:** "Insurance Strategies"	**Livelihood:** Accelerated depletion/erosion of strategies and assest that will lead to high food consumption gaps **Coping:** "Crisis Strategies"	**Livelihood:** Extreme depletion/ liquidation of strategies and assests that will lead to very high food consumption gaps **Coping:** "Distress Strategies"	**Livelihood:** Near complete collapse of strategies and assets **Coping:** effectively no ability to cope
Contributing Factors		*For Contributing Factors, specific indicators and thresholds for inferring Phase need to be determined and analysed according to the unique causes and livelihood context of household groups. General descriptions are provided below. See IPC Analytical Framwork for further guidance on key aspects of availability, access, utilization, and stability.*				
	Food Availability, Access, Utilization, and Stability	• Adequate to meet food consumption requirements and short-term stable; • Safe Water ≥15 litres pppd	• Borderline adequate to meet food consumption requirements; • Safe Water marginally ≥15 litres pppd	• Highly inadequate to meet food consumption requirements; • Safe Water 7.5 to 15 litres pppd	• Very highly inadequate to meet food consumption requirements; • Safe Water 4 to 7.5 litres pppd	• Extremely inadequate to meet food consumption requirements; • Safe Water <4 litres pppd
	Hazards and Vulnerability	None or minimal effects of hazards and vulnerability on livelihoods and food consumption	Effects of hazards and vulnerability stress livelihoods and food consumption	Effects of hazards and vulnerability result in loss of assets and/or significant food consumption deficits	Effects of hazards and vulnerability result in large loss of livelihood assets and/ or food consumption deficits	Effects of hazards and vulnerability result in near complete collapse of livelihood assets and/ or near complete food consumption deficits

*The acronyms for the commonly used methodologies included in the reference table include: HDDS (Household Dietary Diversity Score), FCS (Food Consumption Score), HHS (Household Hunger Score), CSI (Coping Strategies Index), and HEA (Household Economy Approach).

FIGURE 18.3 The IPC Household Group Reference Tables
Source: IPC Global Partners (2012)

Indicators collected at area level are included in former, whereas indicators collected at the household level are included in the latter Reference Table. The IPC Acute Food Insecurity Reference Tables (Figure 18.2) provides Reference Outcomes and Priority Response Objectives for the five Phases of Acute Food Insecurity for the population in a given area.

214   Jannie Armstrong et al.

The Priority Response Objectives provide specific objectives for each of the Phases on the Acute Reference Table. The priority response objectives for each phase include:

Phase 1: Build Resilience and Disaster Risk Reduction
Phase 2: Disaster Risk Reduction and Protect Livelihoods
Phase 3: Protect Livelihoods, Reduce Food Consumption Gaps, and Reduce Acute Malnutrition
Phase 4: Save Lives and Livelihoods
Phase 5: Prevent Widespread Death and Total Collapse of Livelihoods.

Unless otherwise stated, the analysis is based on the whole population in the area. Within a given area, there can be multiple groups of households experiencing different phases of food insecurity. As described in the section above on the Analytical Framework, reference outcomes include food consumption, livelihood change, nutritional status, and mortality, with indicators and cut-offs identified for nutritional status and mortality.

The Household Group Reference Table includes both single indicators and commonly used methodologies that have been calibrated to the common IPC scale. Indicative Cut-offs for each indicator are included in Figure 18.2.

18.3.2.1 Household outcomes

- Food Quantity – this refers to the global standard convention of 2,100 kcal per person per day
- Household Dietary Diversity Score (HDDS) – indicates the quality of food consumption and, as a proxy measure of access to food
- Food Consumption Score (FCS) – developed by WFP, indicates aspects of quantity and quality of food consumption
- Household Hunger Score (HHS) – developed by Food and Nutrition Technical Assistance (FANTA) based on perceptions of food insecurity at household levels
- Coping Strategies Index (CSI) – developed by Maxwell and Caldwell (2008), tracks changes in household behaviours, indicating degrees of food insecurity compared over time or compared against a baseline
- Household Economy Approach (HEA) – developed by Save the Children (SCF, 2008), examines livelihood strategies and the impact of shocks on food consumption and other livelihood needs

18.3.2.2 Livelihood change

Livelihoods and changes to those livelihoods are context-specific, and universal thresholds do not exist. Therefore, general descriptions are used in conjunction with a typology of coping strategies that identifies three main levels:

1. Insurance strategies (reversible coping, preserving productive assets, reduced food intake, etc.);
2. Crisis strategies (irreversible coping threatening future livelihoods, the sale of productive assets, etc.)
3. Distress strategies (starvation and death, the absence of coping mechanisms).

18.3.2.3 Contributing factors

The Reference Table, following the IPC Analytical Framework, divides contributing factors into Hazards and Vulnerability and the four dimensions of food security (food availability, access, utilization and stability).

As with livelihood changes, contributing factors that result in food security outcomes vary greatly from one situation to the next. For example, a vital livelihood strategy for pastoralist populations may be of little consequence for smallholder agricultural producers, but government policy on land may affect both populations, but to differing degrees. Given this diversity of context and consequence, the IPC Reference Table only provides general descriptions, not hard thresholds, for contributing factors.

IPC analysts must evaluate relevant indicators in the context to infer what outcomes, and thus what Phase, they equate to. All of the data is then compiled into analysis worksheets, organised, documented and analysed to build the evidence base necessary to classify the severity of acute food insecurity and identify immediate causes. These, in turn, form the basis from which the conclusions of an IPC analysis are presented to decision makers.

Finally, while the IPC Reference Tables propose general strategic objectives for responses to each Phase, the IPC is a situation analysis and does not monitor or evaluate the efficacy of measures taken in response to the needs of the populations identified by the IPC.

18.4 Discussion

The presentation of the IPC Analytical Framework and Reference Tables above represents a useful entry point for discussion of a number of the IPC's contribution to analytical approaches to food security. The Analytical Framework is one of the first (and most durable) substantive attempts to create a causal framework for food security which works in all contexts. While there have been extensive efforts to generate working definitions of food security (notably the Rome Declaration (FAO, 1996) and Committee for World Food Security (2012)), analytical modelling has tended to be *ad hoc* for the purposes of individual reports or publications (Shaw, 2007), and is, as a consequence, rarely taken up as standard by other users. The collaborative nature of the IPC's design and development meant that by the time the overall analytical model was developed, its adoption (or endorsement of its general validity, at a minimum) was baked in, by virtue of the collaborative inputs of its participating organisations.

216 Jannie Armstrong et al.

Although a synthesis of existing frameworks, the IPC Analytical Framework is more than the sum of its parts. It introduces reflexivity into the modelling that makes for a stronger conceptual whole: other models of food security (Shaw's (2007), 'eye of the storm' being one such example, propose a concentric or hierarchical model, in which food security is the apex outcome of a sequence of contributing factors. The IPC model presents food security as an on-going cycle of changes and feedback loops. The model proposes that food security outcomes (expressed as IPC phases) then become the baseline from which further changes will emanate. This captures better the aspect of food security that Coates et al. (2006) describe as a 'managed process'; the fact that households themselves are active participants in the overall experience of food security and not passive recipients of macro-level change.

The Reference Tables underscore the IPC as an analytical approach for use at the country level, in that they provide in quantitative and qualitative detail, how to take the bundle of data accumulated during the analysis process, and convert that into a series of conclusions which are descriptive, credible and transparent. This represents the praxis between theoretical approaches to defining and analysing food security, with the expediency and pragmatism required at the level of application. Crucially, the IPC reference tables situate data in relation to each other, underscoring the need for data from a range of sectors (and not just pertinent to one dimension of food security), but more importantly, provides the basis for a conclusion, giving the analysts a firm, evidence-based grounding to explain how they reached their findings.

Taken together, these tools provide a working template that supports a blend of qualitative and quantitative analysis, which is both globally consistent and standard, which provides the analyst with the requisite formats and analytical approaches to provide data to decision-makers meaningfully contextualised *in situ*. Moreover, the IPC approach removes some of the opacity from the analysis process, by making clear what the internal logic of the analytical approach has been, how data has been used and why. This supports food security analysis as a public, transparent and rigorous process.

18.5 Conclusions

In the intervening years since the Analytical Framework and Reference Tables presented here were published in 2012, the IPC has expanded to include scales for chronic food insecurity and acute malnutrition. Countries applying the IPC analytical approach may now do so using one or more of the three classification scales, and efforts are underway to allow for integrated analysis of multiple scales simultaneously. For all scales, subject-specific reference tables have been developed, reflective of the key factors pertinent to the scope of inquiry for each topic.

A revised and updated Technical Manual 3.0 will present an integrated conceptual framework, which brings together food security and nutrition into a unified model. While of general interest to food security researchers, for the analyst, the two tools presented here are entry points for the analysis to be conducted; but the real work begins with putting those tools into action. The process is undertaken using additional tools such as analysis worksheets, online data management systems, communications templates, and quality assurance measures which enacted in later stages of the overall analysis process. With global working groups and technical review processes well in place, these tools are under a constant and iterative process of review and peer-led scrutiny, informed by experience of the application of these tools at the national level. We have concentrated on presenting these two tools in particular as we believe they provide the best snapshot of the overall conceptual approach which guides the IPC.

Note

1 The authors acknowledge the important contribution of Nick Haan to the development of the IPC as a whole and Technical Manual 2.0 in particular.

References

Coates, J., Frongillo, E.A., Rogers, B.L., Webb, P., Wilde, P.E. and Houser, R. (2006) 'Commonalities in the experience of household food insecurity across cultures: what are measures missing?', *The Journal of Nutrition*, vol 136, no. 5, pp. 1438–1448.

Department for International Development (DFID) (1999) *Sustainable Livelihoods Guidance Sheets*. DFID, London.

Dilley, M. and Boudreau, T.E. (2001) 'Coming to terms with vulnerability: a critique of the food security definition', *Food Policy*, vol 26, no. 3, pp. 229–247.

FAO (1996) 'Rome Declaration on World Food Security and World Food Summit Plan of Action', World Food Summit 13–17 November 1996, FAO, Rome.

FAO (2008) 'An introduction to the basic concepts of food security', Food Security Information for Action. Practical Guides, FAO, Rome.

FAO (2017) *The State of Food Security and Nutrition in the World 2017: Building Resilience for Peace and Food Security*. FAO, Rome.

Frankenberger, T. (1992) 'Indicators and data collection methods for assessing household food security' in S. Maxwell and T.R. Frankenberger (eds) *Household food Security: Concepts, Indicators, and Methods*. United Nations Children's Fund and International Fund for Agricultural Development, New York and Rome.

Food Security Information Network (FSIN) (2017) *Global Report on Food Crises 2017*. FSIN, Rome.

IPC Global Partners. (2012) *Integrated Food Security Phase Classification Technical Manual Version 2.0: Evidence and Standards for Better Food Security Decisions*. FAO, Rome.

IPC Global Partners. (2015) *Addendum to IPC Technical Manual Version 2.0: IPC Tools and Procedures for Classification of Chronic Food Insecurity*. FAO, Rome.

IPC Global Steering Committee. (2016). *Guidelines on Key Parameters for IPC Famine Classification*. FAO, Rome.

Jones, A.D., Ngure, F.M., Pelto, G. and Young, S.L. (2013) 'What are we assessing when we measure food security? A compendium and review of current metrics', *Advances in Nutrition*, vol 4, no. 5, pp. 481–505.

Maxwell, D. and Caldwell, R. (2008) 'The coping strategies index: field methods manual' http://home.wfp.org/stellent/groups/public/documents/manual_guide_proced/wfp211058. pdf.

Save the Children Fund (SCF) (2000) *Household Economy Approach: A Resource Manual for Practitioners*. Save the Children UK, London.

SCF (2008) *The Household Economy Approach: A Guide for Programme Planners and Policymakers*. Save the Children UK, London.

Shaw, D.J. (2007) *World Food Security: A History since 1945*. Palgrave Macmillan, New York.

Turner, B.L., Kasperson, R.E., Matson, P.A., Mccarthy, J.J., Corell, R.W., Christensen, L., Eckley, N., Kasperson, J.X., Luers, A. and Martello, M.L. (2003) 'A framework for vulnerability analysis in sustainability science', *Proceedings of the National Academy of Sciences*, vol 100, no. 14, pp. 8074–8079.

UNICEF (1990) *A UNICEF Policy Review: Strategy for Improved Nutrition of Children and Women in Developing Countries*. UNICEF, New York.

White, G.F. and Haas, J.E. (1975) *Assessment of Research on Natural Hazards*. Massachusetts Institute of Technology Press, Cambridge.

PART IV

Practical insights for implementation, monitoring and evaluation

19

SHAPING FOOD SECURITY AGENDAS

Notes from the field on challenges, solutions and promising ideas

Angela M. McIntyre, Jannie Armstrong, Suresh C. Babu, Yergelem Beraki, Duncan Boughton, Boaz B. Keizire, Michael Roberto Kenyi Legge, Lailà Lokosang, Bongeka Mdleleni, Rufaro Musvaire, Leila Oliveira, Luca Russo, Jeanette Sprinkhuizen and Duncan Stewart

19.1 Introduction

This chapter explores the "soft" side of food security policymaking and research. It is informed by a series of discussions with key food policymakers and researchers, aimed at exploring real-world experiences and lessons learned while navigating a rapidly changing global policy landscape. Chosen from academic institutions, think tanks, international and regional development agencies and community development organisations, the participants were asked to share challenges and successes encountered in the wide, global arena of food security policy, implementation and evaluation. Experienced policymakers, researchers and program managers share experiences and lessons around governance, coordination and accountability, drawn from their personal involvement in shaping food security agendas. The contexts include regime-changes and post-conflict recovery and peacebuilding, high-level trade and policy negotiations, places experiencing the severe effects of climate change and financial crises, and interactions with top government officials and rural communities alike.

19.2 Background

A key strategy of the sustainable development agenda is described by some authors as "governance through goals," in which goals, once agreed upon through a widely inclusive process, are left to be pursued by whatever means available to states. The success of the SDGs, therefore, depends on states' progress on formalising commitments, domesticating agendas and aligning sectoral policies, coordinating programs and measuring progress (Biermann, Kanie and Kim, 2017). For food security policymakers, multi-sectoral coordination challenges, policy contradictions and divergent agendas are nothing new.

Tensions between stakeholder agendas, institutional culture clashes and power differentials occur across government sectors like health, agriculture, water, energy and finance, but also between government agencies, the private sector and civil society at different levels. Beyond borders, relations between low, medium and high-income countries and their myriad international obligations, political alliances and interdependencies complicate coordination (Stafford-Smith et al., 2017).

In the absence of effective coordination, policy contradictions can have adverse effects on food security. "Policy integration", and "integrated food security policies" describe attempts at high levels to ensure policies do not work against each other. At the same time, there is a renewed focus on socio-political contexts and local food systems emphasise a bottom-up approach, more consistent with the ideas of former UN Special Rapporteur on the Right to Food, Olivier De Schutter, who highlighted the importance of processes – more bottom-up and inclusive problem solving – for tackling hunger and malnutrition.

There is no shortage of innovative ideas about food security. Some get the attention of researchers, gain traction among development practitioners, civil society groups and influence policymakers. New models and approaches of the SDG era enrich the food security discussion from technical, political and legal perspectives in their attempts to link the whole of the human development endeavour into a grand, inclusive picture. At the same time, place-based agro-ecological approaches, agricultural innovation systems, social-ecological systems and political ecology models, are needed to demonstrate the impacts of economic fluctuations and political, social and environmental change at the level of individuals and livelihoods (Foran et al., 2014).

The new complexity-oriented approaches raise some critical questions in real-life contexts. What are the implications of the wave of SDG policy "products" and their inclusive processes? Do they adapt to the unique political economies of nations grappling with chronic food insecurity, let alone protracted food crises? Do they translate into diverse local development contexts?

Policies are loaded with value propositions, expectations of capacity and assumptions about political economies. In this chapter, we asked some voices of experience to consider questions related to growing stakeholder fields, new coordination challenges and emerging accountability issues. The views were candid, critical, and sometimes tinged with frustration, but carry the enthusiasm and hope that keeps dedicated food security professionals doing what they do. Participants remain anonymous, but in some instances, their roles and types of agencies are revealed.

19.3 Coordination: how many stakeholders and meetings are enough?

Most of the participants agreed that the call for multisectoral and cross-disciplinary approaches has resulted in more stakeholders than ever involved in food security governance. Several development agency workers suggested that because of this, there are also more meetings than ever and it is hard to get around to the actual work of implementation. This "gathering of tribes" as it was called by one participant, has almost become an end in itself. Attendance is mandatory to receive financial support and to maintain standing in the community, but the discussions seemed to sometimes overlook constraints on implementation, to ignore political realities and be disconnected from those struggling for livelihoods on the ground. Some of these real coordination challenges are described below.

In countries in conflict, weak government leadership means successful coordination is attributable to local conditions – the absence of resource conflicts, peace and stability and committed NGO partners – than it is on national-level policy. At the subnational level, state governing bodies with high capacity have taken leadership in food security coordination and governance where national structures are weak. Scaling up local and sub-national coordination efforts needs to be met with much greater resource commitments from above. This high degree of decentralisation, however, can make the transition to more stable governance difficult.

Working within country usually means dealing with policy silos. Occasionally, though, there are multiple, fully autonomous structures, for example, governments and non-state actors controlling geographical territories in conflict settings. For example, policy coordination roles in Somalia can involve dealing with three governments: Federal Government of Somalia, Somaliland and Puntland. The high turnover of political party leaders in governments makes follow-through very difficult.

In humanitarian crises, the presence of numerous humanitarian actors means at least two distinctive, high-level centres of coordination, governments, in charge of the longer-term development agendas' and humanitarian assistance actors. The two have very different information needs and objectives. Humanitarian action is aimed at preventing food crises from worsening – preventing people who are experiencing severe, acute food insecurity from slipping over the edge into famine. This involves precise targeting of very specific objectives, in a way that does not exacerbate conflict and considers the root problems of marginalisation and access to resources. The majority of humanitarian emergencies are conflict-driven, with over 60% of people faced with food crises living in conflict-affected contexts. Governments are part of conflict dynamics. Transitioning from an "emergency" agenda to long-term development agenda and rebuilding resilience increases the importance of government's role, but these transitions are long and fragile and require a seamless flow of information, complicated political transitions, sometimes rebuilding or overhauling policy, platforms and governing structures.

Building policy from scratch would seem like an exaggerated notion, were it not for the case of Myanmar, a country that emerged from decades of isolation and embarked on a widespread program of political reform so new that poverty, hunger and malnutrition only came into public discussion around 2016. The first multisectoral plan of action for nutrition was launched in mid-2018. Before this, food security meant rice self-sufficiency and agricultural extension meant government inspections and state requisitions of rice production. In a country with agroecological zones ranging from the Himalayas to the tropics, the needs for agricultural research are vast and the demand for graduates cannot be met, a situation exacerbated by the superior wages offered to qualified people by NGOs and agribusiness. In spite of an encouraging show of high-level political will around food security, things move slowly in a rigidly hierarchical government showing few signs of loosening up. The prior absence of anything resembling food security coordination mechanisms is anything but a blank slate. National and global political economies exert powerful forces even when agendas are decisive. Political and humanitarian crises like the one that unfolded in Myanmar in 2017 cast a shadow over international partnerships – and the hard-won working relationships between individuals that are critical to collaboration – raising the possibility that everything could grind to a halt.

Whether emerging from conflict, isolation, or, in the case of South Africa, from apartheid, no country presents an empty landscape for food security policy coordination, however new the idea. Political economies confound the most progressive policies and the best intentions. Malnutrition in South Africa, a country with a relatively high GDP, one of the farthest-reaching social protection programs on the continent and the right to food guaranteed in its constitutions, seems an intractable problem. With more than 160 publicly funded programs aimed at addressing food insecurity, South Africa retains childhood malnutrition levels that are higher than some of its neighbours.

Where the government seems to have lost its agency, though, South Africa's homegrown private sector is stepping in. This is a shift from the multinationals with largely extractive agendas found across the continent in the mining, oil and gas and agricultural sectors. Corporate social investment is on the rise in South Africa because companies perceive that socio-economic growth is good for business. Local philanthropic foundations and NGOs are deeply involved in sectors like early childhood development. In one instance, a major player in grape production has adopted its own Sustainable Development Goal agenda, re-working its value chains and benchmarking progress against the competition. Action to change obesogenic food environments is appearing on corporate agendas in South Africa, while their counterparts in high-income countries continue to fight against food labelling and added-sugar legislation. The idea of companies doing good by citizens is encouraging, but is a patchy substitute for coordinated action and commitment in a country that has failed for decades to shake off its childhood stunting problem.

Policies can support or hinder the agency of actors in different ways. Efforts to build resilience, according to one academic and public health practitioner, need to work in confluence to address multiple developmental problems in ways that empower people and enhance agency. Family planning, early childhood development, control and treatment of infectious diseases, housing, transportation and other services that act as social determinants can either amplify or dampen down the impacts of food security interventions. Social protection measures such as cash transfers do not lift people out of poverty in the absence of wider social transformation.

There is a critical mass of resilience and self-determination necessary to support development, according to a seasoned policy advisor, who warned of the danger of prolonged dependency on technical, financial and even government, support. Broad educational improvements lead people to take the initiative in finding their own solutions. India has many examples of both grassroots agrarian activism, but also of commercial farmers banding together to contract their own technical support. In other scenarios, though, dependency on NGOs for technical assistance, on government inputs and donor funding, as well as the burden of political leverage that these bring gives countries an illusion of resilience when in fact livelihoods are extremely vulnerable to political and economic changes. In the words of a senior African policy advisor, resilience does not build in these situations because when capacity does not grow, we are "pouring water into a pot with holes".

19.4 Accountability: do we see ourselves in policy?

The conversations with these extraordinary food security practitioners resounded with empathy. They put themselves in the roles of different food security stakeholders, fluidly changing perspectives – from the breastfeeding mother, to the extension worker to the Minister of Agriculture – to critique different aspects of the food security policy landscape. This ability develops with prolonged immersion in complexity and with hands-on work in the most challenging settings. In itself, this breeds accountability – a deep sense of responsibility and purpose derived from knowing fully the impact of what we do, and the consequences of mistakes and poor judgment.

A major challenge to accountability is the rapid rate of policy turnover. Before there is even a chance to think about the impact of one initiative, there is another in its place, being promoted by a fresh set of policymakers in new coordinating forums, introducing new models and approaches and new reporting requirements demanding different data. A kind of productivism afflicts the policy business, which is responsible for a crisis of accountability in international development and food security.

It was not surprising, therefore, that critique was levelled at the trend towards the slew of evolving complex analytical models, frameworks, novel approaches and descriptive terminology. These are seen to have an influence on policy even though they are driven by academic incentives for the publication of more papers and the need to show evidence of (albeit often superficial) policy engagement. Researchers and consultants can problematise food security in ways that ensure that they are seen as the purveyors of the solutions, in a self-perpetuating policy-document industry where there is no real ownership of the problems, but a vast selection of aggressively-promoted advice on offer. In effect, this makes food security more complex, rather than unraveling its threads, getting to root causes and offering plausible and sustainable solutions.

The idea of ownership has been around a long time and is widely acknowledged to be important in policymaking. But what does it actually mean? Clearly, policies should be designed by people with theoretical understanding of food security and malnutrition, political economies, food systems and the drivers of food insecurity. But should they be designed by people who have no direct experience in these contexts and no vested interest in policy outcomes and impacts? A smallholder farmer struggling with unpredictable weather certainly has relevant experience. An extension worker equipped with little more than 50-year-old knowledge of a single crop also has relevant experience. Someone working in a district-level agricultural office with a defunct, antiquated irrigation system is a key stakeholder. A child eating a school meal, a nutritionist explaining breastfeeding to a group of mothers, a Minister of Agriculture advocating for budget increases – the possible list of food security stakeholders with vested interested is endless. Even the most vulnerable recipients of food assistance have agency and are assumed to be acting in particular ways. But are they represented in the expanding stakeholder field? Accountability is tied to ownership, which depends on actors seeing their interests reflected in policy, with particular roles, responsibilities, assets, capacities and challenges.

Capacity is built on existing assets and agency – the ability to effect change grows by enhancing capabilities and responding to changing environments. At the highest levels, in an example offered by a regional advisor, the African Union has used its convening power to build consensus and drive economic transformation in directions that will improve food security, changing itself from a purely political forum to a highly technical one. The idea that existing assets should form the basis of new development applies on many levels. This recognition makes policies relevant and inclusive of different actors, from politicians to service providers, to citizens. We need to see ourselves, our potential, and our interests, reflected in policies.

Sometimes accountability is linked to how actors do not want to see themselves. Recently, the UNSC passed Resolution 2417, recognising denial of humanitarian assistance or access to livelihoods as a war crime. This is an important accountability measure, as no government welcomes this accusation. Public information has taken on a central role in accountability in responding to food crises. The international donor community has been inconsistent in responding to humanitarian emergencies, also for political reasons. In the 2011 Somali food crisis, 200,000 lives were lost because massive humanitarian assistance was mobilised only after the IPC Famine Declaration of July 2011. Several analysts attributed the slow and low level of responses on part to geopolitical considerations; Somalia at that time was largely under the control of the Al Shabab extremist group (Maxwell and Fitzpatrick, 2012). A similar situation was avoided in 2017 when ongoing improvements in the provision of information made the danger of famine public, and the response this time was swifter. Making coordinated and accountable calls on food crises are the outcome of a consensus-building process, requiring rigorous information gathering, common parameters and thresholds. The IPC, a globally recognised information system that elicits commitments from donors, has dramatically improved accountability over past decades (see Chapter 18 for details on this approach).

National governments need to be "in the driver's seat" of food security coordination. In many countries, tackling malnutrition has been taken on by presidents' offices, acting as a hub for food security advisors placed in different ministries. Others have enhanced accountability through democratic governance, for example by training parliamentarians (in Rwanda) and journalists (in Malawi) in concepts and issues relating to food security.

Some conceptual shifts are also still needed in practice. One thought-provoking observation was "we talk about building resilience but keep on addressing the vulnerability". Building resilience is a technical problem with profound implications for process. If assets are to be built and capabilities enhanced, it will not be achieved with top-down deliberations. Trying to change broad patterns of deficit interventions from a standard menu of solutions that can be handed out as necessity arises is unlikely to enhance capacity, where there is wide diversity and communities are ecologically, culturally and socially unique. But community engagement, gathering data and building consensus at this level is often beyond the capacity of many governments; it is time-consuming and expensive, and offers few short-term incentives.

Much more attention is needed to community-level stakeholder engagement in policy processes. Many of the local, lateral influences on food security are overlooked, and, in the absence of good information, are filled by logical leaps and assumptions. Information gathering and research tend to be extractive undertakings from which results are rarely brought back to communities, who are treated as passive recipients and beneficiaries, and whose livelihoods are not seen as works in progress, but as futile struggles. Unless we can engage communities in defining problems, the problems will continue to be defined by the external purveyors of solutions. Communities want ownership of processes and to be respected partners in finding solutions, which is not the present situation: "We are not walking the journey with them, communicating downward – that is accountability". Mechanisms such as a beneficiary complaint system, have potential for enhancing accountability by "keeping partners on their toes".

If we do not understand why things go wrong, we probably do not understand why they go right. Nearly unanimously, the participants in these discussions cited the failure to assess policy impacts. This is related to the inadequacy of planning, monitoring and evaluation tools for assessing policy impact. One of the most compelling arguments for engaging on different scales was simple – we have a limited understanding of why things fail or why they are successful unless we examine dynamics at all levels. In the example of a "bottleneck analysis" to understand low treatment recovery rates of malnourished children, committees at the national, subnational and district levels follow a template of inquiry that includes data analysis. The perspective of the beneficiaries and caregivers oftentimes reveal the root causes of "bottlenecks" for example, an intra-household food distribution pattern where a mother shares the therapeutic food meant for a malnourished child with other children in the home. This results in a dilution of benefits that negates the entire purpose of getting life-saving nourishment to the most vulnerable children. A multitude of influences the level of individuals and

228 Angela M. McIntyre et al.

families in their socio-cultural contexts add up to the discernible patterns we recognise as hunger and malnutrition, and these same influences must be considered in finding solutions.

19.5 Conclusion

With little in the way of introduction and few guiding questions, the participants in this relatively brief consultation weave a coherent story. It begins with hunger and malnutrition. Concerned people in governments, development agencies, NGOs and advocacy groups, academics and sometimes citizens and private sector actors see a need for change. Because food security is complex and cannot be tackled without addressing its constituent parts, they seek to better understand problems, gathering information, which, it is hoped, reflects reality. Together they build hopeful hypotheses, called "policies" and postulate ways of turning them into actions that seem feasible at the time, and are likely to produce desirable outcomes. The more diverse, experienced and invested are these stakeholders, the stronger and more enduring the consensus and the more empirical evidence incorporated into design, so it is assumed, the better the policy. Over the years, the checks and balances in this process have improved, technology has revolutionised the ways information is used and the best academic minds and some powerful politicians have become champions of food security. But coordination seems also to require a great deal of contextual knowledge of political economies, empathic communication and community engagement that no degree of theoretical sophistication, more ingenious models or quantities of data can substitute.

The flaws in our policies, strategies and plans reveal themselves almost from the outset. Unpredictable events move things off course; governments change, variables are overlooked and sometimes catastrophes, like conflicts and natural disasters, derail things completely. Then come the real tests of accountability: what happens when things go a little wrong, or perhaps catastrophically wrong? Can we rely on stakeholders to stand by their commitments, to accept mutual responsibility when there are miscalculations and when the outcomes are disappointing? Does failure provoke reflection and rethinking about how to set things back on course, or does it create denial and avoidance? Accountability requires a degree of underlying trust and solid relationships that no sanctions, punitive measures or incentives can replace. Perhaps, then, the real value of stakeholder diversity and inclusion is in increasing the chances that someone is there in times of doubt and need, as well as times of optimism and prosperity.

References

Biermann, F., Kanie, N. and Kim, R. E. (2017) 'Global governance by goal-setting: the novel approach of the UN Sustainable Development Goals', *Current Opinion in Environmental Sustainability*. Elsevier B.V., 26–27, pp. 26–31.

Foran, T., Butler, J., Williams, L., Wanjura, W., Hall, A., Carter, L. and Carberry, P. (2014) 'Taking complexity in food systems seriously: An interdisciplinary analysis', *World Development*. Elsevier Ltd, 61, pp. 85–101.

Lambek, N. and Claeys, P. (2016) 'Institutionalizing a Fully Realised Right To Food: Progress, Limitations, and Lessons Learned From Emerging Alternative Policy Models.', *Vermont Law Review*, 40(4), pp. 743–789.

Maxwell, D. and Fitzpatrick, M. (2012). 'The 2011 Somalia famine: Context, causes, and complications', *Global Food Security*, 1(1), pp. 5–12.

Stafford-Smith, M., Griggs, D., Gaffney, O., Ullah, F., Reyers, B., Kanie, N., Stigson, B., Shrivastava, P., Leach, M. and O'Connell, D. (2017) 'Integration: the key to implementing the Sustainable Development Goals', *Sustainability Science*. Springer Japan, 12(6), pp. 911–919.

20

WHAT NEXT FOR EVIDENCE-BASED FOOD SECURITY POLICY ANALYSIS?

Sheryl L. Hendriks

20.1 Conclusions

Food security continues to deprive people across the globe of opportunity and well-being. It is entrenched by poverty and inequality and exacerbated by an increasing number of wide reaching shocks and stresses. A number of food security-related incidences over the past decade have challenged our thinking about food security causes and the impact of shocks and stresses on food supply and household consumption. More than ever before, we need a comprehensive understanding of the complexity and the impact of the multiple dimensions of food security in the everyday lives of people. If we are, as the SDG agenda intends, not to leave anyone behind by development efforts, we need to find innovative and integrative ways of evaluating the causes, contexts and impacts of food insecurity and identify possible sustainable solutions and address policy incoherence and inadequacy. These processes must be sufficiently sophisticated to avoid proposing solutions that would generate unintended consequences and inclusionary to be of practical value.

The chapters of this book attempt to build a sound theoretical basis for evidence-based food security planning, monitoring and evaluation to strengthen university-level and professional development training on the fundamental understanding of food security policy analysis; essential elements to ensure sound policies and the appropriate measures to evaluate the impact of actions aimed at attaining SDG2 in particular. While it does not attempt to cover the more discipline-specific empirical elements and approaches, it attempts to fill an identified gap in policy, academia and practise regarding food security analysis, evaluation and impact assessment for improved policy making. It fills a significant gap in the guidance of how to design, review and revise comprehensive policy analysis to build a cadre of professionals equipped with the tools to undertake rigorous policy analysis in the era of evidence-based planning and impact-driven through the SDGs and the new era of mutual accountability.

20.2 Looking forward

The complexity of food security demands the application of systems analysis that is inclusive of development stakeholders (including beneficiaries). Systems analysis can help identify multiple solutions required to address the complexity and avoid unintended negative consequences and possible trade-offs between economic, health, social and environmental objectives. Some of the most pressing contemporary issues facing food security policy, evaluation and impact assessment are presented in the chapters of the book. However, ongoing theoretical and conceptual development is necessary to tackle the complexity and ensure that practical, sustainable solutions are identified that have minimal trade-offs for society, the environment and development. Ongoing capacity development and professional development are essential to build a cadre of well-grounded and up-to-date professionals to deal with the complexity and inform research and policy about the daily realities of the food insecure.

INDEX

Page numbers in italics refer to figures. Page numbers in bold refer to tables.

AAAA *see* Addis Ababa Action Agenda (AAAA)

access to food 4, 10–11, 14, 19, 22, 29, 169; addressing 37–8; based on food consumption data 179–89; based on self-reported behaviours and experiences 189–97; improving 31–9, 62, 115, 117; indicators of 177, 179–89, 189–97; inequality of 26; women's 144–5

accountability 58, 112–13, 139, 225–8

Acute Malnutrition Classification (ACM), of food crisis 63

Addis Ababa Action Agenda (AAAA) 133

Agenda 21 133, 158

AGRA (A Green Revolution in Africa) 21, 135

Agricultural Growth Linkages in Sub-Saharan Africa (Delgado) 114

agriculture 26, 42; and food security 45, 86, 105; and food systems, 22, 118, 136, 137; nutrition-sensitive actions in 45, 46; policies 45–6, 91–2, 98, **150**

Agriculture Sector Food Security Policy (Nigeria) 4

Analyzing Food Security Using Household Survey Data: Streamlined Analysis with ADePT Software (Moltedo) 115

Andrews, M.S. 192

Armstrong, Jannie 206, 221

Babu, Suresh C. 41, 46, 49, 88, 90, 94, 112, 113, 115, 221

Beijing Fourth Conference on Women 143

Beraki, Yergelem 221

Bickel, G.W. 192

Bill and Melinda Gates Gender Toolkits and Checklist 146

biophysical drivers, of food system changes 25–7

Body Mass Index (BMI) 43, 185

Bohle, H.G. 125

Boughton, Duncan 221

Brem-Wilson, J. 133

'broken food system' hypothesis 53, 54

Busan Partnership for Effective Development Co-operation (2011) 132

Cafiero, Carlo 169, 171, 177, 197

Caldwell, R. 191

CARI *see* Consolidated Approach to Report Indicators of Food Security (CARI)

Carlson, S.J. 192

Caron, P. 133

Carter, T.R. 125

Catholic Relief Service (CRS), *Pathway to Prosperity approach* 20

CCHIP *see* Community Childhood Hunger Identification Project (CCHIP)

CEDAW *see* UN Convention on the Elimination of All Forms of Discrimination against Women 1981 (CEDAW)

CGIAR (Consortium of International Agricultural Research Centres) initiative 105
civil society 134
climate change 7, 36, 61, 161
Coates, J. 170, 192, 216
Combs, D.L. 125
Committee for World Food Security 215
Community Childhood Hunger Identification Project (CCHIP) 191
Comparative (or Reduced) Coping Strategy Index (rCSI) 190–1
comprehensive development approaches 132–4
Consolidated Approach to Report Indicators of Food Security (CARI) **128**
Convention on Biological Diversity 163; Article 8(j) 158; Article 10(c) 158
coordination, of food security agendas 222–5
Coping Strategy Index (CSI) 190–2, 215
Cost of Hunger in Africa Study 114
Cost of Malnutrition: Why policy is urgent, The (GloPan) 114
Covenant on Economic, Social and Cultural Rights: Article 9 34; General Comment No. 19 34
CRS *see* Catholic Relief Service (CRS)
CSI *see* Coping Strategy Index (CSI)
Current Population Survey (1995) 191

De Schutter, O. 31, 222
de Zeeuw, H. 135
Delgado, C.L. 114
Devereux, S. 19
dietary diversity, indicators of 186–9
dietary energy consumption 183–6
Doss, C.R. 38
Drechsel, P. 135
Drèze, J. 35

EAR cut point method 181
Early Warning System (EWS) 115
EBFS *see* experience-based food security measurement scales (EBFS)
EBIA *see* Escala Brasileira de Insegurança Alimentar (EBIA)
economic drivers, of food system changes 28–9
Economics of Iron Deficiency (Horton and Ross) 114
Economics of Reducing Malnutrition in Sub-Saharan Africa, The (Hoddinott) 114
ELCSA *see* Escala Latinoamericana y caribena de seguridad alimentaria (ELCSA)
Emergency Food Security Assessment Handbook (EFSA) (second edition) (World Food Group) 114

EMSA *see* Escala Mexicana de Seguridad Alimentaria (EMSA)
enabling criteria 139
entitlement failures 35
entitlement theory 35
environmental degradation 26
environmental drivers, of food system changes 25–7
Escala Brasileira de Insegurança Alimentar (EBIA) 193, 196, 201
Escala Latinoamericana y caribena de seguridad alimentaria (ELCSA) 193, 196, 201
Escala Mexicana de Seguridad Alimentaria (EMSA) 193, 201
evidence-based food security policy analysis 230–1
evidence-based policymaking 5, 88–9
EWS *see* Early Warning System (EWS)
experience-based food security measurement scales (EBFS): Food Insecurity Experience Scale 195–7; Household Food Insecurity Access Scale 194–5; Household Hunger Scale 195; Latin American EBFSs 193–4; Rasch model 191–3; US Household Food Security Survey Module 191–3

Fabian Commission 35
FANTA *see* Food and Nutrition Technical Assistance (FANTA) Project
FAO *see* Food and Agricultural Organisation of the United Nations (FAO)
FBS *see* Food Balance Sheets (FBS)
FCS *see* Food Consumption Score (FCS)
Feed the Future 201
FHI360 186
FIES *see* Food Insecurity Experience Scale (FIES)
Fischer, G.H. 192
fish sector 26
Food and Agricultural Organisation of the United Nations (FAO) 198; adequacy of dietary energy consumption 184–6; annual State of Food Insecurity reports 21; climate change and risk of food insecurity 25; cultural indicators of IPs food and agroecological systems 160, 163; Food Balance Sheets 171–6; food security 4, 16; framework for gender analysis 149, **150**; gender mainstreaming 146; right to adequate food 33; State of Food Security and Nutrition Report 42; "Voices of the Hungry" project 195; Voluntary Guidelines to Support the Progressive Realisation to Adequate Food in the Context of National Food Security (2004) 34

234 Index

Food and Nutrition Technical Assistance (FANTA) Project 188, 194, 215
food assistance: contemporary policy issues in 61–72; definition of 62; solutions and innovations in 68–70, *70*, **71**; systemic problems in 66–8
food availability: assessments of 171–6; changing nature 24–5, *25*; contemporary policy issues related to 21–30; environment and systems 22–3, *22*; food system changes 24, *25*–7, 28–30; *see also* access to food
Food Balance Sheets (FBS) 171–6, 186; data, uses of 175–6; reliability of 173–5
food consumption 57–8; data-based indicators 179–89, 198; dietary diversity 186–7, *187*–9; dietary energy consumption, adequacy of 183–6; measurement 179–80; nutrient intake, adequacy of 181–2; threshold, choice of 180–1
Food Consumption Score (FCS) 188–9, 192, 198, 201, 215
food crises: causes of 63–5; IPC/CH phase description of 62–3, *62*; policies for preventing and mitigating 70–2, *72*; prevention of 65, 70–2, *72*; risk factors of *64*
food environments 22–3
food insecurity 16; access and 34–6; chronic 17; continuum *16, 18–19*; definition of 64; gender and 142–52; global challenges to 3–4; inequality, impact of 36–7; intensity of *18*; measurement of 169–201; severity *versus* magnitude 19, *19*; systemic problems in 66–8; *see also* measurement, of food insecurity; *individual entries*
Food Insecurity Experience Scale (FIES) 195–7, 201
Food Policy Analysis (Timmer) 114
food security: agendas, shaping 221–8; causal factors 209–10; continuum *16, 18–19*; core elements of 5, 11–12; definition of 4, 10; dimensions of 4, 210; outcomes of 209; strengthening 161–2; terminology 10–11; *see also individual entries*
food security framework: assessment of 110–11, *110*, **116**; evaluation of 112–15, 117–19; monitoring of 111–12, *111*, 115, 117–19
Food Security, Poverty and Nutrition Policy Analysis: Statistical Methods and Applications 115
food sovereignty 162
food systems 22–3; changes, of 4, 25–7, 28–9; conceptual framework for *23*;

diversity of, cultivating 53–9; functional and contextual view of *66*; waste and losses in 29–30
Foreign Agricultural Service of the United States Department of Agriculture 171
Fossi, Filippo 121
Free Prior and Informed Consent (FPIC) 163
Frongillo, E.A. 170, 189

GAFSP *see* Global Agriculture and Food Security Program (GAFSP)
Gajanan, S.N. 46
Gallup World Poll 195
gender: analysis in nutrition policy **150–1**; bias, and inequality 38–9, 70; definition of 142–3; and food security 142–52; mainstreaming 143, 146; and nutrition 145–6
'Gender and Development' approach 143
Gender Integration in Monitoring and Evaluation 146
GIAHS *see* Globally Important Agricultural Heritage Systems (GIAHS)
Gibson, R.S. 181
GIFT *see* Global Individual Food consumption data Tool (GIFT)
Global Agriculture and Food Security Program (GAFSP) 201
global challenges, to food insecurity 3–4, 6
global food price crisis of 2007/8 9, 11–12, 29
Global Hunger and Food Security Initiative 201
Global Individual Food consumption data Tool (GIFT) 182
Global Nutrition Report (2017) 114
Global Panel on Agriculture and Food Systems for Nutrition (GloPan) 41; *Cost of Malnutrition: Why policy is urgent, The* 114; *Economics of Reducing Malnutrition in Sub-Saharan Africa, The* 114
"Global Partnership for Sustainable Development," 133
Global Report on Food Crises 206
Globally Important Agricultural Heritage Systems (GIAHS) 158
GloPan *see* Global Panel on Agriculture and Food Systems for Nutrition (GloPan)
Goldman, I. 113
Gouws, Francette 31
government organizations, policy coherence for 78–9
Graham, Chelsea 61
Grindle, M. 92
Guide for Conducting and Managing Gender Assessments in the Health Sector 146

Haggblade, Steven 88, 90, 94
Hallam, J.A. 46
HCS *see* household consumption surveys (HCS)
HDDS *see* Household Dietary Diversity Score (HDDS)
HEA *see* Household Economy Approach (HEA)
Hendriks, Sheryl L. 3, 9, 14, 16, 21, 22, 88, 90, 109, 230
Herforth, A. 118
HFIAS *see* Household Food Insecurity Access Scale (HFIAS)
HHS *see* Household Hunger Scale (HHS)
High Level Panel of Experts on Food Security and Nutrition (HLPE) 36–9: food system changes 21, 24, 28–9; multi-stakeholder partnerships 134–6, 138, 139; *Social protection for food security* 38; *Sustainable fisheries and aquaculture for food security and nutrition* 26
Hoddinott, J. 126
Horton, S. 114
household consumption surveys (HCS): dietary diversity, indicators of 187–9; dietary energy consumption, adequacy of 183–4
Household Dietary Diversity Score (HDDS) 188–9, 192, 198, 214
Household Economy Approach (HEA) **127**, 215
Household Food Insecurity Access Scale (HFIAS) 194–6
household food insecurity indicators, taxonomy of 197–201, **199–200**; food consumption data-based indicators 198; self-reported experience-based indicators 198, 201
Household Hunger Scale (HHS) 195, 215
household-level approaches, to vulnerability estimation **128**
Household Vulnerability Index (HVI) **128**
Howe, P. 19
Human Rights Based Approach (HRBA) 161
Hunger and Climate Vulnerability Index **127**
Hunger and Public Action 35
HVI *see* Household Vulnerability Index (HVI)

IAP *see* Inter-Academy Partnership (IAP)
ICCPR *see* International Covenant on Civil and Political Rights (ICCPR)

ICESCR *see* International Covenant on Economic, Social and Cultural Rights (ICESCR)
IFAD (International Fund for Agricultural Development) 161, 196
ILO Convention 107 158
ILO Convention 169 158
Inclusive Sustainable Partnerships for Development (ISP4D) Framework 136–8, *137*
Indigenous Peoples (IPs) 157, 158, 163: definition of 155–6; food insecurity among 159–60; inclusion and engagement with 155–63; principles and approaches to strengthen food security 161–2; role in biocultural diversity and associated knowledge systems 157–8; ways forward 160–1
inequality 26, 28; gender 38–9, 70; impact on food insecurity 36–7
Integrated Food Security Phase Classification (IPC) 170, 201, 206–17; Analytical Framework 208–11, *208*, 215, 216; contributing factors 215; Famine Declaration of July 2011 226; of food crisis 62–3, *62*; household outcomes 214; key parameters for classification 210–11; livelihood change 214–15; Reference Tables 209–15, *212*, *213*; Technical Manual 2.0 207, 211
Inter-Academy Partnership (IAP) 21, 22, 26
International Conference on Nutrition (2014) 12
International Covenant on Civil and Political Rights (ICCPR) 163; Article 1 160
International Covenant on Economic, Social and Cultural Rights (ICESCR) 32, 163: Article 1 160; Article 11.1 32–3; Article 11.2 32, 33; General Comment No. 12 37; on social protection 37–8, **38**
International Fund for Agricultural Development 163
Investment Framework to Reach the Global Nutrition Targets: Investing in Nutrition the Foundation for Development (World Bank Group) 114
IPC *see* Integrated Food Security Phase Classification (IPC)
IPs *see* Indigenous Peoples (IPs)
IRT *see* Item Response Theory (IRT)
ISP4D *see* Inclusive Sustainable Partnerships for Development (ISP4D) Framework
Item Response Theory (IRT) 171

236 Index

Jones, A.D. 170, 206
Josling, T. 31

Kalafatic, Carol 155
Kaleidoscope Model (KM) 88–98, *90*;
  adoption of 96; agenda setting for 96–7;
  design of 96; diagnostic tools for 90–3,
  92, *93*; evaluation and reform of 97–8;
  implementation of 97; testable hypotheses
  for 93–5, **95, 97**
Keizire, Boaz B. 221
Kennedy, G. 186
"Kihamba" system 157
KM *see* Kaleidoscope Model (KM)
Kon Guidelines 163
Korpi-Salmela, Kaija 206
Krantz, D. H. 178

Lancet 96
latent trait measurement 171, 178, 179
Latin American EBFSs 193–4
Legge, Michael Roberto Kenyi 221
Leroy, J.L. 170
Levinson, F.J. 118
life course approach, to malnutrition
  44–5, *44*
Lokosang, Lailà 221
Lopez, Jose 206
losses, in food system 29–30
Luce, D. 178

Mabuza, Nosipho 133
Makhura, Moraka N. 133, 136, 140
Malabo Montpellier Panel (MMP) 21, 133
Malawi Growth and Development Strategy
  III 152
Malawi Nutrition Policy 152
malnutrition 224; life course approach to
  44–5, *44*; nutrition transition 42, 43–4;
  policy discourse and changes 45–6, **47–8**;
  policy imperatives to reduce 41–50;
  targets for improving 41; as universal
  problem 42–3
Marine Protected Areas 26
Mason, N. 90
Mather, D. 90
Maxwell, D. 191
Mayne, J. 103
McIntyre, Angela M. 41, 53, 100, 221
MDGs *see* Millennium Development Goals
  (MDGs)
Mdleleni, Bongeka 221
measurement, of food insecurity 169–201;
  access to food based on food
  consumption data, 179–89; Food Balance

Sheets 171–6; household food insecurity
  indicators 197–201, **199–200**;
  measurement errors 178–9; reliability of
  177–9; self-reported behaviours and
  experiences, indicators of access to food
  based on 189–97; validity of 177–9
Medium Term Strategic Framework
  (MTSF) *see* National Growth and
  Development Strategy (NGDS)
micronutrient deficiency 105, 106
Millennium Development Goals (MDGs)
  184, 198; Target 1C 185
Minimum Dietary Diversity: for Women
  (MDD-W) 186, 187; indicator for
  Children age 6–23 months (MDD-C) 186
Mkandawire, Elizabeth 142
MMP *see* Malabo Montpellier Panel (MMP)
Molenaar, I.W. 192
Moltedo, A. 115
monoculture, rise of 55
Motta, Lorenzo 61
MOVE framework **127**
MTSF *see* Medium Term Strategic
  Framework (MTSF)
multi-stakeholder partnerships (MSPs):
  advantages and challenges of 135–6;
  coordinated FSN institutional systems
  138–9; definition of 133–4; institutional
  architecture for food security 136–8
Musvaire, Rufaro 221
mutual accountability 113

National Agriculture and Food Security
  Investment Plans (Africa) 138
National Development Plan (NDP) 80
National Growth and Development Strategy
  (NGDS) 80
National Research Council 193
National Vision *see* National Development
  Plan (NDP)
NDP *see* National Development Plan
  (NDP)
Ndyetabula, D. 90
negative nutrition transitions, mitigation of
  53–9; 'broken food system' hypothesis
  54; food consumption 57–8; greater
  diversity 58–9; monoculture, rise of 55;
  policy silos and nutrition paradoxes 55–7
NGDS *see* National Growth and
  Development Strategy (NGDS)
Nkwana, Hunadi Mapula 109
Nord, M. 171
nutrient intake, adequacy of 181–2
nutrition: economics 46, 49; gender and
  145–6; paradoxes 55–7; transitions 42,

43–4, 53–9; *see also* malnutrition; negative nutrition transitions, mitigation of
Nutrition Economics: Principles and Policy Applications (Babu) 115

OHCHR (Office of the High Commissioner for Human Rights): General Comment No. 19 34
Oliveira, Leila 206, 221
Olivier, Nic J.J. 31, 77
Olivier, Nico J.J. 31, 77
Omamo, Steven Were 61

Paris Declaration for Aid Effectiveness 88
Participatory Wealth Ranking **128**
Pathway to Prosperity approach (Catholic Relief Service) 20
policy: alignment 85; articulation 79–85, *81–3*, **85**; coherence 77–87; convergence 85; development loop/cycle *83*; integration 85, 222; silos 55–7, 223
policymaking process 88–98; evidence-based 88–9
political drivers, of food system changes 28–9
population-level approaches, to vulnerability estimation **127**
Potato Park 162
PoU *see* prevalence of undernourishment (PoU)
Poverty and Famine 34–5
PPPs *see* Public Private Partnerships (PPPs)
Pretorius, Beulah 41
prevalence of undernourishment (PoU) 184–6
Prevalent Vulnerability Index (PVI) **127**
private sector 134
process oriented criteria 139
Public Private Partnerships (PPPs) 138
public sector 134
PVI *see* Prevalent Vulnerability Index (PVI)

Quisumbing, A. 126

Radimer, K.L. 189–91
Rasch model 191–4
rCSI *see* Comparative (or Reduced) Coping Strategy Index (rCSI)
Regional Economic Communities (RECs) 80
Resnick, Danielle 88, 90, 93
results oriented qualities 139
right of self-determination 159, 163
right to food 32–4
Rio Declaration 159

risk management 122–3, **123**
Rome Declaration 215
Ross, J. 114
Russo, Luca 221

Sassi, M. 170
Save the Children Fund (SCF) 214
SAVI *see* Southern African Vulnerability Initiative (SAVI)
Scaling Up Nutrition: What Will It Cost? 114
SCF *see* Save the Children Fund (SCF)
Schönfeldt, Hettie C. 41
SDGs *see* Sustainable Development Goals (SDGs)
SEAGA *see* Socio-Economic and Gender Analysis (SEAGA)
self-determination 225
self-reported behaviours and experiences, indicators of access to food based on 189–97, 198, 201; Comparative (or Reduced) Coping Strategy Index 190–1; experience-based food security measurement scales 191–4
Sen, A. 11, 31, 34–5, 38, 169
SNAP *see* Supplementary Nutrition Assistance Program (SNAP)
social drivers, of food system changes 28–9
social protection 37–8, **38**
Social protection for food security (HLPE) 38
Social Vulnerability Index (SVI) **127**
Socio-Economic and Gender Analysis (SEAGA) 146
South Asia 3
Southern African Vulnerability Initiative (SAVI) **128**
Sprinkhuizen, Jeanette 221
starvation 19, 35
State of Food Insecurity: Building climate resilience for food security and nutrition 24
State of Food Security and Nutrition Report (FAO) 42
Stewart, Duncan 221
Stockholm Resilience Centre 14
Supplementary Nutrition Assistance Program (SNAP) 193
SUSENAS 184
Sustainable Development Goals (SDGs) 11, 132, 221; agenda, reducing inequalities 32, 230; on food assistance 61; on food crisis 65; on gender 142; on Indigenous Peoples 160–1; links to food *15*; on malnutrition 42, 49; policy coherence 77–8, 88; population growth and 24; target setting 3–6, 100–1, 110, 222

238 Index

Sustainable fisheries and aquaculture for food security and nutrition (HLPE) 26
Sustainable Livelihoods Approach 209–10
SVI *see* Social Vulnerability Index (SVI)
systemic problems, in food insecurity/assistance 67, *69*; bad year scenario 67–8; good year scenario 66–7; last mile scenario 68

theories of change (ToC) 100–7; applications to food security research and development 105–7, *106*; challenges and limitations of 104–5; elements of 102–4, *103*; impact on development planning, monitoring and evaluation 101–2; target setting in SDG era 100–1
threshold, choice of 180–1
Timmer, C.P. 114
ToC *see* theories of change (ToC)
2030 Agenda for Sustainable Development 196
2100 kcal approach 183–4

UN Committee on Economic, Social and Cultural Rights (UN CESCR) Committee: General Comment No. 12 33
UN Committee on World Food Security 21
UN Convention on the Elimination of All Forms of Discrimination against Women 1981 (CEDAW) 33
UN Convention on the Rights of the Child (1989) 33–4
UN Convention to Combat Desertification 159
UN Declaration on the Rights of Indigenous Peoples (UNDRIP) 159, 161, 163
UN Development Group Guidelines 163
UN General Assembly 162, 163
UN General Assembly Resolution 67/174 (2012) 34
UN General Assembly's Millennium Declaration (2000) 34
UN Special Rapporteur on the Right to Food 222
UN Statistical Commission 201
UNDRIP *see* UN Declaration on the Rights of Indigenous Peoples (UNDRIP)
UNICEF 96; Conceptual Framework for Child Under Nutrition 10
United Nations High Commissioner for Human Rights 33

United States Department of Agriculture (USDA): Foreign Agricultural Service 171
Universal Declaration of Human Rights (1948); Article 25 32
Universal Declaration on the Eradication of Hunger and Malnutrition (1974) 34
UNSC: Resolution 2417 226
urbanisation 24
US Household Food Security Survey Module (US HFSSM) 191–3, 201
USAID (United States Agency for International Development) 194; Guide to Gender Integration and Analysis 146

Vienna Declaration and Programme of Action-World Conference on Human Rights 159
vulnerability frameworks 123–6, *124*, *125*
vulnerable populations, identification of 126–9, **127–8**

waste, in food system 29–30
WDDS *see* Women's Dietary Diversity Score (WDDS)
weather-related crises, increasing number of extreme *25*
WEF *see* World Economic Forum 2016 (WEF)
WFP *see* World Food Program (WFP)
What Will It Cost? (Scaling Up Nutrition) 114
WHO *see* World Health Organization (WHO)
'Women in Development' approach 142–3
Women's Dietary Diversity Score (WDDS) 186
World Bank Group: *Investment Framework to Reach the Global Nutrition Targets* 114
World Economic Forum 2016 (WEF) 125
World Food Program (WFP) 69, 188, 196; *Emergency Food Security Assessment Handbook (EFSA)* (second edition) 114
World Food Summit (1996) 10, 11, 33, 185
World Health Organization (WHO) 41; Gender Assessment Tool 146; second Global Nutrition Policy review 45; severity indices **63**
World Risk Index **127**
World Summit for Children (1990) 96